# SEX SCANDAL AMERICA

## Politics & the Ritual of Public Shaming

Also by David Rosen:

*Off-Hollywood: The Making & Marketing of Independent Films*

# SEX SCANDAL AMERICA

---

## Politics & the Ritual of Public Shaming

# David Rosen

KPH

First Hard Cover Edition 2009
The Key Publishing House Inc.
Toronto, Canada
Website: www.thekeypublish.com
E-mail: info@thekeypublish.com

ISBN 978-0-9782526-8-7 hardcover

Cover design Olga Lagounova
Copyediting Jennifer South
Typeset and indexing Velin Saramov

Library and Archives Canada Cataloguing in Publication

Rosen, David,
        Sex scandal America : politics & the ritual of public shaming /
David Rosen.

Includes bibliographical references and index.
ISBN 978-0-9782526-8-7

        1. Sex scandals--United States--History. 2. Politicians--Sexual behavior--
United States--History. 3. Celebrities--Sexual behavior--United States--History. 4.
Sex customs--United States--History. 5. United States--Moral conditions. I. Title.

HQ18.U5 R685 2009              306.770973              C2009-901368-1

Printed and bound in USA. This book is printed on paper suitable for recycling
and made from fully sustained forest sources.

Published in association with The Key Research Centre (www.thekeyresearch.org).
The Key Publishing promotes freedom of thought and expression, and peaceful
coexistence among the people of the world. Our publications provide knowledge
that brings tolerance, respect, mutual understanding and harmony among human
society.

Other books by David Rosen
*Off-Hollywood: The Making and Marketing of Independent Films*

# TABLE OF CONTENTS

# PREFACE

**M**uch of life is chance. It marks the moment of conception and birth, of gender and place of birth, of physical and mental abilities, and finally death. This book is a result of similar chance.

One day in the fall of '08, I received an unexpected email from Key Publishing. They had been reading my articles at the political website, CounterPunch, and contacted me about writing a book about sex scandals.

At CounterPunch, I regularly rail about the politics of sexuality, about the sexual humiliation of detainees, rape as a weapon of war, abstinence imposed on teens, the plight of sex workers and, of course, the sex scandals that add a humorous dimension to American political and cultural life. I received hundreds of emails in response to these articles, but The Key's email was the first from a publisher.

The folks at CounterPunch and Key know that sex scandals have a deeper story than their fifteen minutes of headline sensationalism. They also know that many Americans know very little of the real history of their country, particularly its sexual history. Thus, they welcomed articles and a book that place the history of sex and sex scandals in a critical context.

The modern culture industry effectively obliterates from the present both meaning and history. Thus, the sex scandal involving Eliot Spitzer serves the same social function as the drug scandal involving Yankee slugger Alex Rodriguez. They are interchangeable, equally distracting and titillating. But sex scandal has a history that illuminates not only a peculiar past, but the formation of an equally unique present. Scandals mark out the boundaries of acceptable conduct, and especially sexual conduct.

Much of what is written about American sex scandals fails to consider the social function they serve or how this function has changed since America's founding four centuries ago. In many of the popular historical studies, websites and published articles discussing sex scandals, the scandals are presented in informative and entertaining manners, as nothing is as enjoyable as the undoing of hypocrites. However, without placing these scandals in a more rigorous, critical context, they remain mere gossip, tales of personal foibles and individual failings instead of revealing a deeper truth about America.

Since the nation's founding, sex scandals have been morality tales to punish and/or shame the perpetrator. They are rituals setting the boundaries of acceptable sexual practice. During the colonial period, especially among Puritans, the "outing" of someone who committed an unacceptable sexual act often led to a religious-civil hearing and severe punishment. Punishment often included a public admission in a church or town square, corporal punishment such as branding, whipping or hanging and social humiliation like that made famous by Nathaniel Hawthorne in his 1850 play, *The Scarlet Letter*.

Four centuries later, the nature of shaming rituals associated with sex scandals has changed. Corporal punishment has been replaced by the spectacle of nonstop media hounding. Shaming has become a form of entertainment, meant to distract or fascinate the public—a twenty-first century gladiator sport with the camera replacing the lion. Nevertheless, public shaming, especially directed toward political and cultural figures, has been a powerful force used to impose and maintain social control. As evident in the experiences of Spitzer and John Edwards, nearly all politicians caught in a sex scandal bow to public shame and quickly retreat from the media spotlight.

The nature of sex scandals has changed since the first days of the nation's founding. Barack Obama, the child of an inter-racial marriage, is president; Sarah Palin, a vice presidential candidate, is the mother of a daughter who had an out-of-wedlock child; Ronald Reagan, a divorcee, was elected president; Thomas Jefferson's relation with Sally Hemings or John Kennedy's affairs with Marilyn Monroe and many others are part of presidential lore; and Bill Clinton's "sex" with Monica Lewinsky was a political and not a sex scandal. Sex and sex scandals have changed as the nation changed.

Two types of perpetrators get caught up in sex scandals today: Those living a lie and those living out a lifestyle. The vast majority who get outed fall into the former category, most notably the politicians, celebrities and other worthies who make up much of this book's subject matter. These are people who feel that they have something to hide, a sexual secret that (if exposed) would compromise, falsify or undercut their public self-representation, thus upsetting their personal life fiction.

There is, however, a second group who get outed. This group includes politicians like Palin who faced down the criticism (as a bad parent and thus a poor candidate) following news of her daughter's pregnancy. But it also includes Alan Richmond and Barney Frank, two '70s congressmen who refused to be shamed when outed over their homosexuality; after being exposed in headline-grabbing scandals, they both secured reelection, a vote of acceptance by their respective constituencies. If marriage was no longer seen as a property relation and people were free to have "open" marriages, would adultery be a crime? And if adultery was no longer subject to public shaming, what would become of sex scandals?

A decade or so ago I worked for one of the most advanced computer-aided design (CAD) companies; the company's mathematically accurate software helped in the building of the International Space Station. However, many at the company wondered how such software could become a mass-market product. Of course, I suggested, it has to do with pornography.

Porn graphically powered the transition from film to tape, from movie theatres to homevideo. Thus could advanced CAD technology help fashion a new sexual media, a sexualized virtual reality? So began a study in the relationship between sexuality, technology and politics that informs the articles that appeared at CounterPunch and in this book.

CounterPunch is an eclectic and critical domain of political discourse. I was a regular reader when, in 2006, I sent in an article on the then-scandal of the day, Mark Foley's relations with youthful Congressional pages. I was overjoyed when Alexander Cockburn, Jeffrey St. Clair and their compatriots accepted my submissions.

Much of the material in this book comes from articles which first appeared in CounterPunch.

I would like to acknowledge the invaluable assistance and support extended by a group of friends without whom this book would not have been written. First and foremost, Linda Mockler helped me find my active voice; for a writer, the third-person passive voice is quicksand.

A handful of "comrades" (in the Spanish Civil War sense) provided critical engagement that helped give direction to my thinking: Peter Hamilton, Donald Smith and Sandy Rosenberg. Still others contributed to the ongoing discussion I've had about the nature of sexual life, including Ed Ifshin, Howie Swerdloff, John Simmons and Chris Carlsson. And for those who helped me settle on a name for this book, Titus Levi, Mark Powelson, Jamie Canton, Don Gilbreath and Bruce Kushnick, this one works.

A special appreciation is extended to Charles Pengelly for his friendship, support and invaluable editorial validation.

Nothing was harder than developing the cover, something that I hope is sleazy but subtle. Translating words to images is no easy trick, so I want to extend my appreciation to Joanne D'Allura, who helped me think through and conceive a visual representation of what I hope to say. And also to Olga Lagunova, who realized our vision.

Finally, to Madeline, Irma, Jessie and Dara, who prove that love remains, as always, a conscious decision and not an accident of birth.

This book is dedicated to George William "Bill" Rose, a writer, translator, editor, educator, revolutionary, co-father and friend who made a difference and remains alive in my heart.

David Rosen
New York, April 2009

# INTRODUCTION: SEX SCANDALS IN AMERICA

Americans love sex scandals, and nothing better tells the story of America than sex scandals.

Nothing captivates the nation's attention more than the exposure of an illicit tryst involving a president or congressperson, tycoon or celebrity. The scandals preceding the 2008 election involving John Edwards and Eliot Spitzer, like earlier ones involving Larry Craig and David Vitter, made front-page headlines, but played only a minor role in the election outcome. However, the rash of sex scandals involving Mark Foley, Don Sherwood and Rev. Ted Haggard contributed to the outcome of the 2006 election as Bill Clinton's Oval Office intimacy with Monica Lewinsky helped propel George W. Bush into the White House in 2000.

Sex scandals are not new to Washington's political class. Gary Hart's tryst with Donna Rice might have cost him the 1998 presidential nomination. The 1970's adulterous affairs of powerful Congressmen Wilbur Mills and Wayne Hays with their respective mistresses, Fanne Fox and Elizabeth Ray, led to public disgrace and the end of their long political careers. The outings of Gary Studds, who had sex with a male page, and Barney Frank, who facilitated his male lover's gay prostitution ring, seem lost in the mist of the political past. However, Edward "Ted" Kennedy's fateful car ride with Mary Jo Kopechne in Chappaquiddick, MA, on the night of July 18, 1969, is still the Achilles' heal to an otherwise notable career of public service.

Clinton's dalliances seem relatively innocent when compared to other presidential indiscretions, many of which have been effectively hidden over the last two hundred years. For example, little media attention was paid to the sexual accusations leveled against George W. Bush. Once upon a time, the extra-marital sexual relations of former presidents were discreetly hidden, understood to be outside the bounds of acceptable journalism. As evident in the 2008 electoral contest, unproven sex scandals were raised about both major party candidates, Barack Obama and John McCain, but quickly disappeared under careful public scrutiny. However, they illustrate the deeper changes that mark sex scandals today: They are political acts and no longer merely moral judgments.

*Sex Scandal America* tells the story of sex scandals that have enveloped presidents and many other public notables. It does this by laying out the history of scandals from the country's earliest settlement to today, from Pocahontas and the Puritans to George W. Bush. It shows that scandals do not take place in an historical vacuum, but acquire their meaning as part of the larger sexual culture in which they occur. In doing so, the book reveals how the nature of scandal has changed over the four centuries since Europeans first settled the New World.

The scandal is a public spectacle intended to serve two contradictory social functions. First and foremost, a scandal is a morality tale, a public ritual intended to punish or shame the perpetrator. Second, particularly over the last century, the scandal has changed, increasingly becoming a form of entertainment, intended to distract or fascinate the public. The shift in the social function of the scandal is a measure of how moral values of the secular marketplace are increasingly replacing the power of religious tradition. Nothing demonstrates this better than the evolution of scandals involving political figures.

John F. Kennedy's affairs with Marilyn Monroe and Angie Dickinson; Inga Arvad, a Danish journalist; the stripper, Blaze Starr; Judith Exner Campbell, mistress to mob boss Sam Giancana; and White House secretaries Priscilla Weir and Jill Cowan and still other women have moved from scandal to presidential lore. Other presidential liaisons, once carefully hidden, are now public secrets. What are we to make of Franklin Roosevelt's love affair with Lucy Mercer; Warren Harding's affairs with Carrie Fulton Phillips and Nan Britton; and Andrew Jackson's bigamist marriage to Rachel Donelson Jackson? How many Americans appreciate that at a time when we elected our first African-American president, a gay man was elected to the highest office of the land over one hundred and fifty years earlier? Who remembers James Buchanan and his love affair with Rufus King? And, of course, there is Thomas Jefferson's relationship with Sally Hemings, the African-American slave who was his wife Martha's half-sister and with whom he had six children. Sex scandals are not unfamiliar to the American political tradition.

Sex scandals are regularly featured on TV tabloid shows and gossip rags sold at the supermarket. They are also used to discredit political figures when aired through the mainstream media, as evident in the *New York Times* exposé of John McCain during the '08 campaign.[1] A scandal can also emerge as a local incident that becomes a national preoccupation, involving neither politicians nor celebrities. For example, reporters throughout the country wrote with similar gusto about the alleged rape charges against the Duke lacrosse players in 2006 and the Texas Mormons in 2008.

Scandal can envelop people further down the celebrity totem pole, propelling less public figures into the national spotlight. For example, the love triangle involving NASA astronauts Capt. Lisa Nowak, Cmdr. William Oefelein and Capt. Colleen Shipman became front-page news around the world. The gossip linking CNBC financial reporter, Maria Bartiromo, and the former CEO of Citigroup's wealth management unit, Todd Thompson, made front-page headlines not only in the tabloid press but the business press as well. Yoko Ono's affair with her chauffer, Coral Karsen, ended in an extortion charge. San Francisco's mayor, Gavin Newsom, was caught in an affair with Ruby Rippery-Tourk, the wife of his campaign manager. Detroit's mayor Kwame Kilpatrick's extramarital affair with his chief-of-staff, Christine Beatty, was one of the scandals that drove him from office. Scandals have become everyday occurrences, the stuff of headlines for both local and national media hungry for distraction.

Celebrities, like politicians, are easy targets of sex scandals. Hollywood stars, big-business tycoons, musicians and athletes capture the popular imagination. Stories about the exploits of Paris Hilton and Brittany Spears are today's media fodder, as were tales of Texas Guinan and May West during the 1920s. Michael Jackson's misadventures, like those of Liberace a generation earlier, are the source of ongoing speculation. These are the tip of a sizeable iceberg of scandal.

Disclosure about the illegal and immoral conduct of Roman Catholic priests, first in Boston and then throughout the country, was a peculiar scandal having as much to do with child abuse as a distorted sense of eros. Unlike many scandals, the victims could not be silenced and the media stuck with the story, resulting in dozens of resignations, lawsuits and even some prison sentences. A millennium of sexual exploitation may finally have ended.

The experiences of three New York governors over the last three centuries illustrate the changing nature of sex scandals. Revelations of Spitzer's sex-*posé* with "female companions" secured through the Emperor's Club V.I.P., a call-girl ring, forced his resignation. Spitzer, aka Client 9, reportedly spent $80,000 fulfilling his sexual obsession. Three decades earlier, former governor Nelson Rockefeller is rumored to have had many extra-marital liaisons. However, a front-page scandal broke out when he died of a heart attack in January 1979, naked, having sex with his 27-year-old mistress, Megan Marshak. And then there was Lord Cornbury (Edward Hyde), reputedly New York's most outrageous drag queen. As Britain's governor-general of New York, he is alleged to have opened the General Assembly of 1702 in an exquisite formal gown. He is reputed to have dressed in drag to better represent Queen Anne.

Two sex scandals are associated with Barack Obama during the course of his political career, one a fiction, the other fortuitous. These scandals represent the antinomies of modern politics—the counter forces of mean-spirited intentionality and historically determined chance. The lie involves a scurrilous rumor floated in '08 by the Drudge Report and other right-wing sources claiming that, in 1999, Illinois state-representative Obama had sex and took drugs with Larry Sinclair. In a video posted on YouTube, "Obama's Limo Sex and Drug Party," Sinclair claimed that they met twice, once in a limo and the other at a hotel. However, WhiteHouse.com paid Sinclair $10,000 to take a polygraph test which, it claims, he failed and the story died.[2]

Chance played a different role. Few today recall the scandal that befell the 2004 Illinois GOP senatorial candidate, Jack Ryan, a millionaire playboy. Drawing upon previously-sealed divorce papers, the *Chicago Tribune* reported that Ryan's ex-wife, the TV actress Jeri Ryan, star of "Star Trek" (or, as one commentator called her, "the borg-goddess") and "Shark," "accused him of taking her to sex clubs in New York and Paris, where he tried to coerce her into having sex with him in front of strangers." The revelations forced Ryan to withdraw from the election, leading to Obama's victory.[3] And, as they say, the rest is history.

*Sex Scandal America* employs a loosely structured historical framework to tell the tale of our nation's sometimes darker, sometimes funnier and often sleazier moments of public spectacle. Chapters 1 and 2 follow the earliest colonial settlers through the Revolution generation, assessing the scandals involving Pocahontas and the Puritans, George Washington, Jefferson, Buchanan and Francis Wright, the foremost free-love advocate of the antebellum era. Chapters 3 and 4 focus on the period of American modernization, from the traumatic post-Civil War years through the Great Depression and the end of World War II, recalling the scandals of Harding and Roosevelt, Henry Ward Beecher and Harry Kendall Thaw as well as Mae West, Roscoe "Fatty" Arbuckle, Jack Johnson and Charlie Chaplin. Chapters 5 and 6 examine the half-century between the end of World War II and Clinton's impeachment in 1998 which marks the era in which scandal evolved from a moral injunction to an entertainment sport, involving not only presidents Kennedy, Lyndon Johnson and Richard Nixon, but senators Ted Kennedy, Bob Packwood, Gary Hart and Charles Robb. To help set the historical stage, it discusses more celebrity-oriented scandals involving actors Montgomery Clift and Rock Hudson, sexologist Alfred Kinsey, and, least we forget, religious leaders Jim Bakker, Jimmy Swaggart and Paul Crouch. Finally, the shame of the twentieth century, the pedophile scandals involving the Catholic Church, is reconsidered.

In conclusion, Chapter 7 explores the role of scandals in the era of the Christian right's culture wars. Scandals upended the political careers of conservatives like Foley, Sherwood, Haggard, Vitter and Craig, thus helping undo the Republican Party's electoral fortunes. However, scandals also upended notable liberals like Spitzer and Edwards. The book concludes by speculating that, with Obama's victory and the defeat of the Christian right, the culture wars have finally subsided. Most telling, and as discussed in the Afterword, was the public outing of Republican vice-presidential candidate Sarah Palin's daughter, Bristol, who was revealed to be pregnant from a premarital relation. With the eclipse of the culture wars, can we expect a change in the nature of sex scandal? While scandals surely will continue and capture media attention, for sex still sells, they may lose even more of their moral approbation and set the stage for a new era of American sexual morality.

## References

[1] Jim Rutenberg, et. al, "For McCain, Self-Confidence on Ethics Poses Its Own Risk," *New York Times*, February 21, 2008.

[2] Seth Colter Walls, "Obama Accuser Larry Sinclair Holds Stupefying Press Conference," *Huffington Post*, June 18, 2001; "Sleaze Charge: 'I Took Drugs, had Homo Sex with Obama," WorldNet-Daily, February 17, 2008, http://www.wnd.comdeathby1000papercuts. blogspot.com /2008/02.

[3] Rick Pearson and Liam Ford, "GOP Leaders Say They Felt Misled on Ryan," *Chicago Tribune*, June 23, 2004.

# CHAPTER 1. BIRTH OF A NATION

*... in nothing doth the raging power of original sin more discover itself ...*
*than in the ungoverned exorbitancy of fleshly lust.*
Samuel Willard, Puritan minister, 1640—1707 [1]

The New World was besieged by numerous sex scandals during the first seventy-five years of Puritan settlement. For New Englanders and other British colonists up and down the Atlantic Coast, these scandals set the boundaries of acceptable sexual practice. They mostly involved premarital sex (fornication), extramarital sex (adultery), sodomy and interracial sex. Two offenses were most upsetting: bestiality involving young men and sexual witchcraft among older women. Among Puritans, as John Murrin points out, "[b]estiality discredited men in the way that witchcraft discredited women."[2] However, in New England, sex with the devil was the gravest of all sins! Puritan sexual scandals were a terrain of struggle that illuminates, if only in its exaggeration, America's most formative era of sexual identity. It is an identity that, like a threatening shadow, continues to hover over America today.

Mary Johnson, of Wethersfield, Connecticut, was one of ten Puritan women accused of having sex with Satan. In 1648, Johnson allegedly admitted to minister Samuel Stone (and reported by Cotton Mather): "She said her first Familiarity with the Devils came by Discontent" with her role as a servant and that "she was guilty of the Murder of a Child and that she had been guilty of Uncleanness with Men and Devils." Two years earlier, she had been accused of thievery and was publicly whipped. However, for her truly unholy deed of consorting with the devil, she was convicted of witchcraft and executed.[3]

Another resident of Wethersfield, Rebecca Greensmith, admitted having participated in "a meeting under a tree on the green ...

[where] we danced and had a bottle of sack"; she also admitted to Hartford ministers and magistrates that "the Devil had frequently the carnal knowledge of her Body"; in January 1663, she was hung along with her husband, Nathaniel, who denied all accusations until the bitter end.[4] Ann Cole, of Hartford, was a woman reported to have suffered convulsions and fits; she was accused of taking part in "witches' night wandering." Her fate was sealed when she admitted that she allowed Satan to have "frequent carnal knowledge of her."[5]

The historian Richard Frances found that Sarah Parker had made a covenant with the devil due to "her great sin of Committing adultery" and that "the Devil had come to her & kissed her." It is not clear as to her fate.[6] Elizabeth Godman, of New Haven, was socially different from many accused women in that she had a sizable estate estimated at £200 at her death in 1660. However, as a widow with no sons she was vulnerable to a variety of social accusations. Some said she was "a malicious one" because she expressed discontent with religious teachings and practices, challenged the notion of "God's elect" and "… [would] justify [witches] rather than condemn them," practiced black magic, inspired fear in others and of gnashing her teeth and grinning. In 1653 neighbors complained that she "had laine with" Satan and that "Hobbamocke [an alleged Indian 'devil god'] was her husband."[7] Another woman, Mary Parsons, of Springfield, Massachusetts, was disparaged for being "married to a papist". In 1651, she was accused of "being seduced by the devil" and "making a covenant with him." According to her fellow Puritan John Hale:

> she had lost a Child and was exceedingly discontented at it and longed; *Oh that she might see her Child again!* And at last the Devil in likeness of her Child came to her bed side and talked with her, and asked to come into the bed to her, and she received it into the bed to her that night and several nights after, and so entered into covenant with Satan and became a witch.

She was executed.

Still other women faced accusations of consorting with the devil. One woman, Goody Osborne, testified that "a thing like an indian all black" came to her in bed one night and, in the words of one historian, "pulled her by the back of her head toward her door."[9] Another woman, Sarah Bridges, is reported to have signed the devil's book in blood, attended an Andover witches conclave with two hundred-plus witches and "gave her body" to the devil in the form of a man and an animal; surprisingly, she was not executed.[10] Mary Warren, of Salem who earlier had been a servant to Henry Salter of Andover, was accused of suffering dreadful fits, of "yielding" to the devil and signing the devil's book and, even though she confessed to being a witch, was not executed when the witchcraft panic subsided in 1693.[11]

Finally, we come to Bridget Bishop, the first woman at the Salem trials executed for her sins. She was first accused of being a witch in 1679 when her husband died. It was during the Salem trials (and when she was in her fifties) that she faced a second trial for being a witch, for attending a witches gathering at the Parris field, for having a body mark (or what was known as a "witch's teat" or imp) and for giving her body and soul to the devil. She steadfastly insisted on her innocence, but was nevertheless hung.[12]

Three women were accused of having illegitimate children as a result of witchcraft—and were executed. Alice Lake was accused in 1651 by minister John Hale of being "… a single woman play'd the harlot, and being with Child used means to destroy the fruit of her body to conceal her sin and shame;" she was hanged for her sins.[13] Martha Corey was accused of having "had born a bastard mulatto son," of causing pain in others, of having a "black man" (i.e., a specter) whisper in her ear and of participating in witches' sacrament with forty others at Parris' pasture; she denied being a witch, even denied the existence of the devil—and was hung in 1692.[14]

Suzannah Martin, who was born in England and lived in Amesbury, Massachusetts, was first accused of being a witch in 1669. Subsequently, she was accused of having a bastard son and having violent quarrels in her home; she was suspect for challenging male power in court. In 1692 and at age sixty-seven, she was again charged with witchcraft, this time based on the testimony of Bernard Peach, who claimed that during one of her night wanderings Martin sexually assaulted him:

> being in bed on a lords day night he [Peach] heard a [scratching] at the window. He this deponent saw susana martin … com in at the window and jumpt downe upon the flower. Shee was in her hood and scarf and the same dress that shee was in before at metting the

same day. Being com in, she was coming up toward this deponents faced but turned back to his feet and took hold of them and drew up his body into a heape and Lay upon him about an hour and half or 2 hours, in all which taim this deponent coold not stir nor speake... .

She was executed for her sins.[15]

Other women were charged with witchcraft and adultery. Elizabeth Seager, of Hartford was accused of witchcraft in 1662, 1665 and 1666 but was acquitted; she was reported to have slapped a neighbor and was suffering various questionable pains; however, she was also accused and convicted of adultery and blasphemy, but fled to Rhode Island to avoid punishment.[16] Rachel Clinton, who was born in England and lived in Ipswich, Massachusetts, was accused of having adulterous relations including with an indentured servant fourteen years younger and who she eventually married; she was also accused of expressing dissatisfaction with her inheritance settlement from her first husband and bringing the matter to court. In 1692 and at the age of fifty-eight, she was convicted of witchcraft, but pardoned by the governor a year later.[17]

We've come a long way since the British settlers first colonized the New World: People are no longer executed for consorting with the devil. A host of sexual prohibitions, including masturbation, premarital sex, adultery, homosexuality and interracial sex, are no longer considered sins by civil authorities, most moralists and a significant proportion of the public. Prostitution has become a discreet business activity, regulated in two states, and relatively free from moralistic and police harassment. The limits to acceptable sex are based on consent among adults or among similarly aged adolescents over sixteen years. Strong prohibitions, both legal and ethical, attempt to halt nonconsensual sexual acts like rape, pedophilia, incest and bestiality. However, for the early Puritans and other colonists, both Satan and sex were threats to personal and public life—and nothing was worse than sex with the devil.

* * *

On April 5, 1614, Pocahontas, a Powhatan woman and reputed daughter of Chief Powhatan, married the Englishman John Rolfe near Jamestown, Virginia. The marriage took place just eight years after this first permanent English settlement was established in what would become the United States; it is the first recorded interracial marriage in the newly-colonized territory. Sixty-seven years later, in 1681, the first recorded legal marriage between an African man and a European woman is reported to have taken place on William Boarmans' plantation on the western shore of Maryland. The couple—Eleanor Butler, a white servant girl called Irish Nell, and Negro Charles, a black slave—was married by a local Catholic priest.[18]

During the early days of the settlement of the new nation, voluntary and noncommercial sexual relations between whites and people of color were not yet illegal. Nevertheless, colonial male leaders were particularly troubled by such relationships. While they were initially between British males and Native females, as the immigration of both free and indentured European women and the forced importation of African slaves, both male and female, increased, the complexity of such relations multiplied.

Columbia University sociologist Aaron Gullickson argues that "interracial sexual contact likely peaked sometime during the early colonial period when white indentured servants and black slaves were in close contact in large numbers."[19] Complaints about such liaisons drew various forms of protest. One of the most surprising was that of Lord Baltimore, Nell's master, and other local whites. While they did not seek to prevent the marriage between Nell and Charles, they could not understand why a white woman would marry a slave and thus not only lose her own freedom but the freedom of her children.

Equally disturbing, sex between a white woman and a nonwhite man could result in a child that was legally white. This concern found particular expression in what are known as female captivity narratives that helped rally settler resentment against Native people. These tales were popular in the late-seventeenth century and championed women like Mary Rowlandson and Hannah Swarton who escaped capture by Native tribes while preserving their virginity. These tales were intended to undercut or deny the stories of women like Mary Jemison, Frances Slocum and Eunice Williams who, after captivity, chose to marry and live out their lives with Native people.[20]

Bans on interracial marriage arose in the late-seventeenth century. For example, in 1662, nearly a half-century after Pocahontas married Rolfe, the Virginia Assembly established the first law against interracial sex. Thirty years later, in 1691, it passed a much stiffer law banning "negroes, mulattoes and indians intermarrying with English, or other white women, [and] their unlawful accompanying with one another."[21] Other colonies followed with similar bans, as exemplified by the North Carolina colony that, in 1715, adopted laws prohibiting interracial marriages. Now, three-and-a-half centuries later, America has elected its first president of mixed-race origin, a child of once-scandalous interracial sex.

\* \* \*

Pocahontas is one of the great American mythic figures. She has been immortalized in Disney animated children's movies and in Terrence Malik's beautiful film, *The New World* (2005), as well as in comic books and videogames, even toys and wallpaper. She has been effectively whitewashed into a popular-culture icon, the truth about her relatively short and remarkable life—and the scandal she precipitated—has all but been lost.

Pocahontas is the nickname for a girl born Matoaka in 1595 or 1596 upriver from the settlement of "James Towne." According to the Native American scholar, Paula Gunn Allen, the nickname has a variety of meanings, including "wanton," "mischievous," "sportive," "frisky" or "frolicsome." She says the nickname, "at least as it was understood by the English," was related to the rabbit or chipmunk, both considered tricksters by the Powhatan people. More importantly, Pocahontas was of royal blood, a chosen-one with the power of "Dream-Vision"; she was a female visited by spirits that foretold the future. As a child she had a prophetic vision involving the landing of a ship that would change the course of history and the appearance of a strange man whose life she would save.[22]

John Smith, a mercenary soldier and adventurer, was the leader of the Jamestown settlement. Legend and subsequent scholarship tell us that, in 1608, he was captured while attempting to reach Chief Powhaten. The initial settlement at "Fort James," established only a year earlier, was a near disaster, with the British suffering from hunger, illness, loneliness, Native assaults and other privations. Rumors of sodomy among early settlers were not uncommon.[23] In an attempt to survive, Smith ventured forth to find the mighty chief and establish diplomatic relations.

As Allen tells the tale, Smith was captured and brought before the chief in the colony's great house during an important religious ceremony. He was forced to the ground with two warriors holding him down, their spears at the ready. He feared imminent execution, only to be saved at the last moment. Allen dramatically envisions the scene accordingly:

> Pocahontas rises [from the assembled gathering] to her feet and swiftly runs the thirty feet to the center of the Grand House. She hurls her small body upon Smith's, wraps her arms tightly around him, and lays her head over him. Everything stops in a great tableau; only the smoke swirls upward through the roof. Then it is known and a great wail goes up among all the people. They are thanking the spirits, and they begin to dance.[24]

Pocahontas, aged twelve or thirteen, recognized Smith as the fulfillment of her Dream-Vision. Had she not, his life would not have been spared.*

Early English settlers did not know how to relate to Native people, especially to females when it came to intimate matters. Robert Godbeer, in his essential study, *Sexual Revolution in Early America*, paints a compelling portrait of the complex and often contradictory sexual relations that defined this aspect of America's first century-and-a-half of nation formation. On one side, English settlers "were for the most part loath to join in sexual communion with Native Americans." Yet, "Englishmen clearly found Indians beguiling; native women also had a reputation for being hard-working and faithful as wives."[25]

Smith reports that Englishmen who stayed overnight were presented with "a woman fresh painted red with pocones and oil to be his bedfellow." According to Allen, the well-dressed Powhatan woman of the time—anyone at and above puberty—wore a capacious garment that resembled an apron. It was made of a length of cloth that draped downward from the hips, falling over the crotch to a length of maybe ten inches below the navel. And she adds, "the

---

* This incident is much debated. It is based on Smith's account published seventeen years after it allegedly took place and subsequent to Pocahontas' death.

outfit was sans bodice, a fact that undoubtedly contributed to the Englishmen's view of the woman of the *tsenacommacah*, the largest Powhatan community, as uncivilized... ."[26] Smith described an "antic," or wild fete, in which "thirty young women came naked out of the woods (only covered behind and before with a few green leaves), their bodies all painted." And, after performing, "they solemnly invited Smith to their lodging, but no sooner was he within the house, but all the nymphs tormented him more than ever, with crowding, and pressing, and hanging upon him, most tediously crying, love you not me?"[27]

The sexual temptation of Native women was very threatening to upstanding British settlers, especially those alone in an alien land. Many British feared that such intimacy would bring about "cultural degeneration" among settlers in the colonies, whether in Ireland or the New World. The great fear was that sexual relations with "savages" would lead to the erosion of what made the British "civilized." In response to this fear, the British passed the "Laws Divine, Moral, and Marital" in 1610 that called for the death penalty for any settler who raped an Indian woman or ran away with an Indian.[28]

While colonists "perceived Anglo-Indian unions to be degrading and potentially dangerous," sexual relations appear to have flourished. There appears to be a goodly number of reported incidences of sexual intimacies between settlers and Native people, both in the Chesapeake region and further north. For example, Jacob Young, of Maryland, was charged with marrying and fathering children with a woman of the Susquehanna Nation. The Puritan Thomas Morton, when he took over a plantation in 1626, renamed it the Merry Mount and, according to reports from members of the nearby Plymouth Colony, "set up a maypole, drinking and dancing about in many days together, inviting the indian women for their consorts, dancing and frisking together." However, Godbeer notes a singular story of an early female settler in Northampton County, Virginia, who, according to a local doctor, "defiled herself" in a sexual relation with an Indian male.[29]

Given this cultural environment, how did Pocahontas come to marry John Rolfe? After she saved Smith, Pocahontas became his "spiritual guide" (and Smith was given an Indian name, Nantaquod), making regular visits to Fort James, enjoying the friendship of other settlers and serving as a go-between for the British and Chief Powhatan. During this period, Smith returned to England and was replaced by Thomas Dale as leader of the settlement. Also during this period, Pocahontas married Kuocum, a fellow Powahan, and they had a child.

This story, however, takes a strange turn in 1612 when Pocahontas was apparently abducted by an English settler, Samuel Argall (aka Argyall). She was held in captivity in Jamestown for over a year, during which period she met Rolfe, a 28-year-old widower and tobacco planter. As a condition of her release, she agreed to marry Rolfe. What actually happened between them remains a mystery. What is known is that Pocahontas converted to Christianity and was renamed Lady Rebecca. Her appearance radically changed as she adopted British formal dress and, in 1614, married Rolfe.

To legally marry Pocahontas, however, Rolfe had to secure permission from Dale. In 1614, he formally petitioned to marry, arguing that his intent for union with her was not based on an attraction derived from "the ugly sort, who square all men's actions by the base rule of their own filthiness"; he insisted that his intent was due to true love, "not any hungry appetite, to gorge myself with incontinency." He assured Dale that he was motivated by a higher calling than "the unbridled desire of carnal affection." He argued that their marriage would be a form of spiritual redemption. It would save her from evil: "for the converting to the true knowledge of God and Jesus Christ an unbelieving creature, namely Pocahontas." Finally, he pointed out the alliance would strengthen the political relations between the settlers and the Powhatan people.

A couple of years later, Pocahontas and Rolfe traveled to England in search of both financial support for the Virginia colony and to promote his new commercial product, tobacco. She became, as they say, the toast of the town, feted by all. While in England, she had a son, Thomas, in 1617, and shortly thereafter, while beginning the voyage back to the New World, became ill and died.[30]

Following Pocahontas's death, the inherent tensions between the ever-expanding settlers and the Powhatan broke out into open warfare that lasted from 1622 to 1646. It was a period in which social relations, let alone sexual unions, became more and more difficult to achieve. In the end, the Powhatan's people were decimated and a form of colonization was established that defined the dominant white culture's relations to the Native peoples for the next two centuries.

* * *

The Puritans landed in New England in 1620 and, for the first quarter-century of settlement, occasional accusations of witchcraft were raised, but no one was executed. However, during the following half-century, 1647–1693, over two hundred people were accused of witchcraft and about thirty were executed. Most of these alleged witches were women who came from more than thirty communities in Connecticut, Massachusetts and New Hampshire, including Easthampton, Long Island, now part of New York. Following the notorious Salem trials of 1692–1693, convictions and executions for witchcraft essentially ended.

Puritan notions of sin and punishment have cast a long shadow over the nation's conscience. A century-and-a-half after the trials, Nathaniel Hawthorne recalled the Puritan anxiety over adultery in *The Scarlet Letter* (published in 1850) and, a hundred years later, Arthur Miller invoked the trials in *The Crucible* (published in 1953) to challenge anti-Communist hysteria. Today, charges of Puritan repression are still heard against Evangelical and other religious fundamentalists, especially those holding powerful government offices like former attorney generals John Ashcroft and Alberto Gonzales.[31]

Few remember just how troubled were the lives of the early Puritans. Their settlement was inspired by the desire to civilize the New World, to wrest from the devil both the natural world and the aboriginal people, and thus create New Jerusalem. Yet, they found themselves confronted at every turn by formidable threats, in constant fear of nature's uncertainties and in dread of innumerable battles with hostile Native tribes. The New World was a hostile environment in which to create heaven on earth.

Making matters worse, their attempt to establish New Jerusalem was hampered most by the very fragile humans who were expected to accomplish this religiously inspired mission. Humans were seen as imperfect creatures, scarred for all eternity by original sin yet, given the predetermination that directed all of God's actions, capable of being saved and achieving a state of grace. These troubled beings were subject to a nearly inexhaustible list of sins that fell into two broad categories, sins of character and sins of the flesh. Among the former were pride, anger, envy, malice, lying, discontent, dissatisfaction and self-assertion. Among the latter were seduction, lust, bestiality, masturbation, fornication, adultery, incest, polygamy, sodomy and temptations like carnality, drunkenness and licentiousness. Almost anything could be a sin.[32]

Puritan society permitted sexual relationship only within the context of marriage and only between a man and woman for the purpose of procreation. Everything else was sin. Nevertheless, sex was as much a duty as a delight between people who loved one another. As Godbeer argues, "Puritans were both exuberantly permissive and vehemently restrictive. ... Puritans sought not to repress their sexual instincts but to keep them within ordained borders."[33] He stresses that marital sex was crucial in order to populate New England as well as to prevent illicit, non-marital sex. Unfortunately, this intimate aspect of personal life was undermined by the Puritan belief in original sin, a sin reproduced from generation to generation through this very sexual intimacy.

The Puritans fought mightily against the overpowering threats that were as much external as internal, especially sexual threats. They fashioned, in the words of Godbeer, "a culture of sexual surveillance and regulation" to strictly oversee and control interpersonal relations.[34] First and foremost, this surveillance was intended to prevent premarital sex and pregnancy or what was known as bridal pregnancy. It was not uncommon for neighbors to carefully observe interpersonal encounters taking place in homes or in fields, on roadways or in the woods. No place was considered private, beyond the bounds of community monitoring. This control was only intensified given the close physical proximity under which Puritan settlements existed. The personal information garnered through surveillance provided the basis for many of the reported scandals involving alleged witchcraft.

As judgment for a sinner's bad conduct or warning to one so tempted, the Puritans drew upon a wide assortment of punishments to enforce social control. They ranged from the threat of excommunication, disenfranchisement and banishment, to public shaming and whippings, to selling a convicted person's children into bondage, to branding, cutting off body parts (e.g., an ear) and body mutilation (e.g., disfiguring the nose), and, when all else failed, to hanging and even being pressed under rocks until death. Unfortunately, these threats and punishments did not work.[35]

An insight into early New England sex panic is suggested by Kai Erikson's assessment of fornication convictions based on the court records of Essex County, Massachusetts, between 1636 and 1682. In *Wayward Puritans: A Study in the Sociology of Deviance*, Erikson points out that convictions increased among married couples who delivered their first child too soon after their wedding. During the period of 1651–1655, the fornication conviction rate was 0.78 per 100 people and, a decade later, 1661–1665, the rate had fallen to 0.44 per 100; yet, over the following decade fornication convictions more than doubled, reaching, by 1676–1680, 1.02 per 100. Fornication conviction rates suggest the general pattern of sex offenses during the Puritan era. Erickson links the "bulge" in the crime rate to the Puritan campaign against Quakers, but other factors were surely at work.[36]

John Underhill, for example, was excommunicated for fornication in 1640. Mary Hitchcocke, of New Haven, admitted in 1662 "that her way had been very evil & sinful"; and Jacob Moline, also of New Haven in 1662, was whipped. However, in 1669, Bethia Stanly, of Beverly, Massachusetts, repented her sin and was welcomed back into her congregation.[37] During this period, fornication was neither uncommon, nor a terribly serious offense—and it did not result in capital punishment. This would change three decades later during the witchcraft trails.

Puritans distinguished between a sinner, even one convicted of a sexual offense, and a witch. According to historian Elizabeth Reis, "a witch [was] the most egregious of sinners." She insists: "Those who admitted signing [the devil's pact] crossed the forbidden line between sinner and witch." This act, signing the devil's book with one's own blood, marked forsaking God and aligning with Satan. Equally critical, it was a voluntary act, a personal decision, motivated neither by seduction nor temptation.[38]

The sinner and the witch could engage in the same sexual act, but the meaning for each was fundamentally different. For the sinner, sin was a survivable offense and offered a chance for redemption. This was especially true for male as opposed to female sinners. For the witch, however, there was only hanging and eternal damnation.

In addition to fornication, women accused of witchcraft could also be charged with other sex offenses, including adultery, illegitimacy and, the worst, sex with the devil.

* * *

One of the grandest sex scandals of the early colonial era may never have occurred. Rumor has long persisted that Lord Cornbury (Edward Hyde), Britain's governor-general of New York and New Jersey, opened the New York General Assembly of 1702 in an exquisite, formal gown in the Queen Anne style—a hooped gown with an elaborate headdress and carrying a fan. As has become a popular legend, the governor insisted that he dressed in drag to better represent the Queen, his first cousin. Looking back, Lord Cornbury may well have been the nation's most famous drag queen—if he was a transvestite at all.

Shelley Ross, writing in his popular history, *Fall From Grace*, calls the Cornbury affair one of "the most notorious—and bizarre" tales of "sex, scandal, and corruption in American politics." According to Ross, Cornbury "was a thief, a bigot, a grafter, a drunk, and, strange as it was, a transvestite." An image of Cornbury in drag is immortalized in a painting first exhibited in London in 1867 and now held by the New-York Historical Society. Ross' opinion is shared by other scholars, including George Bancroft, a leading nineteenth century historian. A contemporary scholar, Patricia Bonomi, points out that he "is notorious in the historical literature as a moral profligate, sunk in corruption, and perhaps the worst governor Britain ever imposed on an American colony."[39]

Cornbury served as the colonial general during the 1702–1708 period. In addition to his alleged drag outfit worn at the opening of the 1702 Assembly, he reportedly dressed in drag at his wife's funeral in 1707, deeply upsetting his contemporaries. There is even a story that he was arrested as a prostitute.

However, Bonomi argues in her study, *The Lord Cornbury Scandal*, that there is no direct evidence, legal or otherwise, to substantiate these claims, only four letters from three of Cornbury's political opponents. She insists that "the sight of a royal governor parading about the streets, or even the ramparts of the fort, in female dress would have scandalized friend and foe alike." More so, she points out that at the end of the seventeenth century, colonial America moved aggressively against cross dressing. She notes that during the seventeenth century two men were arrested in New York for appearing in public in women's cloths; in 1696, Massachusetts passed a law against cross dressing; and in 1703, a man named John Smith was arrested in Philadelphia for being "MASKT, or Disguised in women's apparel... ." Thus, one of America's grand sex scandals might well have been no scandal at all.[40]

## References

[1] Richard Godbeer, *Sexual Revolution in Early America* (Baltimore: John Hopkins University Press, 2002), 58-61.

[2] John Murrin, "Things Fearful to Name: Bestiality in Early America," in Elizabeth Reis, ed., *American Sexual Stories* (Malden, MA: Blackwell Publishers, 2001), 29.

[3] Carol F. Karlsen, *The Devil in the Shape of a Woman: Witchcraft in Colonial New England* (New York: Vintage Books, 1989), 22-23; Mather quote in John Demos, *Entertaining Satan: Witchcraft and the Culture of Early New England* (New York: Oxford University Press, 2004), 345-46.

[4] Damos, 174 and 352; Karlsen, 25, 28 and 113.

[5] Kai T. Erikson, *Wayward Puritans: A Study in the Sociology of Deviance* (New York: Macmillian, 1966), 194; Mary Beth Norton, *In the Devil's Snare: The Salem Witchcraft Crisis of 1692* (New York: Knopf, 2002), 137-38; Karlsen, 25-26.

[6] Richard Francis, *Judge Sewall's Apology: A Biography* (New York: Harper, 2005), 147-48.

[7] Karlsen, 23, 60-61, 80, 116, 125-27, 138 and 287; Demos, 75, 89, 90, 186, 189, 249 and 295.

[8] Karlsen, 22; Demos, 71, 74, 89, 271-74 and 284.

[9] Francis, 88.

[10] Elizabeth Reis, "The Devil, the Body, and the Feminine Soul in Puritan New England," *The Journal of American History* (vol. 82, issue 1 [January 1995], 10; Norton, 258 and 291.

[11] Reis, 10; Norton, 164, 165 and 167; Richard Godbeer, *The Devil's Dominion: Magic and Religion in Early New England* (New York: Cambridge University Press, 1992), 113.

[12] Norton, 79, 112-13, 195, 204-07, 210 and 214-15; Karlsen, 75 and 259; Demos, 66.

[13] Reis, 125.

[14] Norton, 44-47, 58, 60 and 74-75; Godbeer, *Devil's*, 201; Karlsen, 107-09.

[15] Reis, 12; Norton, 146-47 and 205; Karlsen, 32, 89-94, 108, 117, 137, 140 and 296; Demos, 74.

[16] Karlsen, 26 and 140; Demos, 179, 183, 189 and 216.

[17] Karlsen, 108-09, 128, 140 and 260; Demos, 21-33 and 85-86.

[18] Martha Hodes, *White Women, Black Men: Illicit Sex in the 19th-Century South* (New Haven: Yale University Press, 1997), 19-22.

[19] Aaron Gullickson, "The Significance of Color Declines: A Re-Analysis of Skin Tone Differentials in Post-Civil Rights America," *Social Forces*, September 2005.

[20] Godbeer, 165-68.

[21] Willie Lee Rose, ed., *A Documentary History of Slavery in North America* (University of Georgia Press, 1976), 20—22.

[22] Paula Gunn Allen, *Pocahontas: Medicine Woman, Spy, Entrepreneur, Diplomat* (New York: HarperCollins), 32; see also, pp. 27-81.

[23] Godbeer, 123.

[24] Allen, 50.

[25] Godbeer, 156 and 163.

[26] Allen, 85.

[27] Smith quote in Allen, 88-89.

[28] Godbeer, 160.

[29] Ibid, 163-64.

[30] Allen, 273-87.

[31] See Tristram Hunt, "A Puritan on the Warpath," *The Observer*, September 1, 2002.

[32] Godbeer, 66-68; Kalsen, 119 and 127-30; Reis, 96.

[33] Godbeer, 55.

[34] Ibid, 228.

[35] Reis, 114; Karlsen, 200; Erickson, 117, 119, 122, 149, 187-88 and 197.

[36] Erikson, 171, 174 and 175-76.

[37] Reis, 129-30.

[38] Ibid, 131-32.

[39] Shelley Ross, *Fall From Grace: Sex, Scandal, and Corruption in American Politics from 1702 to the Present* (New York: Ballantine Books, 1988), 3; Patricia U. Bonomi, *The Lord Cornbury Scandals: The Politics of Reputation in British America* (Chapel Hill, NC: University of North Carolina, 1998), 3.

[40] Bonomi, 141.

# CHAPTER 2. REVOLUTIONARY GENERATION

*that hard-to-be-governed passion of youth*
*hurried me frequently into intrigue with low women that fell my way.*
Benjamin Franklin[1]

Thomas Jefferson is warmly remembered as the principal author of the Declaration of Independence and the most cosmopolitan of the Founding Fathers. In January 1772, he married Martha Wayles Skelton and their marriage lasted until her death a decade later. Martha bore Jefferson seven children, a child every year-and-a-half. Only three survived. Jefferson was much devoted to his wife and resigned from Congress in September 1776 to care for her during her final convalescence. She died four months after giving birth to their last child.

According to Jefferson's house slave, Israel Jefferson, "on her death bed," Martha forced him to pledge never to marry again, fearful that her own biological children would lose their privilege. Jefferson lived for another forty years and kept his promise. This promise may explain the most scandalous aspect of Jefferson's sex life. Jefferson was remarkably passionate and brilliant. However, Joseph Ellis, a leading Jefferson biographer, calls him "a kind of male coquette." Ellis and others point out that he had a proclivity for intimacies with married woman. Whether these relations were more than romantic infatuations remains an open question.[2]

Before he married, Jefferson was infatuated with Betsy Walker, the wife of a close friend, John Walker. The couple was so close that Jefferson was an usher at their wedding. Jefferson's infatuation appears to have lasted from 1768 to 1770, during a period when Walker was away on a business trip. Looking back in 1805, John Walker recounted an incident with Jefferson that disturbed him:

He and his wife went on a visit to Col. Cole a mutual acquaintance and distant neighbor. Mr. Jefferson was there. On the lady's retiring to bed he pretended to be sick, complained of a headache [and] left the gentlemen among whom I was. Instead of going to bed as his sickness authorized a belief he stole into my room where my wife was undressing or in bed.

Walker was so distraught by Jefferson's attempt to seduce his wife that he challenged Jefferson to a duel. In the mud-slinging days of early American politics, Jefferson was denounced as a "scoundrel," a "scourge" and "the outcast of America, without abilities and without virtue."[3]

Jefferson's second affair with a married woman took place while he was America's representative in Paris during the mid-1780s. This was a period when he was deeply depressed over his wife's death. In August 1786, he made the acquaintance of Maria Louisa Catherine Cecilia Hadfield Cosway, the 27-year-old wife of England's leading miniaturist, Richard Cosway. A painting of her depicts, in the words of a contemporary, "a golden-haired, languishing Anglo-Italian, graceful to affection, and highly accomplished, especially in music." Ellis describes her as having a "beguiling blend of hauteur and vulnerability," which besotted America's future president.[4]

Maria Cosway, born in England, was raised in Florence by a cultured family. When they met, Jefferson spent weeks with Maria both alone and in the company of others, including her husband, who seems to have encouraged their relations. Richard Cosway was a slight if not effeminate man who apparently had adulterous affairs with both women and men.[5] Months later, when Maria returned to Paris alone, the two again spent considerable time together. Writing in a now-famous twelve-page love letter to Maria, known as "My Head and My Heart," Jefferson made his feelings quite clear: "Had they [philosophers] ever felt the solid pleasure of one generous spasm of the heart, they would exchange for it all the frigid speculations of their lives… ."[6]

Between 1787 and 1789, while Jefferson was posted to Paris, Sarah (Sally) Hemings, a house slave and "body servant" to Jefferson's youngest daughter, came to live in his household. Thus began a relationship lasting thirty-eight years that remains one of the most scandalous affairs in American history.

Unlike subsequent scandals involving presidents, the Jefferson-Hemings affair is controversial because it was not simply interracial, but involved a master and a slave, a slave who bore her master six offspring and a slave never freed by her master. While still denied by some of Jefferson's decedents, most now accept that Jefferson and Hemings bore six children together and had a deep and long-lasting relationship.* While Martha was Jefferson's true wife, Sally may have been the love of his life.

Jefferson had a contradictory attitude toward African-Americans, whether free or slave. His public writings and private correspondence are filled with disparaging comments and dubious "scientific" claims about black inferiority. Yet, there are innumerable stories of how he treated both slave and free African-Americans with respect and dignity. Nevertheless, among the plantation gentry of the period, a slave master was understood to have certain "property rights" that legitimized sexual access to female slaves, and Jefferson took full advantage of this "privilege" in his relationship with Hemings.

Hemings was born in 1773, the daughter of Elizabeth (Betty) Hemings and a nondocumented father. Apparently her father was John Wayles, Jefferson's father-in-law, making Sally Martha's half-sister. Some argue that she was the daughter of an English sea captain. According to one of Jefferson and Hemings' three sons, Madison, Elizabeth was Wayles' "concubine." Martha inherited Elizabeth Hemings' children upon her father's death.[7]

Hemings accompanied Jefferson's daughter to Paris with her brother, James, when she was about fifteen years old. Madison reports that when Jefferson was returning to America, Sally initially refused to return, as slavery laws did not apply in France and she was a free person. "To induce her to do so," writes Madison, "he promised her extraordinary privileges, and made a solemn pledge

---

* The Thomas Jefferson Foundation issued a report in January 2000 finding high probability that Jefferson was the likely father of Hemings' six children; the Thomas Jefferson Heritage Society released a study in April 2001 attempting to refute the Foundation study by proposing that Jefferson's younger brother, Randolph, was the likely father of Hemings' children. Annette Gordon-Reed's recent biography of the Hemings family, *The Hemingses of Monticello: An American Family* (New York: Norton, 2008), finally puts an end to such denials.

that her children should be freed at the age of twenty-one." She returned pregnant, but lost the child a few days after birth. According to Madison, Hemings subsequently served Jefferson at Monticello as chambermaid, seamstress, nursemaid-companion and, later, lady's maid to his daughters. Both Madison and Israel Jefferson refer to her as "Jefferson's concubine."[8]

Hemings appears to have been a very attractive, poised and appealing woman. When visiting England with Jefferson, John and Abigail Adams found her to be "fond of [Jefferson's] child and appears good natured." Isaac Jefferson reports her to be "mighty near white … very handsome, long straight hair down back." And Jefferson's grandson, Thomas Jefferson Randolph, recalls her as "light colored and decidedly good looking."

Four of her children with Jefferson, three males and one female, survived to adulthood and all appeared white in complexion. Jefferson, fulfilling his promise to Hemings, set them free. Beverly and Harriet married white spouses, while Eston and Madison married "colored women"; Madison's wife was a freed slave. Ironically, Hemings was not freed by Jefferson but given "her time" (a form of unofficial freedom so she could live in Virginia) by his daughter, Martha Randolph.

During the antebellum era, scandalous relations across the race line also took place between a white woman and a black man. This is exemplified in relations involving the noted abolitionist Frederick Douglass. Born Frederick Baily, a slave, in 1818 at Holmes Hill Farm, on Maryland's Eastern Shore, Douglass lived in Baltimore before escaping to freedom in 1838 masquerading as a sailor aboard a northbound train. Arriving in New York, he later wrote, "A new world had opened upon me."

Until his death in 1895, Douglass was America's leading voice for African-American freedom. His autobiography, *Narrative of the Life of Frederick Douglass, an American Slave* (with introductions by America's two leading white abolitionists, William Lloyd Garrison and Wendell Phillips) became a best seller. Douglass initially clashed with Lincoln over his support of the fugitive slave laws and, during the Civil War, his commitment to restoring the Union but not ending slavery. However, all was resolved when Lincoln signed the Emancipation Proclamation ending slavery.

In 1838, only recently escaped from slavery, Douglass married Anna Murray, a free black woman from Baltimore to whom he was engaged and who had helped finance his escape. They were together for the next forty-four years and had five children. Anna Douglass is reported to have been illiterate all her life and suffered from various maladies. She appeared to have shared little of Douglass' intellectual and political interests.

Douglass is rumored to have had a number of affairs with white women. In 1848, the first scandal erupted in Rochester when Julia Griffiths began to serve as Douglass' assistant and became his companion. Rumors intensified because Griffiths lived in the same house with Douglass and his family. In the 1850s, rumors again circulated about still other interracial liaisons, including one involving the daughter of a leading British abolitionist.

However, the most important interracial relation was Douglass' intimacy with Ottilie Assing. Born in Germany in 1819, Assing was a half-Jewish immigrant journalist who, like Karl Marx, was a "'49er," a veteran of the Germany revolution of 1849. She was an outspoken abolitionist who met Douglass in 1856 when researching an article for a German newspaper. Thus began a nearly three-decade relationship with him and his family. She was not only his lover, but also a close political advisor, tutor to his children and translator of his works. When diagnosed with cancer in 1884, Assing committed suicide. Anna Douglass died in 1882 and, after observing the traditional two-year period of grieving, Douglass married Helen Pitts, a white woman twenty years his junior. They were together until his death.[9]

\* \* \*

Few Americans fully appreciate how *revolutionary* the American Revolution really was. While much has been written about the Founding Fathers, little has been said about the insurgent cultural changes that came in its wake. It was a movement that defined the nation over its first century. It was driven by the powerful tension that pitted traditional Christians against those who welcomed social reform. This tension often exploded into sexual scandal.

"The ferment of the Revolution period," argues the historian Milton Rugoff, "resulted in greater social freedom, however temporary." During the two decades following the Revolution, an insurgent sexual ardor spread through all social institutions. "Men wore skin tight pantaloons and displayed their thighs by cutting down the skirt of the coat to narrow tails," notes Rugoff. "Women abandoned corsets and bared their arms, shoulders and parts of their breasts."[10]

Abigail Adams' complaint about the scandalous goings-on in the 1790s in the nation's capital, Philadelphia, offers insight into the new cultural climate. Alarmed by more risqué women's fashions and people's deportment at late-night dances, parties and other galas, Adams fretted:

> The style of dress ... is really an outrage upon all decency. ...Most [ladies] wear their clothes too scant upon the body and too full upon the bosom for my fancy. Not content with the show which nature bestows, they borrow from art and literally look like nursing mothers.[11]

The concern of this upright Calvinist symbolized the threat to traditional propriety felt by many in early America.

It seems nearly impossible today to imagine what the quality of life was like during the decades immediately following the Revolution. For most people, independence had been long in coming. After the Revolution, many were filled with a boldness drawn as much from their own revolution as that of the French that took place in 1789. It fueled a palatable sense of optimism for many colonists, except African slaves and Native people.

Many complained that young people no longer listened to their parents, that church authority was being undermined by secular society and the intimacy of rural and small-town life was giving way to the more promiscuous anonymity of city life. Small-town institutions of social control were replaced by the city's opportunities for illicit conduct. For many, an American sexual revolution was underway.

The most profound freedom the Revolution ushered in was that of the new man. In the words of historian Howard Chudacoff, "notions of Lockean individualism, which gave precedence to the autonomous being in relation to external institutions such as the state, laws, the economy, replaced the corporate communalism that characterized colonial society."[12] A new person, a new man, was taking shape.

But his "new" man was, in many ways, not unlike the oldest of men, driven by many of the deepest desires that date from the first settlement of the colonies. These desires often found expression in illicit sexual relations. Often, a too-intimate friendship between a man and a woman was grounds for suspicion, suggesting more scandalous goings-on. This suspicion fell upon America's first president, George Washington.

Mystery surrounds Washington's sexuality. One of his biographers, James Thomas Flexner, paints this portrait: Washington was "... probably sterile [and] is said to have been a eunuch, even a woman in disguise; [yet] he is said to have been the 'stallion of the Potomac.'"[13]

Washington and his older half-brother, Lawrence, were very close to the family of William Fairfax, a nobleman with an impressive estate, Belvoir, in Mount Vernon, Virginia. The Fairfax clan essentially adopted George and his brother. They were so close that Lawrence married Fairfax's daughter, Anne, and George was a fast friend of Fairfax's son, George William.

George, for his part, married the 26-year-old widow, Martha Dandridge Curtis, on Twelfth Night, January 12, 1759, a festive holiday. While George and Martha never had children, they did raise her two children from her previous marriage. The fortune she inherited (including slaves) was valued at over one hundred thousand dollars, a considerable amount for the time. This inheritance permitted Washington to both pursue the life of a gentleman soldier and politician, and to acquire significant land holdings in the wilderness territories.

The intimacy between Washington and George William Fairfax's wife, Sally, is the subject of much speculation. Sally was the daughter of Colonel Wilson Cray, one of Virginia's wealthiest men. He owned one of the grand family estates, Ceelys on the James, and was a member of the colony's House of Burgesses. Sally, his eldest daughter, was a well educated, handsome, strong willed and engaging woman.

Mrs. Fairfax seems to have been the love of Washington's life. As Martha Washington's biographer, Helen Bryan, notes, in 1758, while engaged to Martha, Washington's flirtatious relations with Fairfax "crystallized into a full-blown love affair."[14] Fairfax spent many days attending to Washington when he was bedridden with dysentery for six months. However, as his wedding approached, Washington essentially broke off with her, writing:

> You have drawn me, dear madam, or rather I have drawn myself, into an honest confession of a simple Fact—misconstrue not my meaning—doubt it not, nor expose it—The world has no business to know the object of my Love—declared in this manner to you— when I want to conceal.

Bryan believes that this letter suggests "a strong hint that something had been going on between them." Nevertheless, once married, Washington and Mrs. Fairfax remained on friendly terms.[15]

Various rumors circulated about the deep affection between Washington and Mrs. Fairfax. Bryan argues that Sally and her husband could not conceive a child and "they may have hoped that George [Washington] would father a child for them and save the Fairfax title for George William." However, no pregnancy resulted from either the Fairfax or the Washington marriages.[16]

Washington's interest in Mrs. Fairfax was not the only alleged affair that haunts his reputation. During the war, many rumors, often attributed to British propaganda, circulated suggesting that he engaged in a number of illicit relations. One rumor alleged that he had a mistress, Mary Gibbons, a New Jersey woman. Another claimed that he kept a corporal's wife as a mistress at his camp. Still another alleged that he had an adulterous liaison with Lucy Posey, wife of John Posey, a neighbor from Mount Vernon, and fathered her son, Thomas Posey. Some said the boy bore a striking resemblance to Washington. Finally, there was the persistent rumor that Washington fathered a son, West Ford, with Venus Ford, a house slave at his brother's plantation, Bushfield.[17]

Washington was not the only Founding Father who courted scandal. Much has been made of Benjamin Franklin's popularity both in London and Paris during the Revolution. In London, he seems to have had an ongoing affair with his landlady, Margaret Stevenson, and possibly with her 18-year-old daughter, Mary (Polly), as well.

According to Walter Isaacson's recent biography, "[a]mong his reputation was that of a legendary and lecherous old lover who had many mistresses among the ladies in Paris." Franklin's intrigues with Madams Brillon de Jouy and Anne-Catherine Helvért have been much commented upon. The Parisian salon scene shocked the Adams, in particular Franklin's conduct. Abigail was also offended by Madame Helvért, the widow of a very rich financier and philosopher, who hosted a famous salon:

> ... she carried on the chief of the conversation at dinner, frequently locking her hand into the Doctor's [Franklin], and sometime spreading her arms of both the gentlemen's chairs, then throwing her arms carelessly upon the Doctor's neck. ... I was highly disgusted, and never wish for an acquaintance with ladies of this caste.

Isaacson insists that these relations were not sexual, "only of his mind and soul."[18] Sure.

A man of deep passion and Quaker beliefs, Franklin took Deborah Read, an abandoned wife, as his common-law wife in 1730. Pennsylvania did not permit women to petition for divorce because of abandonment. Thus, the Franklins never formalized their marriage. Early in their marriage, Franklin brought home an illegitimate son, William, whom he had fathered with another woman for Deborah to raise. In 1755, when he was forty-nine years, Franklin had a well-publicized affair with Katherine Ray, then twenty-four. Franklin is fondly remembered as the most libertine of the Founding Fathers.[19]

The adulterous affair and blackmail scheme involving Alexander Hamilton makes Bill Clinton's indiscretions with Monica Lewinsky seem banal. The sexual dalliances of Clinton and Hamilton were both exploited for partisan political ends, becoming national scandals. However, where Clinton's intimacies with Lewinsky, Gennifer Flowers and Juanita Broaddrick bespeaks a sexuality of excess, Hamilton's was what his biographer, Ron Chernow, calls "sexual obsession."

And obsession it was, for nothing else explains Hamilton's adulterous fall from grace. While living in Philadelphia with his wife and children, Hamilton was approached by a young damsel in distress. She claimed to be a New Yorker, recently relocated to the nation's capital and was so seductive that Hamilton agreed to visit her at her home that evening. After having sex, he left money for her. Thus began a sexual liaison that lasted over two years, ending in a blackmail scheme that compromised America's Secretary of the Treasury. He was, as Chernow states, "conned by a pair of lowlife tricksters," Maria and James Reynolds.[20]

\* \* \*

Nation formation from the Revolution to the Civil War can be divided into two phases. The first, 1787 to 1819, was witness to post-revolutionary exuberance, driven as much by a spirit of national liberation as by the rapid growth of cities and the transition to a money economy. This period witnessed Eli Whitney's introduction of the cotton engine or "gin" and the "America System" of production based on the division of labor, interchangeable parts and use of unskilled labor. It saw the Colt Works apply the system to the manufacturing of muskets, not only transforming rifle production, but foreshadowing by a century Henry Ford's industrial revolution.[21]

The second phase, 1820 to 1860, saw the erosion of the earlier exuberance and its replacement with a mounting sense of trepidation. Early optimism began to erode in the wake of the British-imposed embargo of 1806–1807, the resulting War of 1812 and the nation's first depression, the Panic of 1819. The panic resulted from America's competitive, dual currency system (i.e., federal and various state forms of legal tender) and the questionable practices of the Second Bank. It was a sobering experience for a young nation.[22]

Accompanying this economic and political freefall, a sense of disillusionment spread throughout the country. It concerned the central questions of what it meant to be an American: Would individual freedom be applied equally to all of the nation's peoples, be they property owners, property-less white adult males or females, African free-people and slaves or Native people? The nation was changing; its future was in question.

As the earlier exuberance began to fade, a new religious passion spread through the land, that of a powerful evangelical movement. Often called the Second Awakening or the Great Revival, it sought the spiritual renewal of American morality. It began in upstate New York and spread rapidly throughout the country, especially in the rural west. It replaced the deism of the Founding Fathers with fundamentalist fervor as the nation's religious ethos. Its spirit of renewal contributed to the rise of the temperance movement in the 1820s, the abolitionist movement of the thirties, the feminist movement of the forties and the communitarian and "free-love" movements that sprung up throughout the era.

Amidst this widespread social upheaval, America saw the flowering of the first free-love movement and the establishing of a remarkable number of short-lived free-love communities. Robert Owen and Frances ("Fanny") Wright were two of its earliest champions. Others include Stephen Pearl Andrews, an anarchist who formed Modern Times, on Long Island, NY, and Berlin Heights, near Cleveland, OH; Mary Gove Nichols and Thomas Low Nichols, who founded Memnonia, near Yellow Springs, OH; and John Noyes, the founder of the Oneida community in upstate New York. A number of utopian religious sects emerged that, as historians John D'Emilion and Estelle Freedman note, "established a distinctive alternative to the norm of monogamous, marital sexuality. Shakers chose celibacy; Mormons practiced polygamy[;] and the follows of John Humphrey Noyes at the Oneida community engaged in a 'complex marriage.'"[23]

\* \* \*

Now forgotten, Frances Wright was the most scandalous woman in America during the antebellum era. Born in Scotland in 1795, she was a respected author, on a first-name basis with John Stuart Mill, Jeremy Bentham and Mary Wollstonecraft Shelley. She was a confidante of the Marquis de Lafayette, who scandalized his family by his open infatuation with her (calling her fondly, "my dear Fanny"), and accompanied him on part of his travels in America. Looking back at his youth, Walt Whitman fondly recalled seeing Wright: "I never felt so glowingly toward any other woman. ... She possessed herself of me body and soul."[24]

Wright lived in America for six years, 1825 to 1831, and had a series of profound adventures. She met and regularly corresponded with Thomas Jefferson, strongly challenging him over his acceptance of slavery. She joined utopian socialist Robert Owen's "cooperative village" at New Harmony, IN, fiercely opposing him over slavery. Breaking with Owen, she joined his son, Robert Dale Owen, and her sister, Camilla, to found Nashoba, the Chickasaw word that means Wolf River, a radical utopian community in rural Tennessee.

Wright was a sought-after speaker, one of only a few public women in early-nineteenth century America. She was a true radical, championing abolition, advocating free love and assailing religion. She took an unequivocal stand for the equality of the sexes:

> No woman can forfeit her individual rights or independent existence, and not assert over her any right or power whatsoever, beyond what she may exercise over her free and voluntary affections; nor, on the other hand, may any woman assert claims to the society or peculiar protection of any individual of the other sex, beyond what mutual inclination dictates and sanctions.[25]

Wright was so prominent that she was invited to give Cincinnati's 1828 July Fourth keynote address, thus credited with being one of the first woman to give a major public address in America.

With the help of Andrew Jackson, Wright purchased nearly one thousand acres in rural western Tennessee in 1826 in order to establish a utopian community. At that time, Memphis, the largest nearby settlement, was a tiny fur-trading outpost with only, as she reports, "a dozen log cabins." At Nashoba, she attempted to create a community that would not merely challenge deep-seated racial practices and beliefs and do so south of the Mason-Dixon line, but also challenge fundamental Christian values and sexual mores. In addition, she sought to make it a financially self-sufficient operation.

Nashoba was a mixed community of women and men, married and unmarried, black and white, free and slave, adult and child. It was an historically unprecedented attempt to remake civil society. It was doomed to failure by the forces of its inherent and irreconcilable contradictions as well as by the material conditions under which it operated. From all accounts, it seemed to have been a miserable place, with only a handful of poorly constructed and furnished houses, a well for water and ill-tended gardens and domesticated animals.

At Nashoba, on June 16, 1827, James Richardson and Josephine Lolotte declared themselves married and began to live together. Their arrangement is important now, nearly two centuries later, because Lolotte was a free black woman and Richardson a free white man. Equally important, because Nashoba was a radical experiment in terms of interracial relations and free love, in living together Richardson and Lolotte declared not only their love and sexual desire for one another, but entered into a binding commitment outside the sanctity of church and state.

Richardson was an immigrant Scotsman who was Nashoba's storekeeper, doctor and operations overseer. Lolotte was the daughter of Mam'selle Lolotte (Larieu), a free woman of color from New Orleans who oversaw the raising of the children. Josephine is described as "a young and attractive girl of marriageable age," "a young quadroon girl." One historian noted that they were bound to each other by a "natural affinity."[26]

The community's dependence on slavery was its deepest contradiction. The slaves were expected to generate profit, but were accused of being poor laborers. All slaves were under Richardson's supervision. He sent an article about the community to Benjamin Lundy, a leading abolitionist and publisher of the influential *Genius of Universal Emancipation*; Wright was away and surely would have not sent it. Lundy published the article that created a firestorm within the abolitionist movement. While the poor treatment of slaves was denounced (especially flogging) and the failure to have locks on women's rooms assailed, it was the explicit acceptance of free love between blacks and whites that most scandalized abolitionists.

Wright and her brave compatriots had crossed the race line, the Grand Canyon of sexual intimacy, confronting the deepest fears, and fantasies, of the American experience. As two biographers would later declare, the Lolotte and Richardson arrangement was "[a] free union of two persons without marriage! Sexual relations between a white man and a colored woman, on exactly the same terms of free choice and mutual inclination which might be expected among whites."[27]

Nashoba failed in 1828 and was transformed into a society of small capitalists. In 1830, Wright freed Nashoba's slaves in Haiti.[28] After Nashoba, she moved with Dale Owen to New York and opened the Hall of Science, where hundreds regularly attended their lectures (including the impressionable Whitman) and where, according to one historian, "the first books of reform [female] physiology and birth control were openly distributed." So threatening was her message that she was denounced as the "Priestess of Beelzebub" and the "Red Harlot of Infidelity."[29]

\* \* \*

The alleged homosexuality of James Buchanan and Abraham Lincoln is a more ambiguous subject, since our twenty-first century notions of sexuality are not applicable to nineteenth century same-sex intimacies. Then, it was not uncommon for same-sex strangers to share a bed for a night when staying at a small-town inn. "Bundling" (people sharing a bed at a rural household) was common among strangers traveling in the wilderness or to isolated settlements. However, as in the cases of Buchanan and Lincoln, it was uncommon for male (or female) acquaintances of financial means to share an urban home.

Buchanan, nicknamed "Old Buck," was America's fifteenth and most "out" president. He lived in Washington, DC, for many years with William Rufus King, an Alabama senator. The two men were considered inseparable and were the object of much mockery. Jackson dubbed King "Miss Nancy" and Aaron Brown, a prominent Democrat, wrote to Mrs. James K. Polk, referring to him as Buchanan's "better half," "his wife" and "Aunt Fancy ... rigged out in her best clothes."

In 1844, when King was minister to France, Buchanan wrote a mutual friend, Mrs. James Roosevelt:

> I am now 'solitary and alone,' having no companion in the house with me. I have gone a wooing to several gentlemen, but have not succeeded with any one of them. I feel that it is not good for man to be alone; and should not be astonished to find myself married to some old maid who can nurse me when I am sick, provide good dinners for me when I am well, and not expect from me any very ardent or romantic affection.

Their "friendship" ended when King died in 1853.[30]

Some Buchanan scholars look askance at allegations about his homosexuality. "The best speculation about the sexuality of the non-shaven Buchanan, who in his portraits has eunuch like, endomorphic features of body and face as the low hairline characteristic of asexual men with low levels of testosterone," insists Jean Baker, "is that he had little interest in sex."[31] Sure.

Questions about Abraham Lincoln's sexuality have been raised at various times. Most recently, C.A. Tripp questions in his book, *The Intimate World of Abraham Lincoln*, whether Lincoln was gay. A former Kinsey researcher and author of *The Homosexual Matrix*, Tripp's book renews the argument hinted at by Carl Sandburg in his famous 1926 biography. Sandburg, using code words of the day for homosexuality, suggested something more about Lincoln, "a streak of lavender and soft spots as May violets."[32]

There are numerous stories of Lincoln as a circuit lawyer sleeping in a shared bed at small inns as he made his away around Illinois. Tripp suggests that Lincoln may have had sexual liaisons with an early acquaintance, A.Y. Ellis, and his law partner, Henry C. Whitney, as well as with Capt. David V. Derickson, a soldier attached to the Pennsylvania regiment guarding Mary Lincoln. The chief evidence Tripp presents is Lincoln's relationship with Joshua Speed, a 22-year-old shopkeeper. Lincoln arrived in Springfield, IL, in 1837 as a 28-year-old lawyer with high hopes and little money. He sought accommodations at Speed's general store and Speed invited him to share his bed upstairs. They lived together, in the same household, for the next four years.[33] *

* * *

The sex scandals that took place in the decades between the Revolution and Civil War involved many of the sins that obsessed the Colonial era—and still concern many today. Premarital liaisons, adultery, illegitimate children, interracial encounters, obscenity and sodomy challenge deeply-felt Christian moral beliefs. The scandals involving Washington, Franklin, Hamilton, Jefferson, Douglass, Wright and Buchanan were but the tip of a sizeable iceberg of forbidden sex that was remaking America.

This iceberg of scandal included still other social worthies. Andrew Jackson, known to all as "Old Hickory" and celebrated for his victory over the British in the Battle of New Orleans during the War of 1812, fell in love with Rachel Robards, a married woman separated

---

* It should be noted that most leading Lincoln scholars, particularly David Herbert Donald in *We Are Lincoln Men* (New York: Simon and Schuster, 2003), assail the Tripp thesis.

from her husband. Described as a pipe-smoking, gun-toting frontier woman, Robards married Jackson before her divorce was finalized, thus making her technically a bigamist—and the subject of much back-biting from proper society ladies.[34]

Then there was Richard Johnson, vice president under Martin Van Buren, who fathered two children with a slave, Julia Chinn. Unlike Jefferson and many other slave owners, he acknowledged his common-law marriage to Chinn and accepted their two daughters as his own children. His openness about a relationship many considered scandalous, if not immoral, cost him the 1829 Kentucky Senate race.[35]

Scandals also involved celebrities, particularly America's first grand sex star, Lola Montez. Born Eliza Rosanna Gilbert in Ireland, Montez was one of Europe's most celebrated courtesans. She had a scandalous affair with Franz Listz and was the mistress of Ludwig I of Bavaria. During her first visit to America between 1851 to 1853, her notorious reputation, explicit sex appeal, provocative dance and theatrical performances were celebrated by the penny press whereever she traveled. She set the standard for subsequent celebrity scandals.[36]

America was a raucous nation during the century following the Revolution. In the post-revolution decades, Philadelphia and other cities fostered urban life distinguished by a "genuine libertine atmosphere." Walking city streets, especially after dark, one could pass innumerable taverns and brothels or "bawdy houses," get drunk on plentiful and cheap corn liquor, and meet numerous "ladies of pleasure." This libertine culture was fostered by three conditions of emerging modernity: social anonymity, a decline in church-based social control and an increase in wage labor which put money in people's pockets.

One unintended consequence of the new urban culture was the significant increase in casual sex, including premarital relations, adulterous liaisons, commercial exchanges and homoerotic intimacies. Many of these encounters became major political scandals, while others remained local affairs or private matters. Cities allowed both men and women to play out their wilder desires. "Insistence by city-dwellers that they should be 'free and independent' to establish and dissolve marital relations in whatever manner suited them," notes the historian Richard Godbeer, "was doubtless encouraged by the spirit of the revolutionary period."[37]

America's new "freedoms" came with a risky downside. It fostered innumerable anonymous sexual encounters, many of them involving sexual abuse and rape. It also led to many premarital pregnancies that often ended in common-law marriages or abandonments. Unfortunately, because many women had little else to sell but their bodies, there was an increase in female commercial sex. With the increase in casual sex and prostitution, there was a corresponding increase in out-of-wedlock births and venereal disease. While some primitive contraceptives were available, they often proved ineffective, too expensive or unavailable for most people. Sex was not free.

## References

[1] Benjamin Franklin, *The Autobiography of Benjamin Franklin* (Chicago: R.R. Donnelly, 1915), 103.

[2] Joseph J. Ellis, *American Sphinx: The Character of Thomas Jefferson* (New York: Knopf, 2005), 193.

[3] Walker quote in Shelly Ross, *Fall From Grace: Sex, Scandal, and Corruption in American Politics from 1702 to the Present* (New York: Ballantine Books, 1988), 33-34.

[4] Ellis, 93.

[5] Claude G. Bowers, *The Young Jefferson: 1743-1789* (Boston: Houghton Mifflin, 1945), 447.

[6] Jefferson quote in Ellis, 95.

[7] Annette Gordon-Reed, *Thomas Jefferson and Sally Hemings: An American Controversy* (Charlottesville, VA: University of Virginia Press, 1997), 245-46.

[8] Gordon-Reed, 246; Madison quote in Gordon-Reed, 246; Jefferson quote in Gordon-Reed, 252.

[9] William S. McFeely, *Frederick Douglass* (New York: Norton, 1991), 183-86 and 310-22.

[10] Milton Rugoff, *Prudery and Passion* (New York: G.P. Putnam's Sons, 1971), 27-28 and 104.

[11] Adams quote in Ron Chernow, *Alexander Hamilton* (New York: Penguin Press, 2004), 362-63.

[12] Ibid, 27.

[13] James Thomas Flexner, *Washington: The Indispensable Man* (Boston: Little Brown, 1974), 367.

[14] Helen Bryan, *Martha Washington: First Lady of Liberty* (New York: John Wiley, 2002), 112.

[15] Washington quote in Bryan, 115; Ibid, 128.

[16] Ibid, 112.

[17] Ibid, 113, 272-73 and 305-06.

[18] Walter Isaacson, *Benjamin Franklin: An American Life* (New York: Simon & Schuster, 2003), 356; Adams quote in Isaacson, 365.

[19] Ross, 7-10; Richard Godbeer, *Sexual Revolution in Early America* (Baltimore: Johns Hopkins University Press, 2002), 310.

[20] Chernow, 362-66.

[21] Edward C. Kirkland, *A History of American Economic Life* (New York: Appleton-Century-Croft, 1969), 218-19; Siegfried Giedion, *Mechanization Takes Command: A Contribution to Anonymous History* (New York: Norton, 1969), 48-49.

[22] Margaret Myers, *A Financial History of the United States* (New York: Columbia University Press, 1970), 84-98; David Reynolds, *Walt Whitman's America: A Cultural Biography* (New York: Knopf, 1995), 54.

[23] John D'Emilio and Estelle B. Freedmam, *Intimate Matters: A History of Sexuality in America* (New York: Harper & Row, 1988), 113-16.

[24] Whitman quote in Reynolds, 36.

[25] Wright quote in John C. Spurlock, *Free Love: Marriage and Middle-Class Radicalism in America, 1825-1860* (New York: New York University Press, 1988), 50.

[26] A.J.G. Perkins and Theresa Wolfson, *Frances Wright: Free Enquirer—The Study of a Temperament* (New York: Harper & Brothers, 1939), 166 and 170.

[27] Ibid, 169.

[28] Celia Morris Eckhardt, *Fanny Wright - Rebel in America* (Cambridge: Harvard University Press, 1984), 164; Spurlock, 40.

[29] Perkins and Wolfson, 208; Helen Lefkowitz Horowtiz, *Rereading Sex: Battles over Sexual Knowledge and Suppression in Nineteenth-Century America* (New York: Knopf, 2002), 45.

[30] George Ticknor Curtis, *The Life of James Buchanan: Fifteenth President of the United States* (New York: Harper Brothers, 1883), 519.

[31] Jean H. Baker, *James Buchanan* (New York: Times Books, 2004), 26.

[32] Baker quote in C.A. Tripp, *The Intimate World of Abraham Lincoln* (New York: Free Press, 2005), xi.

[33] Tripp, 125-61.

[34] H.W. Brands, *Andrew Jackson: His Life and Times* (New York: Doubleday, 2005), 62-65 and 401.

[35] Ross, 64-70.

[36] Bruce Seymour, *Lola Montez: A Life* (New Haven: Yale University Press, 1996), 285-91.

[37] Godbeer, 313.

# CHAPTER 3. MAKING OF MODERN AMERICA

*Beneath this face that appears so impassive hell's tides continually run,*
*Lust and wickedness are acceptable to me,*
*I walk with delinquents with passionate love.*
*I feel I am of them—I belong to those convicts and prostitutes*
*And henceforth I will not deny them—for how can I deny myself.*
Walt Whitman[1]

On December 16, 1896, a most scandalous event took place in New York and involved one of the nation's first sex stars, "Little Egypt." An Algerian, born Ashea Waba and living in New York as "Mrs. Harper," Little Egypt was to be the featured female performer at a very special "bachelor" dinner party. Things got out of hand, so what actually took place remains a mystery. Little Egypt had earned a scandalous reputation performing at the 1893 Chicago Exposition. She performed with Fatima (Fahreda Mahzar) and other women with stage names like Houri, Husaria, Farida and Maryeta, and represented the erotic fantasy of all that was foreign. She was so enticing that she helped launch the new movie industry, becoming W.K.L. Dickson's "first Mutoscope hit." She was professionally represented by no less a legendary theatrical figure than Oscar Hammerstein I.*

On this particular evening, Herbert Barnum Seeley, a well-to-do nephew of the legendary P.T. Barnum, hosted an intimate get-together for his brother, Clinton. The twenty gentlemen who attended wore their finest formal wear. The evening's entertainment highlight was to be a series of performances by very attractive female performance artists, featuring Little Egypt. In keeping with the customs of the day among upper-class male partygoers, these performers were subject to the male gaze and catcalls as well as lascivious touching. As Seeley later explained to the police, Little Egypt "just wiggled a bit, this way and that, and it was uninteresting, as they had all seen this sort of thing before. There were cries of 'Take it off!' and so forth." When the police arrived, with the press in tow, the female performers—naked but for their overcoats—were ushered out a back door.[2]

Modern urban life is raw. During the momentous decades between the end of the Civil War to the end of World War I, the city became a battleground over cultural values. Urban life was marked by an experience of ever-intensifying sights and sounds and smells, touches and terrors. It embodied a rawness fueled by the overcrowding of congested, clamorous neighborhoods. It was exaggerated by the mixing of a rapidly diversifying population comprised of American whites migrating from rural and small-town backgrounds, former African-American slaves migrating from the South and an influx of immigrants from Europe, Asia and Latin America. Urban dwellers encountered one another on congested streets, in tenement buildings, at workplaces, in hectic stores, at crowded amusement parks and throbbing dance halls, dark movie theatres and jammed subway cars. This intensified intimacy reverberated in the increasingly mechanized forms of labor, be it in manufacturing or the service sectors, the leading domains of male and female wage labor. This rawness defined the existence of modern Americans. This was no truer than at night, or for those caught up in a scandal.

The city was a setting in which the forces of moral rectitude battled to preserve what they believed to be Christian virtue. Led by Anthony Comstock, a new generation of American Puritans fought against prostitution and "white slavery," obscene literature and birth control, race mixing, homosexuality and alcohol consumption. Their efforts found expression in the Comstock laws banning obscene materials and the Mann Act barring interstate sexual commerce. They culminated in the passage of the Nineteenth Amendment prohibiting the manufacture, distribution, sale and consumption of alcohol. Theirs was a heroic effort that, like the recent culture wars, proved an historic failure.

---

* Thomas Edison featured Fatima in one of his early peep shows. [Ian Christie, *The Last Machine: Early Cinema and the Birth of the Modern World* (London: British Film Institute, 1994), 73.]

During this era, cities were bustling, especially at night when illicit sexual life flourished. One night in New York in 1904 on a nondescript block on Thirty-third Street between First and Second Avenue, sex was alive. Manhattan merged with Brooklyn in 1898, Gotham now claimed nearly three-and-one-half million inhabitants and was America's first modern metropolis. That night, three hundred men, many well-dressed and sporting the latest fashions, crowded into the dimly-lit back room of the Tecumseh Hall & Hotel, a shabby, second-rate establishment.

Their collective gaze was focused on a tiny, darkened stage where live sex performances were taking place. This show was "between a black man and a white woman, between two women, and between a woman and a man in women's clothes." Salacious catcalls likely rang out; hushed, heavy breathing may have underscored the room's mounting tension. A few spectators were probably discreetly holding their erect sex organs; others may have exposed themselves and were aggressively bringing themselves to orgasmic relief. However overcrowded and overheated, drink abounded as did the mixed scents of tobacco smoke and the unmistakable excitement of men engaged in what was considered a scandalous sexual experience.

Located on a street bound by small warehouses and row houses, the Tecumseh saloon traditionally catered to union meetings and similar social events. But tonight it hosts a rather more entertaining performance. The men in attendance were lured, most likely, to the Tecumseh through discreetly whispered word-of-mouth enticements and calling cards placed at select saloons, dance halls and hotels catering to prostitutes. These cathouses were mostly located in the "Tenderloin" of the West twenties and thirties, in what was popularly known as "Satan's Circus." Each man in the audience paid $2.50 to get in—a not insignificant sum for the day, about $55 in today's money. Looking back, one can only wonder if they got their money's worth?[3]

Additional late-night temptation could be found on New York's Broadway, known as the Gay White Way. It was, recalls Lloyd Morris, "… a city in itself, the domain of a society that flourishes through the night and dissolves at dawn." "Mingling with the crowds that surged up and down Broadway under the garish lights," he adds, "you saw streetwalkers and confidence men; 'guns,' or thieves; 'dips,' or pickpockets; 'moll-buzzers' who rifled women's handbags; pan-handlers, dope-fiends, male prostitutes; detectives who the under-world called 'fly-cops' or 'elbows.'"[4] Sixth Avenue, between Four-teenth Street and Thirty-fourth Street, was known as "Ladies Mile" during the day and became, at night, the "whore's promenade." One block further west, Seventh Avenue was home to black prostitutes and popularly known as "African Broadway." For many, the modern metropolis was defined by sexual excitement. New York had become Sodom on the Hudson.[5]

A different version of the New York story was being played out in cities throughout the country. In New Orleans, the most cosmo-politan of southern cities, a regular in the know or a visitor with the right contacts could attend the private parties hosted by Emma Johnson, one of the city's most renowned prostitutes, madams and sexual performance artists. Described as "long, rangy," Johnson was, according to one of her biographers, "probably the most wan-ton of Storyville's sinners."* She was a lesbian, "... [who] exercised a strange power over many of her sex and took pride in the fact... ."

Johnson was marked as "savage and full of hate ... [who] ma[de] up for her lack of beauty with fierce energy and a daredevil willing-ness to engage in any form of erotic misconduct the mind of man or woman could dream up." Equally compelling, she "care[d] nothing for life or human emotions, a hard, masculine type who was possi-bly the closest approach to pure evil the Crescent City ever harbored, sadistic and unprincipled, this virago was selling children of both sexes into slavery years before Storyville came into being."

Johnson achieved her legendary status by "offering unbelievably lewd 'shows' every night in her notorious studio on Basin Street... ." As early as the 1880s when she lived on Gasquet Street, she put on private productions in which she starred. "Wealthy men of the town, not in the least inclined to partake of her favors," notes historian Al Rose, "proved eager to spend their money with her for laughs, paying her more and more just to find out how depraved she could be."[6]

---

* Storyville, New Orleans's legendary red-light district, was a regulated zone of legal prostitution, drinking and gambling that existed from 1898 to 1917.

Perhaps it was the very depravity, *scandalousness*, of her performances that allowed Emma Johnson to escape the common fate that marked the lives of all too many Storyville sex workers. Each "inhabitant would stand in the doorway in what she considered her most fetching attitude and hope to entice customers by word, deed, gesture, attire (or lack of it), or any combination of these... ." At Basin and Iberville Streets, in the heart of Storyville, crib girls could earn a dollar a "trick." In less desirable locations, further down Iberville, for example, the price could drop to a dime. In the French Quarter, by the 1910s, "[l]ittle cabarets sprang up in storefronts or in the front rooms of buildings; the lewder programs, like the 'freak shows,' kinky displays of eroticism, were relegated to the back rooms."[7]

* * *

America was a divided nation following the Civil War. In the North, prosperity reigned. Factories and farms boomed during the war, fueled by the needs of war production and the simple fact that the war took place principally in the South. It was an era that can be divided into three segments: First, the immediate post-war period of Reconstruction that lasted until 1877; second, the period Samuel Clements (Mark Twain) dubbed the "Gilded Age" which lasted until the Panic of 1893; and third, the Progressive era which culminated in World War I. It witnessed America's great industrial development, marked by the explosive growth of the continental railroads, the building of huge iron and steel mills, the commercialization of oil and the adoption of a vast factory system of production. It was, on the one hand, the triumph of "robber barons" like John D. Rockefeller and Andrew Carnegie, and, on the other, great class polarization leading to major social upheavals like the Haymarket Riot of 1886 and the Pullman Strike of 1894.

The South, however, was a different story. Its cities were in shambles, factories destroyed and plantations lay in waste. It faced a formal period of Union occupation, Reconstruction, and recovery dragging on well into the twentieth century. It experienced decades of stunted economic growth and regressive social development. Returning defeated Confederate soldiers were adrift, often unable to care for themselves or their families. Former slaves were ostensibly free, but confronted historically unprecedented challenges, including Jim Crow racism, as they navigated the challenges of the wage-labor system.

The period between 1865 and 1919 was a tumultuous era in American history. It witnessed the final restructuring of the nation from a still predominately homogeneous white rural and small-town agricultural and manufacturing country (with freed African-American slaves in the South) to a heterogeneous, urban industrial nation with aspirations for worldwide influence. It witnessed an end to the long "Indian" wars, the final Anglo-European conquest of North America. Equally fundamental, it witnessed the restructuring of the American character, especially notions of self-worth and experiences of sexuality.

For us, a century later, it seems almost impossible to imagine just how raucous and over-powering this new America was becoming. The modern American metropolis is, first and foremost, an unprecedented sensuous experience. It was an experience made vivid with the introduction of electricity, the underlying, enabling technology of the modern age.

Social differences further intensified the experience of modern urban life. The most recent city dwellers came from small towns where everything was similar and certain; they entered a new culture in which nearly everything was different and uncertain. Difference was at once threatening and inviting, and was present at the workplace, in commercial establishments and leisure activities as well as in intimate human encounters, particularly sexual ones. Personal sexual practice was being intensified and, with it, the nation's sexual culture. As scholars acknowledged, "More and more of life, it seemed, was intent on keeping Americans in a state of constant sexual excitement."[8]

* * *

Not unlike today, the decades between the Civil War and World War I witnessed numerous scandals involving not only presidents and legislators, but leading barons of industry, artists, preachers and other social worthies. Each invited its share of press attention, clucking from the morally upstanding and envy from those who only wished they had the nerve or social prominence to do the same. So much changes, so much remains the same.

The greatest scandal of the era involved Grover Cleveland who was, like James Buchanan, a bachelor when he became president in 1885. Cleveland, New York's governor and originally from Buffalo, faced a scandal that makes Bill Clinton's indiscretions seem tame. In the midst of the 1884 campaign, a local Buffalo preacher, Rev. George H. Ball, D.D., drew national attention to an earlier episode in Cleveland's career. Ball insisted the scandal made the candidate morally unfit to hold the nation's highest office. The Democratic candidate was reputed to have had an affair with a widow and mother of two, Marie Crofts Halpin, and have sired an out-of-wedlock child with her. As Rev. Ball stated, the election issue was

> not between two great [political] parties but between the brothel and the family, between indecency and decency, between lust and law, between the essence of barbarism and the first principles of civilization, between the degradation of women and due honor, protection and love of our mothers, sisters and daughters.

Ball further insisted that Cleveland's affair with Mrs. Halpin was not an isolated incident, but that he had "still more proof of debaucheries too horrible to relate and too vile to be readily believed."[9]

The Republicans backing James Blaine played up the scandal. Partisan Republic newspapers like the *Boston Journal,* preachers like Henry Ward Beecher, no stranger to scandal*, and even suffragette Lucy Stone's *Women's Journal* denounced Cleveland's behavior. The scandal became the basis for competing campaign chants: Republicans shouting, "Ma! Ma! Where's my Pa!," and Democrats rejoining, "He's gone to the White House! Ha! Ha! Ha!". The problem with the 1884 revelations about Cleveland's "scandal" was that it was well known to both local and state voters, and was no longer a concern among Democrats.

Mrs. Halpin had moved to Buffalo in 1871 in search of work, leaving her children with relatives. She found employment with a fashionable dry-goods shop and, due to her good looks and convivial personality, made her way into "better" society. She became especially close to, in fact quite intimate with, two of the cities most powerful men, Cleveland, who became mayor, and his best friend

---

* See below for discussion of the Beecher-Tilton affair.

and law partner, Oscar Folsom. In September 1874, Mrs. Halpin gave birth to a son who she artfully named Oscar Folsom Cleveland, encouraging much speculation. While never admitting paternity, Cleveland agreed to provide for the child's upkeep.[10]

Cleveland was a bachelor when elected president and brought to the office a reputation as a lady's man. When Cleveland took office he invited his sister, Rose, to serve as First Lady. Rose was a nineteenth-century "spinster," an unmarried woman with a successful career as a teacher, novelist and literary critic. In 1889, following her brother's marriage, she began a romantic friendship with Mrs. Evangeline Simpson, a wealthy 30-year-old woman. The two women exchanged a series of love letters. In one, Rose admits: "I tremble at the thought of you" and "I dare not think of your arms." Simpson replies, calling Cleveland "my Clevy, my Viking, my Everything." After Simpson's husband died, the women moved to Italy in 1910 and lived together until Cleveland's death in 1918.

However, the gravest scandal to haunt Cleveland presidency was his love affair and marriage to Francis "Frank" Folsom. Some moralists thought the affair indecent. They objected to the fact that he was twenty-seven years older than his future wife and that he had known her her whole life. He had even served as her legal guardian. Frank was the daughter of his long-time legal partner and best friend, Oscar. As historian Alyn Brodsky observes, "After all, he [Cleveland] had dandled her as an infant, bought her first baby carriage, and kept a concerned avuncular eye on her since she was ten."[11] Frank called him "Uncle Cleve" and, after her father died, Cleveland became the executor of her estate.

Folsom was twenty-two years old when she married Cleveland, then forty-nine years old. She was an educated, worldly woman from the rising bourgeoisie. A college graduate, she had spent nine months on the continent before their marriage. She is described as poised, sophisticated and attractive, embodying much of the social contradictions of the era. She supported education and social-welfare programs for the poor, especially African-Americans. She also advocated abstinence from alcohol, but engaged in social drinking. She is the only First Lady to hold the position in two non-sequential presidencies.[12]

Cleveland was not alone among America's political class succumbing to sexual scandal. James Garfield suffered two scandals, one traumatic, the other fatal. The scandal that haunted Garfield involved an extramarital affair he appears to have had with a "Mrs. Calhoun" two decades earlier. While a general in the Civil War, he suffered greatly, both physically and emotionally, during the bloody struggle. His adulterous affair apparently took place in October 1862 during a visit to New York while, as he wrote, he was living through "years of darkness." When his wife, Lucretia, discovered the affair, they worked out their differences.[13] However, Garfield is one of the very few (but still too many) presidents who have been assassinated. After only four months in office, he was shot in July 1881 by Charles Guiteau, a disgruntled office seeker. He died in September and was succeeded by Chester A. Arthur.

Other prominent figures of the day who attracted national attention for their scandalous ways were William Breckinridge, William Taulbee, Arthur Brown and William Sharon. Their tales of woe sound very contemporary when juxtaposed against the recent exploits of David Vitter and Larry Craig, John Edwards and Eliot Spitzer.

William Campbell Preston Breckinridge, a Kentucky congressman from 1885 to 1895, was undone by an indiscretion that lasted a decade. In 1884, Breckinridge met a 17-year-old college student, Madeline Pollard, on a train and began an affair that ended in a sensational trial that finished his political career. In 1893, Pollard brought suit against the congressman for abandonment and the story of the liaison became national headlines.

The young Wesleyan student fell in love with the older man and relocated to Lexington, KY, and Washington, DC, in pursuit of her lover. Married and a father, Breckinridge paid for Pollard's further education and upkeep and got her a federal job. They had an out-of-wedlock child and, after his first wife died, Breckinridge refused to marry her. This precipitated a suit against him. In a Washington, DC, trial that lasted a month, the jury ruled in Pollard's favor and awarded her a significant financial judgment. Breckinridge returned to Kentucky to seek reelection and was defeated.[14]

A few years earlier, a fellow Kentucky congressman, William Preston Taulbee, met a far worse fate as a result of a sexual scandal. In 1887, *The Louisville Times* ran a story entitled, "Kentucky's Silver-Tongued Taulbee Caught in Flagrante, or Thereabouts, with Brown-

Haired Miss Dodge." Other newspapers picked up the story and elaborated upon the congressman's lunchtime romps. In disgrace, Taulbee's wife of seventeen years divorced him and he did not seek re-election. According to writer Shelley Ross, Taulbee retreated into a miserable private life "where he remained in a terrible state of mind."

Over the following years, Taulbee occasionally crossed paths with Charles Kincaid, the author of the story that led to his downfall. Witnesses say that Taulbee repeatedly insulted Kincaid when they met and things got out of control in 1890 at the U.S. Capitol. On that day, February 28th, after exchanging insults, the two men fought. Kincaid, a diminutive man only five feet tall, was no match for the rugged Kentuckian. Beaten and enraged, the writer went home, returned with a handgun and, finding Taulbee entering the House dining hall, shot his adversary. Standing over Taublee's body, Kincaid admitting to onlookers, "I did it." The former congressman died eleven days later.[15]

Another member of Congress to die at the hands of a sexual adversary was Arthur Brown, one of Utah's first senators. However, in his case, his jealous lover, Mrs. Anne Bradley, shot the senator. Brown met Bradley in 1898 and had an on-again, off-again affair with her until his murder in 1906. Newspaper reports made much of Brown's infatuation with the young woman and his repeated promises to divorce his wife and marry her. Bradley believed him. She divorced her husband and had an out-of-wedlock child with the senator. Learning of his affair, the senator's wife had Bradley arrested on adultery charges.

Amidst the mounting tension, the senator and his mistress ran off for a secret get-away, only to be followed by his wife and her attorney. The two women had a dramatic face-to-face confrontation and Mrs. Brown threatened to kill Bradley if she saw her husband again. Unfortunately, Mrs. Brown shortly thereafter died of cancer and, to only Bradley's surprise, the senator refused to finally marry her. Bradley found out that the senator was having an affair with another woman, a young starlet, Annie Adams Kiskadden, the daughter of the then-famous actress, Maude Adams. In a rage, Bradley shot the senator. At her trial, and adding even more drama to a grand scandal, Bradley was acquitted.[16]

Another grand political scandal of the Gilded Age involved William Sharon who, over a decade, had a much-litigated "marriage" to Sarah Althea Hill. Sharon was a successful California banker and real-estate developer who became a Nevada senator in 1875. He was a wealthy 60-year-old widower in 1880 when he was smitten with this young beauty. He is reported to have offered her, first, $500 and, then, $1,000 a month to be his mistress, but she refused. They finally agreed to marry, but from here the story involves years of litigation, death threats, a knife fight in a courtroom and the arrest of a U.S. justice.

Their marriage, however, had a peculiar twist to it. In order to avoid a pending paternity suit brought by yet another damsel he was seeing, Sharon signed an agreement to marry Hill. However, the agreement was technically not a formal marriage contract. Losing interest in his "bride" after a year or so, the senator tried to annul the agreement, precipitating a court case that would drag on for a decade. Claims and counter-claims flew between them; reconciliation efforts failed; Hill had the senator arrested for adultery with yet another woman. Finally, amidst national press coverage, a divorce trial commenced in March 1884 and, on Christmas Eve, "Mrs. Sharon" got her divorce.

In keeping with American jurisprudence, the senator appealed the state court's decision to the federal bench. The stress of the drawn-out scandal, however, took a toll on Mrs. Sharon. She repeatedly assailed the attorneys and even the judge, pulling out a handgun from her purse and threatening people in the court. Finally, the presiding judge had her searched for a gun when she entered the court room.

Adding still more drama to the media circus, Sharon died on the day the court issued its ruling. It found that the original marriage agreement was a forgery, thus annulling the marriage. Amidst the legal squabbling, Mrs. Sharon married her attorney, David Terry, generating still more press attention. The California Supreme Court issued a separate ruling accepting the original divorce decision, thus legitimizing the marriage.

Sharon's heirs from his first marriage went back to the federal court to overturn the California ruling. In September 1888, U.S. Justice Stephen Field ruled against Mrs. Terry, and denounced her personally. Upset, she retorted that the judge had taken a bribe! The judge ordered her arrested for contempt, her attorney (and husband) jumped to her defense, bowie knife in hand, and the court officers pulled their guns. Both Mr. and Mrs. Terry were sentenced to jail terms for their court conduct.

From here, the Sharon-Hill saga goes from bad to worse. Repeated efforts to overturn the contempt charges failed. Mrs. Terry miscarried, increasing her mania. Mr. Terry challenged Judge Field to a duel, leading to federal marshal protection of the judge. Finally, the California court, with a new set of justices, reversed the original decision, invalidating the Sharon-Hill marriage agreement. Could this scandal get worse?

In August 1889, the Terrys and Field were on the same train from Fresno to San Francisco. Stopping at a local café for breakfast, Field, with his bodyguard, was seated when the Terrys entered. Seeing the judge, Mrs. Terry returned to the train, but her husband approached him in a fury. What happened next remains in doubt. Some say that Terry slapped the judge, others insist that he merely tapped him on the shoulder to get his attention. The judge's bodyguard, ostensibly fearing that Terry would pull out his famous bowie knife, shot and killed the attorney.

Judge Field and his bodyguard were arrested for murder and, after posting bond, released. In a subsequent federal hearing on the incident, both Field and his bodyguard were freed. However, a different fate awaited Mrs. Hill-Sharon-Terry. Although a court refused to convict her of federal charges related to her outburst in Judge Field's court, she was declared insane and committed to a state institution where she spent the last forty-five years of her life. As Ross observes, "It is ironic that what began as an illicit affair between a senator and his mistress became a turning point in constitutional law which had an impact for many decades."[17]

\* \* \*

Scandals during the decades between the Civil War and World War I were not limited to politicians. Business tycoons and their offspring were among the most notorious philanderers and worse. In 1906, Harry Kendall Thaw was a Pittsburgh millionaire playboy who gained notoriety when he married the chorus girl, Evelyn Nesbit. Thaw had a particular predilection for very young teenage girls, what psychiatrists today call an ephebophilia. He is reported to have spent $40,000 "in an establishment of unorthodox sex." Operating under the pseudonym of Professor Reid, "he advertised for training of young girls, age fifteen to seventeen, for stage careers. Using a whip, he raised welts on their naked bodies and paid handsomely for giving the lesson. A Mrs. Reid was paid some seven hundred dollars for her 'training.'"

This activity was but an indulgence of the privileged that has gone on from time immemorial. Thaw's great scandal involved killing famed architect (and another notorious deflowerer of young girls) Stanford White. Thaw was incensed by an apparent affair that White had with Nesbit before they were married! The grand shoot-out took place on June 25, 1906, at Madison Square Garden's roof garden. It was a scandal rooted in jealousy, both real and imagined.

As a teenager, Nesbit was a model for the celebrated artist Charles Dana Gibson and became famous as the "Gibson Girl," the quintessential expression of turn-of-the-century virginal beauty. Thaw seems to have learned of his wife's pre-marital indiscretion after their marriage and, in true patriarchal fashion, blamed White for taking advantage of—i.e., deflowering—the young woman. Rumors circulated that White had lured the impressionable Nesbit to a secret hideaway he had at Madison Square Garden where he raped her. Nothing was proven. And Thaw took his revenge.

During the grand Gilded Age, the Thaw-Nesbit-White triangle was considered the great sex-crime scandal of the period. Thaw pleaded not guilty due to temporary insanity, the first time such a defense had been used. He was found not guilty by reason of insanity and spent the rest of his life in and out of mental institutions.[18]

Decades earlier, financier James Fisk was a bigger-than-life character referred to variously as "Big Jim," "Diamond Jim" and "Jubilee Jim." He gained notoriety due to his role, along with Jay Gould, in what came to be known as the Gold Panic of 1869, a financial scandal that almost brought down the presidency of Ulysses S. Grant.[19] However, it was Fisk's affair with Helen Josephine "Josie" Mansfield, a popular showgirl one writer described as having "a voluptuous figure, luxuriant black hair, and a soft voice," and a love triangle with his partner, Edward Stiles Stokes, which ended with Stokes shooting him in 1872, that garnered great national attention.

Fisk married his youthful sweetheart, Lucy Moore, when they were teenagers. While Fisk called New York home, his wife lived in Boston with a female companion in what some suggest was a lesbian relationship. In New York, Fisk held court in his elaborately-appointed offices at the Erie Railroad headquarters at the Pike Opera House on Twenty-third Street. He built a special passageway between his offices and Mansfield's apartment a few doors up the street. Fisk once boasted:

> I was born to be bad. As to the World, the Flesh and Devil, I'm on good terms with all three. If God Almighty is going to damn us men because we love the woman, then let him go ahead and do it. I'm having a good time now, and if I've got to pay for it hereafter, why … I'll take what's coming to me.

And so he did.

Amidst the affair, Mansfield fell in love with Fisk's business partner, Stokes, who Rugoff calls a "handsome dandy." Mansfield broke off her relationship with Fisk and Stokes left his wife and ended his partnership with Fisk. Rumors spread that the couple attempted to blackmail Fisk, threatening to publish his love letters to Mansfield. Fisk refused to pay and sought the couple's prosecution. In a fury, Stokes, facing bankruptcy, sought out Fisk at the Grand Central Hotel on Broadway and shot him. When the police apprehended him, he screamed out: "I have done for the s-- of a b----- this time."[20]

\* \* \*

The social and economic changes that followed the Civil War were traumatic and far-reaching. In the face of these challenges, a powerful movement emerged that attempted to contain the forces that were perceived as threatening moral order. It railed against vice in every form, be it alcohol consumption, gambling, prostitution, birth control or obscenity in the arts. The Young Men's Christian Association (YMCA) and the Women's Christian Temperance Alliance (WCTA), among others, championed this movement. Its national leader was the ever-upstanding Anthony Comstock. So influential was this former dry-goods salesman that George Bernard Shaw coined the term "Comstockery" to denote overzealous moralistic officials.

In 1868, just three years after the end of the Civil War, the movement secured its first major victory when the New York State legislature passed an incredibly broad law to suppress what was described as obscene materials. The law defined obscene to include all materials and devices that dealt with conception, birth control and other sexual matters, be they medical or erotic. Five years later, the movement was strong enough to have the U.S. Congress enact what became popularly known as the Comstock laws, legislation that stands as the most sweeping, omnibus anti-obscenity laws in American history. These laws, in effect, extended New York State prohibitions to all interstate commerce and communications. They covered nearly every form of exchange then known or anticipated:

> ... no obscene, lewd, or lascivious book, pamphlet, picture, paper, print, or other publication of an indecent character, or any article or thing designed or intended for the prevention of conception or procuring of abortion, nor any article or thing intended or adapted for any indecent or immoral use or nature, nor any written or printed card, circular, book, pamphlet, advertisement or notice or any kind giving information, directly or indirectly, where, or how, or of whom, or by what means either of the thing before mentioned may be obtained or made, nor any letter upon the envelope of which, or post-card upon which indecent or scurrilous epithets may be written or printed, shall be carried in the mail ...[21]

Comstock was appointed a special officer of the U.S. postal system and given the power to seize what he labeled as obscene materials as well as arrest those he identified as pornographers.

The law was so effective that within the first six months of passage, Comstock boasted that it lead to the seizure of 194,000 pictures and photographs, 14,200 stereopticon plates and 134,000 pounds of books and other media. In the 1910s near the end of his life, Comstock claimed that he had destroyed 3,984,063 photographs and 160 tons of "obscene" literature.[22] The laws would remain in force until the mid-1930s, when it was partially reversed by the Supreme Court with regard to medical and scientific materials. It would take another three decades until literature and art were given comparable freedom.*

In the face of the profound changes that were recasting the nation during this period, the older proponents of moral order joined a younger generation championing social purity. These groups included the American Purity Alliance (formed in 1895) and the American Vigilance Committee (the two later consolidated into the American Vigilance Association). In addition, numerous special anti-vice, anti-obscenity, anti-gambling, temperance, anti-immigrant and anti-miscegenation committees flourished throughout the country. Local groups included Chicago's Committee of Fourteen, New York's Committee of Fifteen, the New York Society for the Suppression of Vice and the New England Watch and Ward Society in Boston. These groups drew upon many social notables, from Jane Addams and Grace Dodge to J. P. Morgan and John D. Rockefeller, Jr., for both political influence and financial support.[23]

Much of the uninhibited, assertive sexuality that marked the lustful masculinity of the first half of the nineteenth century was forcefully restricted in the decades following the Civil War. The moral reform efforts of the period forced pornographic literature and entertainment underground, restricted street prostitution, suppressed the free-love movement and changed marriage and courtship practices. Nevertheless, the most important reform of the period was the loosening of the prohibition against masturbation: one of the great sins since biblical days. Enough of this lustful masculinity remained to support a remarkably complex male sexual culture that encouraged the indulgence of some of the most illicit desires.

The men who gathered at the Tecumseh Hall in 1904 vividly expressed a particular form of lustful masculinity. Unknown to them, attending this sex show helped them learn how to effectively discipline their wilder impulses. As Sigmund Freud so argued, instilling (unconscious) restraint on erotic desire is one of the great challenges and achievements of civilization. These men represented a moment where nature was socialized.

---

* The U.S. government has not been above using the old Comstock law when it needed to. For example, as Attorney General, Robert Kennedy relied upon it in his victorious 1962 censorship battle against Ralph Ginsburg and *Eros* magazine. [John Heidenry, *What Wild Ecstasy: The Rise and Fall of the Sexual Revolution* (New York: Simon & Schuster, 1997), 60.]

This process took a particular form during the era of America's modernization. Sexual socialization or enculturalization required, first, an ability to mentally and physically cope with ever-intensifying sexual stimulation saturating social life. The intensification of experience was expressed in increasingly provocative advertising, fashion and popular entertainment. It also required a personal acceptance of restrictions on public sexual engagement. Sexual hookups on the street, at a park or at a public restroom were (and continue to be) illegal. Both noncommercial and commercial sex moved to more private settings such as porn-theatres, bar backrooms, sex clubs and through escort services or madams at a swank bordello, hotel room or private apartment. Illicit or unacceptable sex increasingly moved further underground, off the street, out of sight. It proved successful in reshaping male (and female) sense of sexual fulfillment and helped launch a new sexuality. This process of sexual socialization would take three-quarters of a century to be realized in the post-World War II decades.

The refashioning of male desire was complemented by the emergence of a new, if contradictory, notion of female sexuality. On one side, a powerful Christian, middle-class ethos demanded women express an asexual propriety. Against this traditional value system, an alternative approach emerged expressing a far different notion of female sexuality. It transformed the dowdy matron into the working-girl flapper. It found more explicit expression in the erotic temptation of the burlesque performer, the carnival showgirl and the call-house prostitute. Moralists had long been challenged by assertive female sexuality, whether represented by Frances Wright* or the painted streetwalkers—female "harlots" and male "fairies"—who strolled America's urban byways. The establishment of this new female sexuality was driven as much by an expanding, ever-deepening penetration of the market economy, with its resulting commodification of sexual fantasy, as by the new freedoms women carved out for themselves at the workplace, dance hall and ballot box.

* * *

Sex scandals followed Comstock everywhere he went during the nearly half-century he fought to restrict both sexual expression

---

* On Wright, see Chapter 2, Revolutionary Generation.

and sexual experience. His battles involved a wide range of issues, including birth control and purported obscenity. However, the confrontations receiving the most public attention involved his battles with Victoria Woodhull and her sister, Tennessee Claflin; Walt Whitman and Ezra Heywood; and Madam Restell, America's foremost nineteenth century abortionist.

One of America's great post-Civil War match-ups pitted the country's moral crusader, Comstock, against two indomitable free-love and free-speech advocates, Woodhull and Claflin. Woodhull was an advocate for the end to traditional, patriarchal marriage. Thomas Nast, the great nineteenth century illustrator, dubbed her "Mrs. Satan." Their publication, the *Woodhull & Claflin's Weekly*, generated a national stir with its frank discussions of forbidden topics like women's suffrage, prostitution, sex education and short skirts. In 1872 Woodhull ran for president of the United States on behalf of the Equal Rights Party; the party drafted the absent Frederick Douglass for vice president.

The showdown between Comstock and the Woodhull-Claflin sisters occurred when they published a story about an illicit sexual relation involving the Rev. Henry Ward Beecher. He was one of America's leading theologians, bishop at Brooklyn's Plymouth Congregational Church and served a role analogous to that played by Jim Bakker in the 1980s and Ted Haggard before his outing in 2006.* In 1872, the *Weekly* exposed the details of an affair between the good pastor and one of his parishioners, Mrs. Elizabeth Tilton. Comstock had the sisters arrested, not because of Rev. Beecher's hypocrisy, but because information about his dastardly deeds was available for everyone to read. Both New York and federal authorities charged them with circulating obscene materials. At their trial, the sisters were acquitted when the judge noted that the original Comstock law did not cover newspapers. After more than a year of legal wrangling in which the sisters were repeatedly imprisoned, Woodhull and Claflin were set free, their lives ruined and the obscenity loophole closed.[24]

Another memorable scandal of the Gilded Age involving free speech pitted Comstock against Whitman, America's greatest voice

---

* For more on Bakker, see Chapter 6, Sexual Counter-Revolution, and on Haggard, see Chapter 7, America's Sex Wars.

of creative and sexual freedom. Comstock repeatedly attempted to stop Whitman's creative expression. He had long hated Whitman's verse, once insisting that he had never read more than forty lines of his poetry. He also bragged that he had personally intervened to force Whitman out of his position at the Department of Interior during the Civil War. In a confrontation in the early-eighties, Comstock arrested Heywood for mailing a publication that included two Whitman poems and a contraceptive device called "The Comstock Syringe."

Three years earlier, in 1877, Heywood had been arrested by Comstock for publishing *Cupid's Yokes, or, The Binding Forces of Conjugal Life*. It was an attack on traditional marriage and Comstock's repressive campaign. Heywood was convicted but President Rutherford B. Hayes intervened and pardoning him in 1878. After his pardon, Heywood continued to challenge conventional moral standards. In the 1880s, he was again arrested for publishing an obscene mailing—and again found innocent. Comstock's obsession intensified, arresting Heywood three more times. In 1890, Heywood was finally convicted for publishing a discussion of oral-genital sex. At age sixty-one, he was sentenced to two years of hard labor and forced to serve his full sentence. A broken man, he died shortly after his release.

Whether or not it's true that Comstock never read more than forty lines of Whitman, the censor was obsessed by the poet's erotic sensibility. In 1881, while he was persecuting Heywood, Comstock assisted Boston District Attorney Oliver Stevens in an effort to suppress the publication of *Leaves of Grass* by the Boston publisher, James R. Osgood & Co. Aided by the New England Society for the Suppression of Vice, Stevens formally requested that Osgood edit the manuscript, removing what he—and Comstock—considered obscene passages. Ironically, *Leaves* had been originally published in 1855, twenty-eight years earlier. Osgood requested changes from Whitman, who refused. Osgood pulled the book; America's greatest work of verse was suppressed.

The suppression of *Leaves of Grass* precipitated a fierce national scandal over freedom of expression. While many among "better" society shared Comstock's concerns about vice, they had second thoughts because it was Whitman. He was the author of "Oh Captain, My Captain," the nation's great ode to the fallen Lincoln, a figure who remained part of the living memory of many. Like Einstein a century later, Whitman symbolized wisdom and humility. Charges against *Leaves* were ultimately dropped, as part of one of Heywood's not-guilty decisions.[25]

* * *

In September 1909, Sigmund Freud, accompanied by Sandor Ferenczi and Carl Jung, made his only visit to the United States. He was invited to give a series of lectures at Clark University in Worcester, MA, on his new discipline of psychoanalysis. "As I stepped on to the platform at Worcester … it seemed like the realization of some incredible day-dream," Freud later recalled. "[P]sychoanalysis was no longer a product of delusion, it had become a valuable part of reality."

One of those in attendance was William James, author of *Principles of Psychology* and founder, along with Charles Pierce and John Dewey, of America's new school of philosophy, pragmatism. Writing to a friend, James championed Freud's new approach: "I hope that Freud and his pupils will push their ideas to the utmost limits, so that we may learn what they are. They can't fail to throw light on human nature …" However, remaining suspicious of threatening ideas, he warned: "… but I confess that he made on me personally the impression of a man obsessed with fixed ideas. I can make nothing in my own case with his dream theories; and obviously 'symbolism' is a most dangerous method."[26]

Freud's visit symbolically represents a defining moment of America's modernization, an anchor event in which leading thinkers gathered to consider the challenges posed by the emerging industrial society, especially its internal forces of destabilization. His visit expressed the growing thirst among American intellectuals, medical doctors, jurists, civic leaders, prison officials, education reformers, public-policy advocates, teachers, social workers, writers and ordinary citizens to consider new ideas, better ways to analyze and effectively deal with a host of pressing concerns.

This new intellectual class sought an analysis, the theories and practices, that could help it address what was widely perceived as the most profound yet destabilizing force unleashed by modern life, sexuality. It sought to balance an understanding of a person's past with human personality and provide practical solutions to sexual deviance, the threat unleashed by modernization. These professionals understood that wage labor, combined with urbanization and industrialization, stimulated a powerful demand for personal satisfaction and sexual pleasure.

During the *fin de siecle* era, sexual excess was deeply disturbing to public life. Red-light districts were an eyesore to many Americans. The debauchery of painted women; the smoking, drinking, gambling and whoring by men of every class; the spread of venereal diseases to innocent wives and children were affronts to civic virtue. They were genuine threats to public health and well-being. Something had to be done.

Freud's visit came at a time when American sexuality was being fundamentally and irreversibly transformed. Throughout the country, sexual culture was revolutionized and the human body eroticized. This was especially true for women who were simultaneously disrobed, painted and perfumed. They were expected to be more active through the opportunities of education, work, makeup and the vote; yet, they were being made more visible, yet more passive, in terms of media representation in advertising, burlesque and pornography. For Americans, but especially women, what had traditionally been private was becoming public, explicit and asserted. A new sexuality was being incubated.

\* \* \*

Sexual modernization involves the industrialization of sex. This is reflected in the iconography of erotic display, including fashion, advertising or media. It is also found in increasing venues of sexual practice outside of the home that facilitate illicit relations. Such venues ranged from clubs of live performance, like that at the Tecumseh Hall, burlesque and girl shows. They also included a host of settings in which prostitution flourished such as hotels, apartments, cowyards and speakeasies. Finally, they included gay bathhouses, one of which was owned by the Gershwin family. These venues were the social settings in which scandals were often rooted.

In its hey-day, burlesque was like no other form of sexual performance in American theatre. It most admirably mirrors the evolution of American attitudes towards sexuality during the period stretching from the end of the Civil War to World War I. As historical irony would have it, burlesque made its U.S. debut in New York City in 1868, the same year that New York State adopted the Comstock anti-obscenity laws. On the evening of September 28th, British star Lydia Thompson took to the stage of George Wood's Broadway Theatre to perform in *Ixion*. The eight-hundred-seat house was sold out and the audience was delighted, according to a *New York Times* report, by a star "of the purest type, saucy, blue-eyed, golden-haired and of elegant figure." The production included the dancing of the cancan, only recently introduced in Paris, and "jigs, hornpipes, and parodies of minstrel show numbers." Thompson was a national sensation and, almost single-handedly, instituted a new, popular art form that competed with traditional legitimate theatre.[27]

Burlesque was distinguished from the other popular forms of male entertainment by the appeal of the female performers, stars in the mode established by Thompson. The appeal of the early burlesque performer was founded on a compelling presentation of female identity. It combined what the historian Robert Allen calls "sexual allure and inversive feminine insubordination." He clarifies: "Either half alone could be controlled and made to please without seriously undermining the position of the male spectator. Fused together in a single performer, however, this combination was much more threatening."[28] The original burlesque star directly engaged her male audience, challenging the established masculine prerogative about sexuality, undermining their exclusive control over erotic desire. She foreshadowed the post-feminist pop star of the late-twentieth century.

The burlesque star's performance was in stark contrast to the more legitimate vaudeville and revue theatre of the day, typified by the Ziegfeld Follies. The burlesque performer engaged the male audience, directly and actively, through her sexual display and her provocative stage presence. In contrast, the "Ziegfeld Girl" of the 1910s —often referred to as the "American Girl"—epitomized a de-eroticized femininity that was submissive to the male gaze.[29]

By the time of the 1893 Chicago Exposition, burlesque was becoming increasingly one-dimensional, moving more and more toward sexual explicitness with the incorporation of the belly dance and, in its more extreme expression, the "cooch" or "hootchy-kootchy" dance. With the popularization of jazz during the 1920s, the cooch became the "shimmy." As burlesque became identified by these more caricature forms, "all pretense that the performance was about anything other than sexual pleasure was dispensed with."

According to legend, May Dix performed the first "strip" at the Minsky Brothers' New York theatre. As Allen retells the tale:

> In 1917 they constructed a runway into the auditorium so that patrons could examine cooch dancers more closely. ... May Dix did her dance act in a short black dress with detachable white collar and cuffs. At the end of her song one hot summer night, she removed her collar as she walked offstage, trying to forestall the next laundry bill. Someone in the audience demanded an encore, at the end of which she removed her cuffs as well. 'Between the heat and the applause [reports Morton Minsky], May lost her head, went back for a short chorus, and unbuttoned her bodice as she left the stage again.'*

The striptease was "burlesque's last-ditch and ultimately unsuccessful strategy to stay alive."[30] And it was a scandalous sensation!

The "girl show" was another form of live sexual performance. It first appeared as a sideshow at the 1893 Chicago Exposition and quickly became a feature of touring carnivals bringing live entertainment to small-town and rural America. Smaller and less formal than traveling circuses, touring carnivals met with rapid success between 1902 and 1920. The number of girl shows operating across the nation shot up from seventeen to some two hundred!

"Girl shows are distinguished by how 'strong' the dancers are allowed to perform—in other words, by the extent of sexual abandon of the dancing routines and the degree of genital display," notes Allen. "In the large and more sedate carnivals (those that play state fair dates, for example)," he adds, "the performance

---

* The striptease appears to have made its first appearance at the St. Louis Exposition of 1896 when Omeena performed what was called the "take off." [Robert C. Allen, *Horrible Prettiness: Burlesque and American Culture* (Chapel Hill: University of North Carolina Press, 1991), 230.] There also seems to be considerable overlap between more lower-class vaudeville and extreme burlesque. [Elizabeth Alice Clement, *Trick or Treat: Prostitution and Working-Class Women's Sexuality in New York City, 1900-1932*. (Ph. D. University of Pennsylvania, 1998), 236-44.]

might end with a strip down to the G-string or its removal for a moment just before the dancer leaves the stage." Allen goes on to point out that "[in] the smaller shows, however, where 'stronger' acts are the norm, the performance might end with a gynecological anatomy lesson... ."[31]

These shows often featured the female posture artist. She acted out a "living picture" in which she held a revealing pose (often with minimal clothing) for audience inspection. She would then perform a suggestive dance like the "Butterfly" or the "Serpentine." The carney operator might then deploy the artful technique known as the "girls and grift" con, tapping male desire with the suggestive fantasy of the "cooch" dance. After seeing the more public show, and for an additional fee, "marks" would be invited into back rooms for a special performance. In the early decades of the twentieth century, very few shows involved totally nude exhibitions or explicit sex acts such as fellatio or intercourse. This would come later, first, at sex circuses during Prohibition and, later, at sex clubs after World War II.

* * *

Prostitution, along with gambling, alcohol consumption and other social evils, proliferated in the so-called red-light districts* that operated in cities throughout the country during the latter part of the nineteenth century. As the historian Ruth Rosen writes,

> Some of the more infamous districts in the country, though hardly typical in the smaller cities and towns, had already achieved national reputations as dens of legalized vice: New Orleans's Storyville, San Francisco's Barbary Coast, Denver's Market Street, Baltimore's Block, Chicago's Levee, and New York's Bowery, Five Points, and Tenderloin. [In] these sporting resorts with their streets lined with brothels, saloons, and hotels, the air [was] filled with the odor of tobacco and the sounds of blaring music, [and the windows bore] images of women making obscene gestures... .[32]

---

* The term "red light" is apparently derived from the early days of prostitution in Kansas City when a railroad brakeman posted a red light outside a whorehouse while he was engaged inside. [Ruth Rosen, The Lost Sisterhood: Prostitution in America, 1900-1918 (Baltimore: Johns Hopkins University Press, 1982), 105.]

Prostitution was a nationwide business. It was based on the nature of the urban, small-town or rural setting involved. For example, investigators found 1,800 "vice resorts" in New York, three hundred and seventy-two in Philadelphia, three hundred in Baltimore and even a handful in such small Wisconsin villages as Watertown and Janesville.[33]

Looking at a mid-sized town, John Grigsby, a reporter for the *Toledo Blade*, took an invaluable survey of the city's brothel culture in the summer of 1904—the same year that the three hundred men gathered at New York's Tecumseh Hall. At the heart of the Toledo's red-light district, Lafayette Street, thirty brothels were open every night of the week. They typically operated as back rooms to saloons—saloons often with female bartenders! After a few drinks, the bartender escorted the male customer upstairs for what was claimed to be "promises of rousing sex." Often, these saloon-brothels—the worst ones were known as "creeping joints"—were the site of a shakedown or "bilking." Once the john was fully exposed, the prostitute's male co-conspirator would appear and the john was forced to choose between leaving with his valuables or his clothes.[34]

In early twentieth century, Leadville, CO, was the quintessential rural boom-to-bust mining town of the rapidly disappearing frontier West. Birthplace of the legendary boxer Jack Dempsey, Leadville was home to not only thirty-five brothels, but also one hundred and thirty-nine saloons and a hundred and eighteen gambling establishments. Some of the most famous prostitutes during this mining town's hey-day were "Straight Edge," "Contrary Mary," "The Irish Queen" and "Slantic Ann." These women, let alone the poetry of their nicknames, are long gone.[35]

According to Rosen, "working the streets was considered by many prostitutes to be the most dangerous and brutal form of prostitution." Many of the women who took up streetwalking were "occasional" or "casual" prostitutes, women who were momentarily short of money or facing other hardships, and exploited an opportunity promising relatively easy remuneration. Some prostitutes during this period preferred streetwalking because it freed them from the grip of the middleman (pimp or madam), and thus provided an opportunity to earn more money. In addition, because she had to negotiate each transaction, a streetwalker was able to evaluate a prospective customer. This was especially true for African-American streetwalkers in the 1910s, for they had become "exceedingly public, flagrant, flashy [and were] not presumed to be, or presented as, quasi-respectable, but rather as just the opposite: a whore, a fallen woman."[36]

Dance halls during the pre-World War I era often served as venues for illicit sexual encounters, not unlike the photo studios of the 1950s, massage parlors of the 1970s, lap-dancing bars of the 1990s and gentlemen's clubs of the 2000s. The most notorious of turn-of-the-twentieth century New York dance halls was the Haymarket, located on Sixth Avenue at Thirtieth Street. It publicly enforced the civil law that prohibited "close up dancing" between the often well-to-do male customers and the female dancers, the resident prostitutes. It did, however, offer "curtained galleries behind which discreet [sex] could be practiced." On the balcony level, it offered "cubicles [that] featured sex exhibition or circuses." Another report claimed that the Haymarket had "private rooms for five hundred girls entertaining on the premise."[37]

Venues for *private* assignations between a male customer and a female prostitute included brothels, hotels, tenement apartments, "cribs" and "cowyards." From the latter half of the nineteenth century, American brothels—often called "parlor houses"—sought the gaudy luster of the legendary European bordellos. Many of the more celebrated upper-crust establishments were richly decorated, well-appointed mansions with a self-consciously French decor. Here gangsters and entertainers rubbed shoulders with politicians, business tycoons and "sporting" men of every type.

Among the most famous madams that operated throughout the country during this period were Chicago's Ada and Minna Everleigh; Rosie Hertz, Matilda Hermann and Polly Adler in New York; Jessie Hayman, Tessie Wall, Maude Spenser and Reggie Gamble in San Francisco; Emma Johnson, Lulu White, Josie Arlington, "Voodoo Woman" Julia Jackson and Norma Wallace in New Orleans's Storyville; Mae Field, Corrine B. Gary, Kate Rockwell and Josephine Earp in Alaska and the Klondike; Josie Washburn in Lincoln, NB; and Pauline Tabor in Bowling Green, KY. These were career women for whom very few other entrepreneurial fields were open.

Behind the glamour, however, even the most luxurious houses were sites of brutal sexual exploitation and oppression. The conditions endured by ordinary prostitutes, those serving middle- and working-class men, including male immigrants and men of color, often amounted to sexual slavery. For example, three women working in a New York 50-cent brothel at the end of the nineteenth century reported having intercourse over a two-week period with one hundred and twenty, one hundred and eighty-five and two hundred and seventy-five men, respectively; another is reported to have copulated with forty-nine men in a single day! At still another brothel, on Delancey Street, an "inmate" is reported to have had sexual encounters with fifty-eight different men in one day. These examples do not seem either isolated or exaggerated.[38]

Public settings for prostitution extended from the streets, streetcorners and alleyways, building stoops and doorways plied by a legion of "painted women" to nearly every public space where men and women congregated, including public parks, roadways and docks. Private settings included brothels, hotels and tenements as well as in what one historian calls "camouflaged houses" like massage parlors and manicurist shops. Streetwalkers actively solicited in dance halls, movie theatres and, in the 1920s, speakeasies as well as in bakeries, cafés, cigar stores, delicatessens, lunchrooms and other shops. Indeed, "for many local merchants and businessmen, prostitution was a way to attract customers."[39]

Tenement and apartment prostitution flourished in New York and other cities during this period. Replacing the brothel and reflecting the increase in multi-family dwellings, prostitution in these settings "was the least organized and most casual variety of commercial sex." By the 1910s, it was estimated that in New York 30 percent of all prostitution took place in this kind of setting. Many features of the brothel remained, however: "Prices were similar, medical examinations were required by proprietors, advertising was common, and liquor was sold."[40]

If this period witnessed the industrialization of prostitution, then the "crib"—and ultimately the "cowyard"—represented the mass-manufacturing process as applied to the oldest profession. Though cribs operated in New York, New Orleans and other cities, they achieved their fullest expression in San Francisco. Cribs were tiny spaces or sub-divided cubicles designed to accommodate rapid sexual encounters: this was low-cost, high-turnover sex. On average, as Curt Gentry notes in his richly anecdotal history, *The Madams of San Francisco*, they measured: "H: 6-1/2', L: 6-3/4', and W: 4-1/2'." Stripping the urban sexual transaction to its barest essentials, a crib contained only a bed, a chair and a washbasin.[41]

Cowyards comprised "many cribs assembled under one roof and management." The Municipal and the Nymphia were emblematic of San Francisco's many cowyards. The original Municipal Crib, a three-story building located at 620 Jackson Street in Chinatown, had ninety rooms and was destroyed by the 1906 earthquake; it was rebuilt (and, because of its shape, nicknamed the Big Ship) to accommodate one hundred and thirty cribs. The Nymphia—its original name, Hotel Nymphomania, was prohibited by the police—was a three-story U-shaped building that housed four hundred and fifty cribs.[42]

The crib's female inmates, often Chinese, black or members of another immigrant group, worked under cruel pressure to perform. In San Francisco, crib women were expected to be naked while on duty. At the Nymphia and the Municipal Crib, the prostitutes worked in two shifts. They were expected to pay the proprietor between $2 and $5 for a half-day's rental of the crib. "Anything over that was profit."[43] Good luck!

As with any business of the day, prostitution was defined by a formal structure that was both historically and physically determined. It was a structure that mirrored American society's evolving class and race relations. As one scholar astutely observed, "[The] type of sexual institution determine[d] to a great extent the amount of financial remuneration a given prostitute could expect."[44]

Prostitution was identified as both a symptom and a cause of the moral decay that was allegedly destroying the nation. It brought together traditionalists and progressives in common cause to fight for its suppression. The success of their campaigns is evident in the increasing influence they had in setting national sexual standards. Their first successful effort was to restrict prostitution to red-light districts. This was followed by the passage of the Mann Act in 1910 outlawing interstate sex commerce.

However, the U.S.'s entry into World War I marked a watershed moment in the sexual radicalization of America. The forces of moral order, especially those known as "social purity activities," sought to use the war to forcefully contain the explosive expansion of sexual indulgence. This was implemented in two distinct campaigns. First, as the war approached, moralistic efforts led to the closing of approximately one hundred and twenty-five red-light districts under the requirements of "war discipline." Second, this was followed by a campaign that involved the arrest, forceful medical testing and/or imprisonment of an estimated 30,000 women for allegedly being carriers of venereal disease and, thus, "domestic enemies" accused of undermining the war effort. The purity campaign also involved a powerful temperance campaign that secured national influence. The movement's first victory was the restriction of alcohol sales to men in uniform. It was followed by the passage of the Eighteenth Amendment that outlawed alcohol production, distribution, sales and consumption just after the war. Together, these initiatives restructured commercial sex, forcing it into more underground settings and more fully under the control of organized crime.[45]

The restructuring of prostitution took place in a number of critical ways. First, the number of streetwalkers significantly declined and prostitutes became less visible in movie theatres, cabarets and other public venues. Second, due to changes in urban demographics, there was a sizable increase in the number of black women engaged in the sex trade. Third, as sex workers moved indoors, there was a re-emergence of intermediaries like cadets (e.g., taxi-drivers and hotel doormen), madams, pimps and other "go-betweens" facilitating sexual solicitation. Finally, in the face of intensified police harassment, prostitutes turned to these intermediaries, especially madams and gangsters, to protect them from arbitrary arrest, most notably through the payment of bribes. These factors contributed to the significant increase in the fees charged by prostitutes during the Roaring Twenties.

Within this restructured environment, the post-war era witnessed fundamental changes in terms of both the public and the private venues of sexual assignation. Within terms of public arena, two unique venues—the taxi-dance hall and the speakeasy—emerged and played important yet very different roles facilitating sexual engagements. Within terms of private venues, the shift from the brothel to the tenement and apartment, combined with the introduction of the telephone, led to the rise of the "call-flat" that, in effect, established a model of sex work that persists to this day.

\* \* \*

The Lafayette Baths was a notorious venue for homoerotic assignations during the World War I era. Located in New York City's East Village, it was one of a handful of bathhouses that catered to an exclusively gay—mostly white—clientele, providing a safe environment for sexual encounters and other forms of socializing. But there were other men's baths that turned a blind eye to sexual activity among their patrons. Indeed, the main thing that distinguishes the Lafayette from other establishments of the time was the anecdotal fact that, on December 29, 1916, the Gershwin family took over its ownership and Ira Gershwin became its manager.[46]

Bathhouses like the Lafayette "constituted a singular gay environment." Men came there to meet other men for explicitly physical, if not overtly sexual purposes. Nudity was normal in this context and bathhouses paradoxically provided their own kind of cover. They were a discreet setting offering relative freedom from public harassment or police arrest.

According to the historian George Chauncey, "gay baths were few in number and served a more limited—and generally more affluent—clientele than most of the other spaces gay men appropriated in the early twentieth century." Besides the Lafayette, other New York gay baths of the era included the Ariston Baths, the Everard, the Mount Morris Baths, the Penn Post Baths, the Produce Exchange Baths and the St. Mark's Bath. Among the gay-tolerant baths were the YMCA, the Claridge and Stauch's.[47]

It is ironic that these establishments were the result of a half century of socially progressive struggle to better the life of immigrants and the poor. Municipalities throughout the country built sex-segregated public baths in order to mitigate the poor sanitary conditions and the dearth of indoor plumbing that typified urban working-class life. Ethnic, fraternal, religious and other organizations also set up bathing facilities with similar aims in mind. It was only gradually that these places developed a gay profile. Nor would it be fair to say that they ever lost their social dimension for, as Chauncey points out, "the baths were also important social centers, where gay men could meet openly, discuss their lives, and build a circle of friends," thus creating "a social world on the basis of a shared and marginalized sexuality."[48]

* * *

The gravest sex scandal during the era of modernization involved the legendary boxer Jack Johnson. The long, drawn-out harassment, arrest, trial and, finally, incarceration of Johnson vividly captures the great saga of race, masculinity and sex—miscegenation*—that has distinguished American cultural life for nearly four centuries.

Johnson emerged onto the boxing scene in Galveston, TX, during the turn-of-the-twentieth century, a period in which boxing, like baseball, was racially segregated. In 1903, he won the title of Negro heavyweight champion and demanded to fight the then reigning "white" champion, James the "Boilermaker" Jeffries. He repeatedly refused to fight the upstart black heavyweight. After Jeffries' unexpected retirement, a series of far less qualified white boxers scrambled for the championship title. Finally, in 1908, a showdown fight between the new champ, Canada's Tommy Burns, and Johnson was held in Australia to sidestep U.S. racial policies. Johnson won a decisive victory, becoming the first African-American world champion.

Johnson's victory fueled a deep racial panic in the States, with sports writers and the (white) public demanding a "Great White Hope" to defeat Johnson. After Johnson defeated a number of challengers, pressure was put on Jeffries to come out of retirement and

---

* The term "miscegenation" was coined in 1863, at the height of the Civil War, by David Cole and George Wakeman, two New York "copperheads," northern supporters of the South. It is derived from the Latin "miscere," to mix, and "genus," race, and was intended to be a scientific-sounding term to demonize race mixing and replace the notion of "amalgamation." Amalgamation had long been used in America and came from European usage, referring to the mixing or blending of two or more distinct ethnic or racial groups through intermarriage or nonsexual cultural exchange. [Leslie M. Harris, "From Abolitionist Amalgamators to 'Rulers of Five Points': The Discourse of Interracial Sex and Reform in Antebellum New York City," in Martha Hodes, ed., *Sex, Love, Race: Crossing the Boundaries in North American History* (New York: New York University Press, 1999), 191.]

regain the title. Tempted by an unprecedented purse of $100,000, a match, billed as the "fight of the century," was set for Reno, NV, on Independence Day, July 4, 1910. Thousands attended the open-air fight and millions across the country listened to the play-by-play reports from telegraphy and radio coverage. Johnson did what no boxer had ever accomplished: he knocked out Jeffries in the fifteenth round.

Johnson's victory precipitated an outbreak of racial violence. Attacks on blacks were reported in cities and towns across the country. African-Americans were beaten, some shot and killed, in New Orleans, Houston, Little Rock and at a construction camp outside Uvalda, GA, as well as in New York, Los Angeles, Boston, Baltimore and St. Louis. However, the real scandal involving Johnson took place after his victory and outside the ring, and concerned federal and state campaigns against his sexual relationships with white women.

Johnson was notorious for his uninhibited flaunting of conventional race relations. He was regularly seen in the company of white women, often prostitutes, who accompanied him to his fights. This provoked outrage not only among white fight fans, but law officials as well.

In 1912, the Chicago office of the newly established federal Bureau of Investigation opened an inquiry into his relations with Lucille Cameron, his 18-year-old companion. Federal officials believed that Johnson had violated the recently passed Mann Act, which prohibited the interstate transportation of women for commercial sex. Based on the trumped-up fear that Johnson would flee the jurisdiction, the fighter was arrested and jailed. However, Cameron's testimony that she was a prostitute before meeting Johnson and that they were lovers, planned to marry and that no money was exchanged in their relations, forced the feds to drop charges against the champion.

However, as the historian David Langum points out, this rebuff seemed to only increase efforts to "get" Johnson. The Taft administration's attorney general, George Wickersham, intervened directly, supporting a thorough investigation into Johnson's relations with other white women. In this renewed effort, federal authorities focused on another of Johnson's white female companions, Belle

Schreiber. Their attention was heightened by a photo in a Boston newspaper entitled: "Jack Johnson and his pretty white wife." This and other equally flimsy evidence provided the basis for a federal indictment of Johnson. As Langum notes, "It would seem almost impossible for Johnson to further outrage white American opinion, but he succeeded in doing so by [his] marriage to Lucille Cameron while awaiting trial for the transportation of Belle Schreiber."[49]

Outraged by his marriage, Schreiber turned against Johnson and became the government's key witness. In May 1913, Johnson was convicted on two counts of violating the Mann Act. His appeal was met with the most bizarre decision. While the appellate court criticized both federal prosecutors and the court, finding "an atmosphere of prejudice ... pervades the record," it nevertheless upheld his conviction for "other immoral purposes." Johnson was sentenced to one year and one day and fined $1,000. When the Supreme Court refused to hear his appeal, he fled the country until 1920. When he retuned, he was imprisoned in Leavenworth Penitentiary and served his full sentence. His career over, Johnson died in a car crash in 1946 a forgotten man.[50]

## References

1 Walt Whitman, *Leaves of Grass*, "Your Felons on Trial in Courts," in *The Complete Poems*, Francis Murphy, ed., (New York: Penguin, 2005), 407.

2 Christine Stansell, *City of Women: Sex and Class in New York*, 1789-1860 (Chicago: University of Illinois Press, 1987), 5-6; David Nasaw, *Going Out: The Rise and Fall of Public Amusements* (New York: Basic Books, 1993), 133; M.H. Dunlop, *Gilded City: Scandal and Sensation in Turn-of-the-Century New York* (New York: William Morrow, 2000), 91 and 167-92.

3 George Chauncey, *Gay New York: Gender, Urban Culture, and the Making of the Gay Male World 1890-1940* (New York: Basic Books, 1994), 42-43.

4 Llyod Morris, *Incredible New York: High Life and Low Life of the Last Hundred Years* (New York: Random House, 1951), 259-60.

5 Edwin G. Burrows and Mike Wallace, *Gotham: A History of New York City to 1898* (New York: Oxford University Press, 1999), 1149.

[6] Shelley Ross, *Fall From Grace: Sex, Scandal, and Corruption in American Politics from 1702 to the Present* (New York: Ballantine Books, 1988), 50-52.

[7] Christine Wiltz, *The Last Madame: A Life in the New Orleans Underworld* (New York: Faber & Faber, 2000), 19.

[8] John D'Emilio and Estelle B. Freedmam, *Intimate Matters: A History of Sexuality in America* (New York: Harper & Row, 1988), 279.

[9] Alyn Brodsky, *Grover Cleveland: A Study in Character* (New York, St. Martins, 2000), 87.

[10] Ibid, 88-92.

[11] Ibid, 160.

[12] Ibid, 159.

[13] Ross, 123-26.

[14] Ibid, 131-35.

[15] Ibid, 135-36.

[16] Ibid, 143-46.

[17] Ibid, 136-43.

[18] Morris, 269; Warren Forma, *They Were Ragtime* (New York: Grosset & Dunlop, 1976), 17.

[19] Ross, 101-03.

[20] Milton Rugoff, *Prudery and Passion* (New York: G.P. Putnam's Sons, 1971), 278-80.

[21] Martha Alschuler, *The Origins of the Law of Obscenity*, Technical Report of the Commission on Obscenity and Pornography (Washington, DC: U.S. Government Printing Office, 1971), 77-81.

[22] Robert Corn-Revere, "New Age Comstockery: Exon vs. The Internet" (Cato Policy Analysis No. 232, June 28, 1995), 4.

[23] Vern L. Bullough, *Science in the Bedroom: A History of Sex Research* (New York: Basic Books, 1994), 104; Jay A. Gertzman, *Bookleggers and Smuthounds: The Trade in Erotica, 1920-1940* (Philadelphia: University of Pennsylvania, 1999), 103-34.

[24] Barbara Goldsmith, *Other Powers: The Age of Suffrage, Spiritualism, and the Scandalous Victoria Woodhull* (New York: Harper Perennial, 1999), 290-97.

[25] David Reynolds, *Walt Whitman's America: A Cultural Biography* (New York: Knopf, 1995), 541-43.

[26] Freud quote in Hendrik M. Ruitenbeck, *Freud in America* (New York: Macmillian, 1966), 32-33.

[27] Robert C. Allen, *Horrible Prettiness: Burlesque and American Culture* (Chapel Hill: University of North Carolina Press, 1991), 12; Times quote in Allen, 14.

[28] Ibid, 271.

[29] Linda Mizejewski, *Ziegfeld Girl: Image and Icon in Culture and Cinema* (Durham, NC: Duke University Press, 1999), 65-88.

[30] Allen, 248; see also Stanley Walker, *The Night Club Era* (Baltimore, MD: Johns Hopkins University Press, 1999 [originally published in 1933]), 205-07.

[31] Allen, 235-36.

[32] Ruth Rosen, *The Lost Sisterhood: Prostitution in America, 1900-1918* (Baltimore: Johns Hopkins University Press, 1982), 79.

[33] D'Emilio and Freedman, 210.

[34] Elizabeth Alice Clement, *Trick or Treat: Prostitution and Working-Class Women's Sexuality in New York City, 1900-1932* (Ph. D., University of Pennsylvania, 1998), 42-43; Roger Kahn, A Flame of Pure Fire: Jack Dempsey and the Roaring '20s (New York: Harcourt Brace, 2000), 51.

[35] Kahn, 71-72.

[36] Rosen, 63; Kevin J. Mumford, *Interzones: Black/White Sex Districts in Chicago and New York in the Early Twentieth Century* (New York: Columbia University Press, 1997), 101.

[37] Warren Forma, *They Were Ragtime* (New York: Grosset & Dunlop, 1976), 16.

[38] Timothy J. Gilfoyle, *City of Eros: New York City, Prostitution, and the Commercialization of Sex, 1790-1920* (New York: Norton, 1992), 291.

[39] Jay A. Gertzman, *Bookleggers and Smuthounds: The Trade in Erotica, 1920-1940* (Philadelphia: University of Pennsylvania, 1999), 241-42.

[40] Gilfoyle, 240.

[41] Curt Gentry, *The Madams of San Francisco: An Irreverent History of the City by The Golden Gate* (Sausalito, CA: Comstock Editions, 1964), 182; Al Rose, *Storyville, New Orleans: Being an Authentic, Illustrated Account of the Notorious Red-Light District* (University, AL: University of Alabama Press, 1980), 74; Rosen, 94-95.

[42] Gentry, 182-83.

[43] Ibid, 183.

[44] Mumford, 97.

[45] Barbara Meil Hobson, *Uneasy Virtue: The Politics of Prostitution and the American Reform Tradition* (Chicago: University of Chicago Press, 1990), 170-79; Clement, 131-45.

[46] Chauncey, 221 and 221n.

[47] Chauncey, 223, 155 and 210-11; see also John Donald Gustav-Wrathall, *Take the Young Stranger by the Hand* (Chicago: University of Chicago Press, 1998), 158-59.

[48] Chauncey, 209 and 224.

[49] David J. Langum, *Crossing Over the Line: Legislating Morality and the Mann Act* (Chicago: University of Chicago Press, 1994), 183.

[50] Ibid, 185.

# CHAPTER 4. A NATION IN CRISIS

*I love your back, I love your breasts*
*Darling to feeling, where my face rests,*
*I love your skin so soft and white,*
*So dear to feel and sweet to bite ...*
*I love your poise of perfect thighs,*
*When they hold me in paradise.*[1]

This is a love poem written by Warren Harding, before he became president, to his lover, Carrie Fulton Phillips. Unfortunately, Carrie, a "blue-eyed, strawberry blond" with whom he had a fifteen-year affair, was not his wife. Harding was married to Florence Kling De Wolfe, know as the Duchess, the daughter of the leading banker and wealthiest citizen of Marion, OH. Five years older than her husband, the Duchess was "a tall, bespectacled, and strong-willed woman... ." Perhaps she was the perfect wife for an ambitious politician, but not as sexually stimulating as a younger woman.

Warren G. Harding was inaugurated the twenty-ninth president of the United States in March 1921. Before he became president and during his short tenure (he died in 1923*), few Americans knew that Harding was a notorious philanderer. Fearing that a revelation would undermine his election, the Republican National Committee in 1920 offered Mrs. Phillips a trip to Europe and $20,000 to keep the story secret.[2] In addition to Mrs. Phillips, Harding had affairs with chorus girls Maize Haywood and Blossom Jones. His most notorious liaison was with Nan Britton, "a slim, pretty, jut-jawed blonde," thirty years younger, and with whom he had an out-of-wedlock child.

While a senator, Harding began his affair with Britton in 1917. She came from Ohio and had met the future president while a student; her parents were family friends of the Hardings. Harding was known for his flirtatious ways and Britton apparently had a teenager's crush on this worldly older man. Some years later, she wrote to him looking for a secretarial job. As she recounted in her memoir, *The President's Daughter*, during an interview with him at his Senate office, he asked her to disrobe so "I can visualize you when you are not here."[3]

Their liaisons were frequent and questionably discreet. Britton regularly accompanied him on campaign trips and, registering (with a separate room) in local hotels under his secretary's name, spent many nights with him. By January 1919, as she recalled, "... we stayed [in his office] quite a while that evening, longer, he said, than it was wise for us to do, because the rules governing guests in a Senate office was rather strict." And adds, "[i]t was here, we both decided afterwards, that our baby girl was conceived."

However, their most outlandish encounters took place some years later in the White House after he assumed the presidency. As Britton recalled,

> ... [H]e introduced me to one place [in the White House] where, he said, he thought we *might* share kisses in safety. This was a small closet in the anteroom, evidently a place for hats and coats, but entirely empty most of the times we used it, for we repaired there many times in the course of my visits to the White House.

She concludes her intimate reflection with remarkable candor, "... and in the darkness of a space not more than five feet square the President of the United States and his adoring sweetheart made love."[4]

Like Woodrow Wilson before him, Harding opposed Prohibition. But where Wilson vetoed the Volstead Act legislating Prohibition's enforcement, Harding objected only that the Amendment was "unwise, impudent, and inconsiderate." As a senator, Harding voted for the Act, but as a private citizen continued to indulge. He kept a private house in Washington, DC, and a personal retreat in nearby Deer Park Creek where he regularly socialized with his cronies. As a politician, he knew how to please his electoral base. And as presi-

---

* Rumors circulated that the First Lady poisoned him.

dent, he winked at the apparent contradiction between enforcing the law requiring Prohibition and honoring it in his private life— much like he winked at the scandals that became known as Teapot Dome.

"It's good I'm not a woman," Harding once admitted. "I would always be pregnant. I can't say No." Harding seems to have been a genuinely sexually passionate man.[5] Representing the newly emerging post-Civil War Midwest bourgeoisie, Harding personified the crisis his class was undergoing. This condition is eloquently depicted in Sherwood Anderson's *Winesburg, Ohio* (published in 1919) and Sinclair Lewis' *Babbitt* (published in 1922). Social convention can be a tyrant, imposing a significant toll of self-repression on those enforcing public virtue. However, the very wealth, power and authority that these people seek to use to enforce social standards provide them the means to subvert these conventions. For Harding, a deep, erotic passion found expression in repeated affairs. This position, his ruling-class privilege, enabled many secrets to remain hidden. Like John Kennedy and Bill Clinton later in the twentieth century, Harding set the standard of sexual morality during a tumultuous period of American history.

\* \* \*

The period between the end of World War I and the end of World War II was one of the most tumultuous eras in American history. It saw a boom that culminated in the collapse of global capitalism followed by an extended depression only ending with world war. It was a period in which the nation was restructured from a still predominately homogeneous white rural and small-town agricultural and manufacturing country (with freed African-American slaves in the South) to a heterogeneous, continental-wide urban industrial nation with worldwide influence. Equally fundamental, the American character was restructured, especially women's notions and experiences of sexuality.

This tumultuous quarter-century embodies three distinct phases, each with its own cultural character. Prohibition lasted from 1920 until its repeal in 1933, but really ended with the stock market crash of 1929. The long Depression that came in the wake of the crash lasted until the early-1940s. And, finally, the World War II era commenced with the bombing of Pearl Harbor on December 7, 1941 and ended with Japan's surrender in 1945. Often overlooked, each phase is distinguished by a unique culture of sexual scandal.

Prohibition began on January 16, 1920, and proved a vain attempt to restrict alcohol production, distribution, sale and consumption. Its failure fostered an illicit and illegal "speakeasy" culture that laid the foundation for modern underground society. The speakeasy was the centerpiece of popular resistance to Prohibition and, with the inter-mixing of women and men, blacks and whites, gays and straights, jazz and, of course, alcohol, often drew together all that was illicit in American life. Speakeasies facilitated a scandalous sexual culture never before experienced in American history.

In the wake of the stock market crash, America was plunged into the Great Depression. The American economy shrunk, millions of people lost their jobs, their homes and their farms. And many took to the road in search of better opportunities. As Robert Goldston points out in *The Great Depression: The United States in the Thirties*, Americans were on the move:

> Many of them hit the road. Accompanied by families, in broken-down cars or, increasingly, alone, jobless workers roamed from town to town, city to city, state to state, seeking work that was unavailable. The transient knew in his bones that things were no better ahead than they had been behind, but somehow the movement itself seemed positive. It was something, however a hopeless thing, to do.[6]

Nevertheless, amidst the economic crisis, two areas of scandal attract-ed popular attention, entertainment censorship and interracial sex.

World War II imposed significant limitations on the nation's sexual culture, particularly because of the absence of men. Millions of men were called to arms to fight a global war. This left women without beaus, but provided an unprecedented opportunity to as-sume a greater role in civic life, especially in the workplace. While at war, servicemen fantasized about what they left behind. They were enticed by the widespread availability of pictures of pinup girls and cheesecake publications. And the nation was awash with sex scandals involving movie stars, and even the president and his wife. Over the last half-century, little seems to have changed.

* * *

"In the speak-easies mixed drinking of mixed drinks was the rule," noted one Prohibition-era wag, "the women bellying up to the bar with the men, skirt short, stockings rolled below the knee, and corsets sometimes checked at the cloak room."[7] Of all the scandals of speakeasy society, the presence of women most deeply threatened those seeking to enforce moral rectitude. The new woman coming onto the historical stage expressed herself in an unprecedentedly sexualized manner.

Traditionally, the active pursuit of sensual pleasure by Western women was confined to the select few. She was not the every-woman; rather, she was of the idle rich or a courtesan, a madwoman or a witch. With the emergence of the consumer mass market and its colonization of personal appearance, entertainment and other aspects of daily life, the fantasy of pleasure was extended to a growing number of women.

The women who entered the speakeasies during Prohibition were the quintessential expression of the "new woman." While the notion of the new woman emerged in the post-Civil War era, it was not until the first decades of the twentieth century that she became a social reality. As American women were urbanized, they joined the labor market and earned an income, received an education (many going to elementary school as well as some to college and even post-graduate study) and fought for and won the vote. But they fought for the right to birth control and to experience new forms of sexual pleasure.

The "appearance industry" of the early-twentieth century was the principal agency for the reconstitution of women's sexual representation. It consisted of the combined power of the cosmetics companies, beauty parlors, garment and shoe manufacturers, department stores, small retailers and mail-order houses, advertising agencies and, last but not least, the popular media of women's magazines, movies and radio.

One of the principal battlegrounds over female sexuality involved her face. For generations, a highly made-up face was a social scandal. Outside the theatre, it signaled a prostitute, a "painted lady." By the 1880s, makeup had begun "to cross from the stage into everyday life." By the turn-of-the-twentieth century, cosmetics, particularly lipstick, came to stand for women's new freedom in an age where "appearances were fluid and social rank unstable." Makeup, as Kathy Peiss points out, "assert[ed] worldliness against insularity and sexual desire against chastity." Cosmetics sales rose tenfold over the two decades between 1909 and 1929. The traditionalist's battle against the "false face" eroded as women, especially younger ones, used makeup to "transform the spectacle of themselves into self-conscious performances." By the time Prohibition arrived, the line between a painted lady and a respectable working girl was gone.[8]

Kissing, and a woman's use of lipstick, played a critical role in both public display and private engagements. It was known as the "petting question" during the first few decades of the twentieth century. Until Prohibition, college co-eds, "nice girls," did not kiss until they were engaged. During the 1920s, "fairly indiscriminate petting was the rule" and nowhere was such "indiscriminate" petting more common than at speakeasies.

Clothing heightened a woman's physical sense of her body and an erotic expression of self. It was "a particularly potent way to display and play with notions of respectability, allure, independence, and status and to assert a distinctive identity and presence."[9] American middle- and upper-class women had been constrained by corsets and trailing skirts throughout the nineteenth century, but no longer. Fashion symbolized the new woman and a transformed femininity. As one scholar noted, "the fashionable flapper was correctly perceived to present a serious challenge to the tenacious influence of American Victorian traditions of feminine behavior and display."[10] The change led to the freeing of the woman's physical movement, her very step. The removal of stays and the lifting of the hemline in skirts and dresses made this possible. And as the hemline rose, ankles and calves became a theatre of exposed flesh erotically framed by shoes and stockings.

\* \* \*

No two women of the era of crisis were both the subjects of sexual scandal and so different from one another as Margaret Sanger and Mae West. One was a champion of women's rights and birth control, the other a provocative vaudeville performer and movie star.

While both women lived long lives that roughly overlapped chronologically, they never met. While each was a first-generation "new woman" and born of white, artisan-class parentage, they had their greatest impact on the lives of the poorer classes and immigrants. While both were arrested and served jail sentences for committing what was labeled "obscene" activities, neither really knew the work and the inherent radicality of the other. Truly, they inhabited vastly different social worlds and this difference underlines the scope of scandal and sexuality that defined America's era of crisis.

Sanger and West, nevertheless, had much in common. Both were married at relatively early ages and had unfulfilled relationships with their respective first husbands. Both were notorious divorcees in an era that frowned on single women of passion and accomplishment. Both were driven and achieved success and fame through their personal talent, one intellectual, the other artistic. Both faced significant challenges from contemporaries and, through tenacity and force of will, fulfilled much of their promise. While both were essentially atheists, each dabbled with mysticism. Finally, both lived out powerful sexual passions and had affairs with some of the most interesting men of their era.

Sanger and West were radical women in, respectively, politics and entertainment. Their respective radicality pushed the limits of accepted sexual practice—Sanger in the domain of sexual performance, West in that of sexual presentation. Sanger's tireless efforts on behalf of a woman's right to birth control enabled a woman to not only better control her body, her pregnancy, but helped her better separate procreation from pleasure. Thus women—and, in turn, men—could partake in sexual relations with greater freedom and greater pleasure. West's role as a stage and screen persona embodied the most radical version of female sexuality, one that integrated sexual allure with inversive subordination. She represented female sexuality its most active and exotic sense.[11] Her attempt to reconcile the apparent differences between passion and power offered an image to women—and, in turn, men—of an alternative model of sexuality that challenged Victorian culture and the conventional appearance industries.

Sanger was born Margaret Louisa Higgins on September 14, 1879, to Irish-immigrant parents in Corning, NY. She died almost eighty-eight years later on September 6, 1966. Her life mirrors the trajectory of first- and second-generation feminism. The efforts of these feminists led to a fundamental shift in American social values and resulted in greater freedom for women. These feminists secured women's formal citizenship through the right to vote (a defining goal of the earliest women's movement led by Elizabeth Cady Stanton); gained family planning and birth control as a woman's and a family's basic right;* and won some of the important basic labor rights, including the eight-hour work day, minimum wage and child-labor protection. The course of how these issues moved from the radical margin of society, advocated by feminists, bohemian and progressive intellectuals, labor organizers and socialists, into the mainstream of academic, medical, legal, business and social life reflects Sanger's accomplishments. In her youth, she was one in struggle with Emma Goldman, Elizabeth Gurley Flynn and Havlock Ellis; in her maturity, she was on a first-name basis with Eleanor Roosevelt, John D. Rockefeller, Jr., and Gandhi.**

Sanger came of age during a period in many ways similar to the social, intellectual and political upheavals that marked the 1960s. She moved with her husband, William Sanger, and their children from the placid suburbs of Westchester, NY, to New York City in 1910. She plunged fully into the rich intellectual, cultural and political life in what Ann Douglas calls "mongrel Manhattan."[12] She joined the Socialist party; wrote columns for *The Call*, *The Huffington Post* of its day; and was a regular at the legendary salons hosted by Mabel Dodge. Those in attendance included political figures like John Reed and Bill Haywood, the artists Arthur Davis, Charles Demuth and Max Weber, and renowned intellectuals like Will Durant and A. A. Brill. Within such a stimulating environment, the obligations of marriage and family became greater and greater restraints on her desire to live a passionate life.

Sanger challenged the powerful traditionalist convention that held that a married mother without means (i.e., a rich husband or

---

* Abortion rights have yet to be so accepted and therefore remain lightening-rod issues for the third generation movement.

** Goldman was a leading advocate for sexual freedom and an anarchist; Flynn, the "rebel girl," was a radical labor organizer; and Ellis was an early sex researcher.

inherited wealth) should not lead an autonomous life, a life separate and distinct from her husband's. Fully exploiting the knowledge and experience gained as a nurse in upstate New York, she became an articulate spokesperson on what was then called "women's issues," particularly family planning and birth control. Ellen Chesler, Sanger's principal biographer, evaluates the significance of her writing during this period:

> For a woman to write about sex was especially provocative. To tackle such subjects as pregnancy and abortion, masturbation, menstruation, and defloration, the materials of Margaret's first forays as a columnist, demanded considerable courage, even though she took a traditional Victorian and conservative view of sexual excess, especially with respect to masturbation, which she condemned as harmful on the grounds that it made the experience of sexual gratification in conventional intercourse more difficult.[13]

She founded and edited *The Women Rebel* and published two critical pamphlets, "What Every Girl Should Know" and "Family Limitation," that directly challenged U.S. obscenity laws. She was arrested and, fearing a trial and possible imprisonment for up to forty-five years, fled to Europe in 1914 with a false passport.

Upon her return to the U.S., the original charges were dropped. She plunged back into her tireless campaign for women's sexual and contraceptive rights. Emboldened by the strong support she received from both the New York progressive community and women of all classes across the country, she opened the nation's first birth control clinic on October 16, 1916, in a small tenement storefront in Brownsville, Brooklyn. The clinic dispensed birth control literature, provided helpful information and supplied contraceptive devices (e.g., pessaries, condoms and douching solutions) to the predominately immigrant and working-class women of the neighborhood. The police raided the clinic, arrested Sanger and closed it down for violating obscenity laws!

Sanger drew inspiration for her birth control clinic from two sources: the network of some five hundred tuberculosis clinics then operating in the U.S. and the efforts underway in Europe to establish socialized public health clinics that she had learned of during her trip. However, while her effort drew support from neighborhood women and progressives, the traditionalists, police and medical community railed against her. Convicted for violating the New York Comstock laws, she went to jail for thirty days. While imprisoned with prostitutes and drug addicts, she educated these women on birth control and other "women's issues."*

Sanger's arrest and trial took place amidst the mounting hysteria that accompanied the U.S. entry into World War I. The war caused a fundamental schism within the progressive community. While many of her more radical comrades, most notably Goldman, stood in pacifist opposition to U.S. involvement in the war and others supported the war effort, Sanger took a third course. She claimed a neutral position, one that placed women's right to birth control above the war and the polarizing positions it engendered. Sanger's compromise would guide her efforts during the subsequent decades of her long and distinguished career.

Sanger's position allowed her to escape the right-wing revenge against the most radical progressives that followed during the postwar Red Scare. While the Palmer Raids and subsequent deportations of radicals (including her oldest comrade-in-arms and rival for influence, Goldman) were underway, Sanger organized the nation's first birth control conference. Held in 1921, it drew distinguished guests such as Winston Churchill and Theodore Dreiser as well as many medical and academic dignitaries. As Chesler notes, "[t]he conference reestablished Margaret as the country's preeminent spokeswoman for birth control."[14]

Sanger attempted to reconcile political belief with practical action. Birth control not only provides a woman with greater power over her life—her body and her pregnancy—but also provides a means by which she can experience greater erotic pleasure. Sanger's political activism and intellectual forcefulness were matched by a strong sexual passion. She advocated for sexual freedom and also

---

* Ironically, the New York State court turned down Sanger's appeal on the grounds that ordinary women should not give out medical information – this should be left to trained doctors. This ruling set the stage for the subsequent opening of legal birth control clinics with medical supervision. [Ellen Chester, *Woman of Valor: Margaret Sanger and the Birth of the Birth Control Movement in America* (New York: Simon & Schuster, 1992), 160.]

practiced it. She appears to have really enjoyed sexual relations. She may well have had affairs, if not of the flesh than of the mind, with some of the leading intellectuals of her day, including Havlock Ellis, H. G. Wells and Lorenzo Portet.* Her relationship with (and subsequent marriage to) Noah Slee, a millionaire manufacturer, started in 1921 as she organized her first U.S. birth control conference. With its success and her marriage to Slee, she abandoned both her radical socialist roots and sexual liaisons outside of marriage as well.

Mary Jane ("Mae") West was born on August 17, 1893, to Irish-English-German immigrant parents in Brooklyn, NY. She died eighty-five years later on November 22, 1978. The trajectory of her life during the first half of the twentieth century mirrors the transformation of modern female sexuality. Her life bears witness to how sexuality has been integrated into the commercial marketplace and the ongoing attempts to subvert this containment. West understood the full consequences of this development perhaps better than any public figure of the period for living her life at the very eye of the storm and, through her very success and scandals, she also became a casualty of it.

"… West's personae played on the margins of bourgeois tolerance and tested its limits," acknowledges the theatre historian Robert Allen, placing her in a unique position among modern female performance artists. He adds, "she created a personae of the glamorous, tough, aggressive, sensual women."[15] She seems, especially in her youth, to have clearly recognized the difficulty of her position. Her critique of the culture industry, expressed as a monologue in her 1927 play, *The Wicked Age*, is spoken in the self-conscious voice of one who has learned deeply from painful experience:

> The basis of any industry that needs immediate attention of the public for success today is based on the exploitation of the female form … Take the theatre, … plays go over that exhibit the woman's body in some way or another. … [L]ook at musical comedies—with their beautiful curtains of living beauties—their tableaux, their

---

* Portet was a disciple of Francisco Ferrer, Spain's leading reformer and educator who had been assassinated by Spanish monarchists in 1909. Sanger may well have had a homo-erotic encounter with Janet de Selincourt, the wife of one of her lovers, Hugh de Selincourt. [Chesler, 186.]

beautiful scenes—everything is an excuse for a horde of almost naked women to parade up and down the stage, to give the out of town buyers a kick ...[16]

The contradiction that West attempted to reconcile—being simultaneously the almost naked woman at center stage of the culture industry and a fierce critic of it—represents not only the dilemma faced by other female performers of the twentieth century, but women in general in an increasingly commercialized sexual culture.

West's sexuality artfully incorporated two forces—exposure and insubordination, or as she put it, "It isn't what you do; it's how you do it!"[17] It seems that her exposure never involved total nudity. While other cabaret, burlesque and carnival girl-show performers exploited the provocativeness of nudity though the striptease, West resisted. Rather, her exposure radiated a certain lewdness of engagement. The lewdness she articulated—in an increasingly exaggerated form—was richly complex. It was expressed in her suggestive clothing, her verbal inflections, her knowing, provocative double entendres, her playful gaze and pose, and her dancing during live shows, especially the cooch and the shimmy. As she so salaciously said to one of her male fans, "Is that a pistol in your pocket or are you just glad to see me?"[18]

West challenged convention through her representation of a radical sexuality, one that, in its self-conscious lewdness, embodied female insubordination. It was a sexuality that refused to lose its critical edge, to give up its demand for fulfillment, to passively accommodate male desire. This forceful and subversive quality represented her greatest challenge to traditionalist's sensibilities, particularly during the 1920s when she was part of the New York theatre scene. Her success propelled her to Hollywood during the Depression, where she became a commercial sex star, reflecting a more stylized, tamer female performer. Her earlier theatrical performances were considered among the most provocative, lascivious, of the period. They were repeatedly closed down by the police as obscene, resulting in her arrest and imprisonment. She became the queen of front-page tabloid scandals.

Like today's inner-city youth drawn to the hip-hop scene, West grew up at a time and in a place in which the theatre was a viable option for the more adventurous. Her turn-of-the-century Brooklyn neighborhood was birthplace to such stars as Clara Bow and Marion Davies.[19] West first performed on-stage at six years of age.* For a young girl with passion, everything seemed possible. As a performer, she came of age during the 1910s and twenties. It was the era just before the triumph of movies, when popular entertainment was live, whether presented in the more legitimate theatre setting or at more informal cabarets and speakeasies.

It was within the contradictory impulses of Prohibition, of suppression and of transgression, that West achieved her legendary status. She pushed the limits of acceptable behavior and was repeatedly arrested for doing so. *Variety* urged her to tone down her shows, but she wouldn't dream of it. She pushed the performance envelope, inviting popular culture to catch up to her. And it did. With the dedication and resolve recognized only after fame is achieved, West ceaselessly worked for over a decade to perfect her talent and to force America to accept a radically different notion of female sexuality. Her work became more salacious and provocative than mainstream vaudeville, but less explicit than burlesque.

West's performances during the 1920s and early-thirties are marked by defiance. A brief review of five of her shows from the mid-twenties is illustrative. *SEX* opened in 1926 and was, as one of West's biographer's declares, "the play that put Mae on the map." Set in a Montreal brothel and featuring "gaudily dressed prostitutes," it was closed down by the police and ruled by the court as "obscene, immoral, and indecent." West was arrested and, along with her producers, received a fine and a ten-day prison sentence.[20]

The 1927 play, *The Drag*, is about how an apparently "normal" man deals with his homosexual desires. As Allen notes, "[t]he characters who suffer in the play are those who deny their true nature or attempt to conceal it." The high point of the show is the third act during which a party is staged with forty gay men in drag. While

---

* West's last film, *Sextette* was completed in 1977 when she was well into her eighties. It featured Timothy Dalton, Tony Curtis, George Hamilton, Walter Pigeon and George Raft as well as such rock stars as Ringo Starr, Alice Cooper and Keith Moon. [Maurice Leonard, *Mae West: Empress of Sex* (New York: Birch Line Press, Carroll Communications, 1991), 386.]

the play ran for two-week rehearsals in Paterson, NJ, West did not open it in New York because the police notified her that they would close it down.[21] *The Wicked Age*, which ran in 1927, is a critique of beauty pageants, especially the "Miss America" pageant then gaining popularity. West attacked pageants as pernicious vehicles that exploited female sexuality for commercial purposes. While beauty pageants date from 1854, when P.T. Barnum first introduced them to attract male customers, they took on a new social role in the 1920s as a legitimizing institution that set the parameters of acceptable female physical display.[22]

*The Pleasure Man* ran in 1928. It depicts a brother's rage at a man who acts in what one critic called "barbaric masculinity" against his sister; it ends with him castrating the sexual villain off-stage. The play achieved such notoriety during rehearsals that it was closed by the police on opening night.[23] Finally, *Diamond Lil*, which also ran in 1928, was West's most successful Broadway effort. Rich with the imagery of the turn-of-the-century urban underworld or tenderloin, it presents an appealing portrait of the demimonde of prostitutes, "white-slave" traders, shoplifters and cocaine addicts.[24]

With her new acclaim on Broadway, West was enticed to Hollywood as the Depression was settling in and studio executives looked to provocative female sexuality to sell tickets. Early female sexuality had been a staple feature since the medium's earliest inception. Stars like Theda Bara and Alla Nazimova had perfected the on-screen form of female glamour.[25] West's films during the 1930s, like *She Done Him Wrong* (1933) and *I'm No Angel* (1933), were essentially extensions of her theatre personae and paired her with such male stars as W. C. Fields, Cary Grant, George Raft and Randolph Scott. Yet, as she achieved greater popularity through movies, her image of sexuality became frozen and she became a caricature of her own once-radical personality. Nevertheless, as a movie star, her reputation and uncompromising explicitness antagonized traditionalist forces of moral order, particularly the Catholic Legion of Decency. Unfortunately, as Allen and others have pointed out, "West's personae became less and less threatening as it became more and more difficult to take her expressive sexuality seriously."[26]

West's once-radical sexuality was fueled by a self-conscious attempt to reconcile her performance arts (both her performances and the plays she wrote) with her personal life. In the formative years on the New York stage, she not only advocated sexual freedom but practiced it—she appears to have really enjoyed sexual relations! And, in particularly, she found sexual passion in the appeal of powerfully physical men. As Leonard notes, "[t]hroughout her life she loved to have sex with boxers on the night they had fought, and frequently did so." Among her conquests were heavyweight champions James J. Corbett and Jack Dempsey.[27] As she became a frozen sexual personae, her sexual liaisons—especially as she aged—became caricatures of all that had been. Sadly, the more she held to fantasy of her original sexuality, the more she seemed a prisoner of the fiction and, thus, lost the very eroticism that once distinguished her.

* * *

Mae West's showgirl inspiration was the legendary speakeasy hostess, Texas Guinan, the queen of Prohibition America. Tex ran New York's most notorious *speak*, the El Fay Club, bankrolled by the gangster Larry Fay. According to Maurice Leonard, Texas "was blonde and blowsy and could match any man in a fist fight." Among her more memorable contributions to popular culture of her day were the catchphrases "Hello suckers!", "Don't give a sucker a break!" and "Give the little girl a big hand!" Her toughness is enshrined in the alleged comment from one of her regulars: "Reach down in your heart, Texas, and get me a piece of cracked ice."[28]

Speakeasies were often run by colorful women (sometimes madams) and men (sometimes gangsters) who attained legendary status like Texas. They were a nearly nation-wide phenomenon that ranged from the fly-by-night "big pigs" or "blind pigs" dispensing diluted alcohol, to drinking clubs in New York like the Pen and Pencil and the Artists and Writers, and to fancy night spots like Helen Morgan's Chez Morgan, Belle Livingstone's Country Club and Gilda Gray's Piccadilly Rendezvous. Most hostesses at speakeasies, cabarets and nightclubs were far less glamorous and threatening than Guinan, but all had one goal: to encourage men to spend money.

The changing sexual representation of women as exemplified by West was not limited to Broadway or Hollywood stars. Prohibition fostered the speakeasy, America's most radical venue of social transgression. As the historian George Chauncey found,

The criminalization of liquor not only drove many respectable middle-class establishments out of the restaurant business, but resulted in the virtual criminalization of nightlife. The proliferation of illegal speakeasies and nightclubs after Prohibition led to the wholesale corruption of policing agencies, the systematic use of payoffs, and the development of crime syndicates that offered protection from the police.

He adds that "[t]he speakeasies eroded the boundaries between respectability and criminality, between public and private, and between commercial space and home life... ." At the speakeasy, a virtual "criminalized demimonde," patrons "entered an intimate theater in which they were expected to play a role."[29]

In keeping with Prohibition policy, Guinan's clubs were regularly closed down and almost immediately reopened under a new name. Her clubs featured a troupe of scantily-clad fan dancers who, because of limited space, often performed provocatively close to the customers. They became a popular nightspot for a virtual who's-who of the city's luminaries. Regulars included entertainers like Al Jolson, Irving Berlin and George Gershwin, who often played impromptu piano; movie stars such as Gloria Swanson, Clara Bow, Rudolph Valentino and John Barrymore; and such well-heeled worthies as Reginald ("Reggie") Vanderbilt, Harry Payne Whitney and Walter Chrysler. Movie stars Ruby Keeler and George Raft got their starts at the club. The Prince of Wales (later Duke of Windsor) visited New York and came to one of her clubs to see what made *speaks* so popular. On one visit, he joined the fight-promoter George "Tex" Rickard* and cowboys from the Ringling Brothers Circus. The patrons cheered the Prince as one of the fellas!

In a thankless effort to enforce Prohibition, the police kept inventing and enforcing new laws to close down *speaks*. In June 1928, one hundred and sixty Prohibition agents raided fifteen New York *speaks*. Of all those arrested, Texas was the only one who challenged her arrest. Her trial became a media circus. Everyone knew that Texas ran an upscale *speak* and wanted her to beat the prohibitionists.

---

* Rickard ran Madison Square Garden in the twenties and is credited with staging the first $1 million boxing match. He was also involved in a notorious sex scandal, see below.

At her trial, one Prohibition agent, James L. White, said he visited the club twelve times but couldn't get in on the thirteenth because it was too crowded. He also admitted spending $360 for food and liquor. She was acquitted.

Texas was again busted in 1929 and charged with "maintaining a nuisance" at her Salon Royale. At her trial, Tex insisted that she functioned only as a hostess, serving as "a singer, dancer, welcomer and wisecracker"; she sought only to bring "sunshine into the lives of tired businessmen." She described one of the stunts that the patrons enjoyed. She had "a guest walk five times around a walking cane while holding it in one hand" and then walk back to his or her table. The patron would lose his/her balance and often fall down. Following a brief, fifty-five minute deliberation, the jury acquitted her. In the Court Room, in true Roaring Twenties' spirit, someone yelled, "Give the little girl a great big hand." At a gala victory party held at her Club Intime, she read a telegram from Congressman (and soon-to-be mayor) Fiorello La Guardia, "Congratulations. We all give the little girl a great big hand. [30]

* * *

Sex scandal played a critical role in shaping the sexual culture of the interwar era of crisis. Scandal was aggressively reinforced by news reports of often-gory sex crimes, especially pedophilia scandals, a staple of the popular press. Many scandals involved celebrities. Others involved noted political figures, especially the president and first lady. However, the scandals provoking the deepest national anxiety involved interracial sexual relations (real or alleged).

Against the ongoing battles over Prohibition, the scandal involving Jack Demsey's promoter, "Tex" Rickard, captured national headlines. On January 22, 1922, Rickard was reputed to have taken seven pre-pubescent girls, from eleven to fifteen years, to New York's Madison Square Garden swimming pool where "he helped undress them before a dip. When they were naked he fondled their breasts and genitals." He also is reported to have taken two of the girls, Anna Hess (age twelve) and Alice Ruck (age fifteen), up to his apartment in the Garden where he plied them with alcohol and sexually assaulted them. Rickard was arrested, went on trial and was acquitted after only ninety minutes.[31]

Other celebrity scandals during the nineteen twenties involved Hollywood's two most famous funnymen, Roscoe "Fatty" Arbuckle and Charlie Chaplin. During the early-twenties, Arbuckle, an over-weight, comic character, was one the highest paid movie stars. His claim to fame was as the first movie star hit in the face with a pie. On an ill-fated 1921 Labor Day weekend jaunt to San Francisco, he hosted an intimate get-together with a number of local party girls in his suite at the St. Francis Hotel. In the spirit of his celebrity, bootlegged liquor flowed freely. One the young starlets, Virginia Rappe, got very sick and was taken to a local "sanatorium" for pregnant women where she died. Arbuckle was arrested and charged with murder.

William Randolph Hearst's *San Francisco Examiner* promoted the Rappe murder as the crime of the decade. The combination of a Hollywood star, illegal drink, the death of an apparently innocent young woman and wild sex fueled popular calls for moral retribu-tion. Arbuckle was subject to three trials and juries acquitted him each time. In the midst of his second trial in February 1922, the movie director William Desmond Taylor was found shot to death in his Hollywood bungalow, adding to the sensation of Prohibition-era scandal. While innocent in the eyes of the law, Arbuckle was con-demned in the court of public opinion and essentially blacklisted by the movie business.[32]

In 1925, another Hollywood funnyman, Charlie Chaplin, faced a scandal over his marriage to Lillita "Lita" McCurray (aka Lita Grey). Chaplin had known McCurray since she was twelve and when she was sixteen he cast her as his co-star in the hit *The Gold Rush*. However, she got pregnant and they fled to Mexico to marry; Chaplin, thirty-five years old, would have faced statutory-rape charges if they attempted to marry in California. The couple divorced in 1927. During the divorce proceedings, Grey's lawyers charged that Chaplin sought to "under-mine and distort plaintiff's normal sexual impulses and desires, de-moralize her standards of decency and degrade her conception of mor-als for the gratification of the defendant's aforesaid unnatural desires." Such "unnatural desires" were rumored to be oral sex and *ménage a trois* with another woman. The court awarded Grey the then-largest di-vorce settlement of $625,000 and $100,000 for each of their two sons.

Stories of Chaplin's divorce sandal were fodder for the nation's tabloids. These news reports led women's clubs to come out in sup-

port of Grey and led many local politicians and civic groups to pro-
pose banning his movies. America's greatest satirist, H.L. Mencken,
caught the spirit of the episode:

> The very morons who worshipped Charlie Chaplin six weeks ago now
> prepare to dance at the stake while he is burned; he is learning some-
> thing of the psychology of the mob. … A public trial involving sexual
> accusations is made a carnival everywhere in the United States.

One of Chaplin's biographers speculates that this affair was the
model for Vladimer Nabakov's *Lolita*.*[33]

While Hearst promoted the Arbuckle case as the murder trial of
the decade, it was the annulment trial between Alice Jones and Leonard Rhinelander that was the sex scandal of the 1920s. Listed in the
*Social Register*, the Rhinelanders were a New York family that traced
its lineage to settlers arriving in the New World in 1696. The Joneses,
on the other hand, were first-generation working class British immigrants who appeared to be "colored." Alice and Leonard dated for
three years before wedding, appeared to be truly in love and willing to
fight social convention in marriage. However, the young Rhinelander
ultimately capitulated to his father's demand to annul the marriage.
But to secure an annulment, Rhinelander needed to prove that Jones
deceived him and falsely presented herself as a white woman.

The trial commenced on November 9, 1925, and drew national
attention. The highpoint of the trial took place when Alice was asked
to disrobe in the judge's chambers and display herself in a semi-nude
fashion to the jurors. As reported in front-page newspaper stories,
often with hand-drawn images, Alice stood weeping and clutching
her mother's arm while jurors examined her. While humiliated, jurors saw Jones to be a woman of color and Rhinelander's claim that
he had been deceived was untenable. The court dismissed his claim
and the couple eventually resolved a mutual annulment.[34]

The Rhinelander-Jones trial was the most compelling sex scandal of the 1920s, but the Scottsboro trial was the most troubling sex

---

* In his autobiography, Chaplin refuses to comment on the Grey affair, not-
ing only "Because we have two sons of whom I am very fond, I will not go
into any detail." [Charlie Chaplin, *My Life* (New York: Simon & Schuster,
1964), 365.]

scandal of the thirties, if not of the twentieth century. In 1931, and in the face of the deepening Depression, nine African-American youths ranging in age from twelve to twenty, were arrested for illegally riding a train in search of work. They were removed by local law enforcement at Scottsboro, AL. The authorities convinced two white women, Victoria Price and Ruby Bates, a minor, to accuse the youths of rape. In keeping with swift southern justice, within two weeks all nine defendants—Haywood Patterson, Roy Wright, Clarence Norris, Andy Wright, Willie Roberson, Charlie Weems, Ozzie Powell, Olen Montgomery and Eugene Williams—were tried and convicted; eight of the youths received the death sentence and the youngest, Williams, received life imprisonment.

Interracial heterosexual sex is one of the deepest taboos in American culture, especially in the South. When such sex is due to alleged rape, especially involving a black male and a white female, particularly an underage girl, southern racism comes to a ferocious boil. According to the historian Nell Irvin Painter, "from 1882 until the early 1950s, reports show, 4,739 people died at the hands of lynch mobs; the actual number may approach 6,000." Painter estimates that "82 percent of lynchings have occurred in the South, where 84 percent of its victims were black and 95 percent male."[35]

One aspect of the Great Depression that made a difference was radical political activism. It was a collective, social response to shared hardship, including racial discrimination. In the wake of the patent racism inflected on the Scottsboro youths, Americans throughout the country mobilized to fight the injustice. Over the next six years, the Scottsboro youths, represented by lawyers from the Communists Party's International Labor Defense and the National Association for the Advancement of Colored People (NAACP), battled southern racism and all-white juries. In three state trials and a successful 1937 appeal to the U.S. Supreme Court, the Scottsboro defendants became an international *cause celeb* and their lives saved! Nevertheless, even after one of the white complaintents, the underage Bates, repudiated her original testimony and admitted that she and Price had made false confessions, the southern juries still convicted the defendants. In the end, all of the Scottsboro defendants eventually got out of prison either by being released, escaping or a pardon. It remains America's ugliest (false!) sex scandal.*[36]

* * *

Since the 1870s, American family planning medical procedures were regulated by federal Comstock laws. Though repeatedly challenged, these laws had their greatest effect on the lives of women and girls facing the problems of birth control, abortion and personal health. They remained in force until Sanger challenged them in 1930 over the importation of Japanese condoms. In 1936, the Supreme Court, in what is know as *U.S. v One Package of Japanese Pessaries*, struck down Comstock restrictions on birth control information and devices for medical purposes. The Court ruled that items used to protect the health of a patient did not fall under federal obscenity laws. This precipitated a national controversy driven by Christian conservatives fearful that the floodgate of illicit sex practices was breached. Like today's concern with abortion, a poll commissioned by *Ladies' Home Journal* found that 79 percent of readers—half of them Catholic—favored loosening birth-control regulations.[37]

During the years of World War II, sex scandals lost the edge as media phenomenon they occupied during the earlier phases of the era of crisis. America was mobilized in a worldwide war. Of course, this did not mean that scandals disappeared. Like earlier periods, scandals often involved celebrities.

One celebrity scandal that captured national attention involved the legendary tennis champion William "Big Bill" Tilden. Within the pro-tennis community, rumors had circulated since the 1920s that he paid special attention to youthful lads. In 1946, his particular sexual deviance was exposed, ending his professional career. Tilden was arrested and convicted of contributing to the delinquency of a minor. The youth, a teenage prostitute, engaged in a voluntary relationship with Tilden, but the tennis star was convicted, sentenced to prison and served seven months of a one-year sentence. In 1949, Tilden was again arrested for sexual advances made on a 16-year-old hitchhiker

---

* The murder of Emmett Till, a 14-year-old, African-American boy from Chicago, on August 20, 1955, for talking with a white girl in Money, MS, shows that racial scandal persisted into the post-World War II era. The 1989 "Central Park jogger" case led to the arrest, trial, conviction and imprisonment of five New York Hispanic and black youths based on alleged "confessions," and from which the youths were finally exonerated in 2002, shows that such false scandals persist into the twenty-first century.

and convicted, sentenced to a year in prison and served ten months. The scandals associated with these arrests ended Tilden's career and he lived out the last few years of his life as a penniless recluse.[38]

Errol Flynn was one of Hollywood's great leading men. He starred in such action-adventure classics as *Captain Blood* (1935) and *The Adventures of Robin Hood* (1938). But he had a reputation for having his way with underage starlets and even fans. In 1942, his particular passion became front-page headlines as double statutory-rape charges were brought against him by two teenage fans, Betty Hansen and Peggy Satterlee. While local gossip suggests that Flynn had voluntary sex with the girls, he steadfastly claimed that he never had sex with them. At trial, the girls gave inconsistent testimony and the actor was acquitted. However, his sexual exploits live on in the memorable phase, "in like Flynn."[39]

The biggest scandal of the war years involved Hollywood's legendary hobo, Chaplin. In 1943, rumors that Chaplin fathered an out-of-wedlock child with the actress Joan Barry were promoted by syndicated gossip columnists Hedda Hopper of the *Los Angeles Times* and Florabel Muir of the *New York Daily News*. In a bitterly-contested paternity suite, Barry's revelations about their affair captured headlines throughout the country. She admitted that around Christmas 1942 she showed up at his house, forced herself in with a gun in hand and went to bed with the actor. While a blood test proved Chaplin was not the father of Barry's child, the Los Angeles court refused to accept the test and ordered him to pay child support.

However, this was only the beginning of an ever-grander scandal that enveloped Chaplin. In her revelations, Barry admitted that Chaplin had paid her and her mother's traveling expenses to return to New York, that she met him when he visited the Big Apple and they had sex together in his hotel room. In 1944, federal authorities charged Chaplin with violating the Mann Act. The Act, originally enacted in 1910, was passed to stem an alleged and wide-scale "white slavery" trade, the interstate transport of women for prostitution. Conviction under the Act could lead to up to twenty-five years in prison and a fine of $25,000. Chaplin believed that he was prosecuted because he was a Hollywood radical who supported America's wartime alliance with Russia. Chaplin was acquitted.[40]

Over the last few decades, Americans have increasingly accepted illicit dalliances by politicians as occupational perks. However, in the pre-Clinton days, rumors of extramarital affairs involving a president or other high officials were discreetly hidden. This is especially evident in the experiences of Franklin Roosevelt and Dwight Eisenhower.

Roosevelt's "friendships" with Lucy Page Mercer, Eleanor's secretary, is openly acknowledged, but its nature is still debated. Eleanor apparently discovered love letters between the two and, in a painful showdown, threatened to divorce FDR if he didn't end his relations with Mercer. However, while ostensibly ending their friendship, FDR continued to occasionally see Mercer; she was with him at Warm Springs just before he died. FDR is rumored to have had affairs with Marguerite Alice (Missy) LeHand, his secretary, and Crown Princess Marta of Norway, who lived at the White House during World War II. Eleanor's own "friendships" with both women and men was the subject of much speculation. She maintained close relationships with Nancy Cook, a carpenter; Marion Dickerman, a teacher; and Lorena Hickok, a leading journalist. Allegations surfaced about her friendships, and rumored affairs, with Earl Miller, a New York State trooper who served as her bodyguard while FDR was governor, and with Joseph Lash, a New Deal activist and biographer of both Eleanor and FDR.[41]

Republicans were not immune from sex scandals, nor from the press hushing them up. Rumors circulated widely that party leader and 1940 presidential candidate, Wendell Wilkie, had a long-term affair with Irita Van Doren, book editor for the *New York Herald Tribune*. He is also reported having affairs with Madame Chiang Kai-Shek and the southern writer, Josephine Pickney.

During the War, Dwight Eisenhower had an affair with Kay Summersby, his English driver. It is said that Ike wanted to resign from the army, divorce his wife and marry Summersby, but General George Marshall told him it would ruin his career. Later, Summersby wrote a book, *Past Forgotten: My Love Affair with Dwight D. Eisenhower*, about their affair. She claimed that she and Ike never had sex: He was impotent due to the pressures of the war!

### References

[1] Harding quote in Roger Kahn, *A Flame of Pure Fire: Jack Dempsey and the Roaring '20s* (New York: Harcourt Brace, 1999), 251-52.

2   John H. Summers, "What Happened to Sex Scandals? Politics and Peccadilloes, Jefferson to Kennedy," *Journal of American History*, December 2000, vol. 87, issue 3, 850.

3   Britton quote in Edward Behr, *Prohibition: Thirteen Years that Changed the Nation* (Arcade, 1996), 110-11.

4   Frances Russell, *The Shadow of Blooming Grove: Warren G. Harding in His Times* (New York: McGraw-Hill, 1968), 466.

5   Harding quote in Kahn, 333.

6   Robert Goldston, *The Great Depression: The United States in the Thirties* (Indianapolis, IN: Bobbs-Merrill, 1968), 50.

7   Quoted in Joan Hoff, *The Twenties: The Critical Issues* (Boston: Little Brown, 1972), 134.

8   Kathy Peiss, *Hope in a Jar: The Making of America's Beauty Culture* (New York: Henry Holt, 1998), 48, 39, 54, 55, 97 and 142.

9   Kathy Peiss, *Cheap Amusements: Working Women and Leisure in Turn-of-the-Century New York* (Philadelphia: Temple University Press, 1986), 3.

10   Angela L. Latham, *Posing a Threat: Flappers, Chorus Girls, and Other Brazen Performers of the American 1920s* (Hanover, NH: Wesleyan University Press, 2000), 21.

11   Robert C. Allen, *Horrible Prettiness: Burlesque and American Culture* (Chapel Hill: University of North Carolina Press, 1991), 281.

12   Ann Douglas, *Terrible Honesty: Mongrel Manhattan in the 1920s* (New York: Noonday Press, 1995), 5.

13   Ellen Chester, *Woman of Valor: Margaret Sanger and the Birth of the Birth Control Movement in American* (New York: Simon & Schuster, 1992), 65-66.

14   Ibid, 201.

15   Allen, 280 and 274; see also Kenneth Anger, *Hollywood Babylon* (New York: Bell, 1991), 182-91.

16   West quote in Latham, 92.

17   West quote in Allen, 274.

18   West quote in Douglas, 47.

19   Maurice Leonard, *Mae West: Empress of Sex* (New York: Birch Line Press, Carroll Communications, 1991), 5.

20   Leonard, 61; Allen, 276 and 277; see also Leonard, 61-85.

21   Allen, 277-79; Leonard, 70-72.

22   Leonard, 77-79; Latham, 91-93.

23  Leonard, 84.

24  Allen, 279-80; Leonard, 80-84.

25  Leonard, 56.

26  Allen, 281.

27  Leonard, 35, 48 and 56.

28  Guinan quotes in Leonard, 53 and 135.

29  George Chauncey, *Gay New York: Gender, Urban Culture, and the Making of the Gay Male World, 1890-1940* (New York: Basic Books, 1994), 308.

30  Louise Berliner, *Texas Guinan: Queen of the Night Club* (Austin: University of Texas, 1993),151.

31  Kahn, 271-78.

32  Anger, 21-30; James P. Petersen, *The Century of Sex: Playboy's History of the Sexual Revolution, 1900-1999* (New York: Grove Press, 1999), 97-100.

33  Mecken quote in Kenneth S. Lynn, *Charlie Chaplin and His Times* (New York: Simon & Schuster, 1997), 311; see also Anger, 79-95 and Petersen, 102-03.

34  Earl Lewis and Heidi Ardizzone, *Love on Trial: An American Scandal in Black and White* (New York: Norton, 2001), 156-74.

35  Nell Irvin Painter, "Who Was Lynched?," *The Nation*, November 11, 1991, vol. 53, issue 16, 577.

36  Dan T. Carter, *Scottsboro: A Tragedy of the American South* (Baton Rouge, LA: Louisiana State University Press, 1979).

37  http://law.jrank.org/pages/13292/United-States-v-One-Package.

38  Timothy G. Gilfoyle, *City of Eros: New York City, Prostitution and the Commercialization of Vice, 1790-1920* (New York: Norton, 1992), 291.

39  Anger, 208-15.

40  Lynn, 432-38; Chaplin, 422-30.

41  Laura Tyson Li, *Madame Chiang Kai-Shek: China's Eternal First Lady* (Open City Books, 2006), 182; *Charles Peters, Five Days in Philadelphia: 1940, Wendell Willkie, FDR and the Political Convention That Won World War II* (Public Affairs, 2006), 193; Joseph Lash, *A World of Love: Eleanor Roosevelt and Her Friends, 1942-1962* (New York: Doubleday, 1984), 385.

# CHAPTER 5. RECOVERY & RENEWAL

*This society turns everything it touches into a potential source of progress and of exploitation, of drudgery and satisfaction, of freedom and of oppression. Sexuality is no exception.*
Herbert Marcuse[1]

In 1958, at a posh party at New York's glamorous Plaza Hotel, celebrities and corporate executives comfortably rubbed shoulders. These social worthies ranged from Lewis S. Rosenstiel, chairman of Schenley Industries, a leading liquor company, to Roy Cohn, former counsel to Sen. Joseph McCarthy, and J. Edgar Hoover, director of the Federal Bureau of Investigation, the nation's top lawman. As gossip has it, Hoover hosted a private get-together in his suite during the evening, where he made a most dramatic appearance.

Susan L. Rosenstiel, the former wife of the Schenley chairman, attended the private soiree. As she reports, "he [Hoover] was wearing a fluffy black dress, very fluffy, with flounces and lace stockings and high heels, and a black curly wig." She adds, "he had makeup on and false eyelashes." She claimed that Cohn introduced Hoover to her as "Mary" and he allegedly responded, "Good evening." She also insists that she saw Hoover go into a bedroom and take off his skirt. There, "young blond boys" had sex with him in bed.[2]

Like Jefferson's interracial relation, Buchanan's homoerotic love affair and Harding's out-of-wedlock child, Hoover's transvestitism is part of popular American lore. Hoover's "deviance" is much debated and, whether real or myth, provides a unique vantage point into the sexuality of the tumultuous 1945–1975 period. Tales of Hoover's transvestitism have their roots in Anthony Summers' 1993 book, *Official and Confidential: The Secret Life of J. Edgar Hoover.* Summers presents Susan Rosenstiel's "gossip" about Hoover's black dress, but

113

tells additional tales where he engaged in sex with young men. She claims that, in 1959, she again attended a gala at the Plaza. This time Hoover wore a red dress, with a black feather boa wrapped around his neck. She also claims that, holding a Bible, Hoover had one of his attending blond young men read a passage as another played with his penis.

Conservatives have fought this depiction of Hoover, somehow thinking his mean-spirited role as FBI director was compromised by his transvestitism. Ronald Kessler, in *The Bureau: The Secret History of the FBI*, presents the most compelling defense of the former FBI chief. He argues that Susan Rosenstiel was a less-than-trustworthy witness, having served time at New York's municipal prison, Riker's Island, in 1971 for perjury. He reports that New York's legendary district attorney, Robert M. Morgenthau, found her a questionable witness, if not mentally incompetent; she believed that Hoover had conspired against her during her divorce proceedings. Finally, he objects to Summers' conclusion that the Mafia blackmailed Hoover because of his fetishistic predilections, effectively halting federal crime investigations; he insists that the prosecution of legendary mob money-man, Myer Lansky, demonstrates Hoover's independence. Anyone who has seen Francis Ford Coppola's classic *Godfather* series will beg to differ.[3]

While the concerns raised by those defending Hoover's reputation may be true (or the evidence questioning Hoover's reputation unsubstantiated), one simple fact stands without question: Clyde Tolson was Hoover's life partner. A fellow FBI agent, Tolson and Hoover were inseparable for more than forty years. They shared a house, dressed in similar outfits, vacationed together and, which says more than anything, are buried alongside one another. What this relationship meant to them remains very much a personal mystery. Like Buchanan's relations to Rufus King and Lincoln's relation to Joshua Speed, homo-social relations may not be homoerotic. Men, and women, can be intimate friends who, like non-incestuous siblings, share the deepest affinity. Without additional empirical proof, Hoover's alleged transvestitism is best seen, particularly in light of his affinity for Tolson during a period in which he led a nationwide moral crusade against homosexuals (and Communists), as the symbolic validation of the drag-queen myth.

Each age engenders its own sex scandals. Among the Puritans, scandals served a moral purpose, to impose shame and enforce social discipline. This persists to today, but in a culturally augmented form. Modern scandals are enhanced with a licentiousness unique to post-war consumer capitalism. Many scandals, exemplified in the antics attributed to Hoover and others during the era of recovery and renewal, were private indulgences, only hinted at or discretely rumored about. Hoover, like John Kennedy, could indulge in his private affairs protected from popular intrusion or judgment, outside the range of media attention. Recalling the privilege of the aristocracy of old, the peculiar sexual eccentricities of social worthies most often remained discreet, private affairs. Nevertheless, if the questionable behavior was sufficiently illicit to be both alluring and criminally unacceptable, even privilege couldn't protect the perpetrator from public scandal. In the wake of the explosive developments of the sexual revolution of the late-1960s and early-seventies, scandal became a distinguishing feature of popular culture and media celebrity.

\* \* \*

The period between the end of World War II and the final withdrawal of U.S. forces from Vietnam marks the most cataclysmic era of American sexual history. This quarter century witnessed considerable social instability. It included a percolating conflict that included major, sustained struggles over foreign policy, Civil Rights, labor relations and popular culture, especially rock-&-roll music. It was also marked by challenges to the meaning of heterosexuality and, in particular, heterosexual masculinity. Much of this conflict has been marginalized within the overall portrait of consumerism and social docility that traditionally characterizes the early-Cold War period. Nevertheless, the underlying forces of opposition were congealing into what, in less than a decade, would erupt into the massive social upheaval of the sixties.

This period was an era that witnessed not only battles over personal freedom, but patriarchal culture itself. In their invaluable history of American sexuality, *Intimate Matters*, John D'Emilio and Estelle Freedman paint a familiar portrait of this traumatic era:

After World War II, the impulse to conform and settle down after years of depression, war, and cold war encouraged a rush of early marriage and saw the birth rate zoom upward. Sexual experimentation appeared lost in a maze of suburban housing developments as a new generation took on family responsibilities and raised more children than their parents had. The erotic seems to disappear under a wave of innocent domesticity, captured in television shows like Father Knows Best or the Hollywood comedies of Rock Hudson and Doris Day.*

Surprising to many, as Janice Irvine astutely observes, "the fifties were a fiercely contradictory decade in which to be a 'deviant.'"[4] And nothing better captured this contradiction than the numerous sex scandals that distinguished the era.

Like the much-rumored scandal involving Hoover, unacceptable sexuality during the post-War period was framed in terms of the new medical notion of "deviance." Deviance took many forms, but all were seen as challenging the dominant notions of heterosexuality and, by extension, national security. Deviance was an expansive category that included child molesters, rapists and lust-murderers; prostitutes and their predominantly heterosexual male customers; adult male homosexuals; transvestites and transsexuals; pornographers of suspect literary and pictorial works as well as their retailers and customers; practitioners of S&M (sadism & masochism), bondage and other fetish indulgences; and even college students involved in panty raids. Deviants included, in effect, anyone who could not be comfortably incorporated into the restrictive confines of an increasingly consumerist, suburban, vision of aesthetics (taste) and sexuality (pleasure). As Jennifer Terry points out, deviant sexuality was a threat: "The nymphomaniacal saboteur, the binding and controlling 'mom,' the male homosexual, and the lesbian were equally dangerous to the average man if he lacked the necessary will-power and vigilance to detect foreign manipulation."[5] Most disturbing, these deviants were seen as threatening to American values as Communists.

---

* Rumors circulated in the 1960s that the all-American Day had an affair with the Los Angeles Dodgers' African-American ball player Maury Wills. [David Kaufman, *Doris Day: The Untold Story of the Girl Next Door* (New York: Virgin Books, 2008), 330-37.]

It is often forgotten that during the post-war period, the U.S. was besieged by what one historian has called a "major sex crime panic." This "panic" lasted from 1949 to 1955 and it was difficult to determine what was meant by a "sex crime." Two contemporary clinicians debated this issue, illustrating the tenor of conflicting opinions. Dr. Paul de River, a psychiatrist, was founder and director of the Los Angeles Police Department's Sex Offense Bureau. He championed the most conservative analysis endorsed by many law-enforcement and psychoanalytical authorities:

> The fact that there is actually no difference between 'criminal sexual deviation or perversion or 'deviation' and what is sometimes referred to as 'common sexual perversion or deviation,' with the exception in the one case the individual has been 'caught' at his perverse practice.

He concluded most emphatically, "Perversion is perversion, whether one is known to practice it or not." In contrast, Mark Adams, MD, pointed out:

> It is now accepted by most authorities that many happily married couples engage in mouth-genital, or anogenital contacts; actions which are considered sex felonies by the law of most states. Countless other individuals, equally respected, commit fornication or adultery. In areas characterized by poor economic backgrounds, incest is, if not common, at least not uncommon. And in many isolated rural districts, human-animal relations have become part of the regional folk lore and humor.[6]

This polarity of debate persists to this day.

The immediate post-war "panic," as one commentator noted, "originated when, after a series of brutal and apparently sexually motivated child murders, major urban newspapers expanded and, in some cases, sensationalized their coverage of child molestation and rape." Between 1953 and 1955, Federal statistics indicate that the number of "sex crimes" increased 17 percent, from forty-six to fifty-four per 100,000.[7] These statistics appear to cover all arrests for sex crimes, including prostitution. The increase contributed to a nationwide fear, especially concerning crimes involving children and young people.

The panic, however, drew force from even more dangerous, disturbing actions. Throughout the nation there were reports of very real sexual and violent attacks and rapes of women. There were also reports of pedophile molestations of children and incidents of "ephebophilia," the abuse of youthful boys and girls, often referred to as pedophilia. However, the most notorious cases of the postwar period included the legendary Los Angeles "Black Dahlia" case and the murder and dismemberment of Dorothy Eggers by her husband.[8] Other cases that became national scandals concerned alleged pedophilia involving an older men and youthful boys, including an assault by former tennis star Bill Tilden against a 15-year-old boy, captured much press headlines.* The most infamous criminal homoerotic episode of the period took place in Boise, ID, in 1955. Three men were arrested for having sex with youths. However, the incident led local authorities to investigate some of 1,500 residents to determine how widespread homosexual practice was.[9]

The most benign expression of panic was a nationwide outbreak of panty raids. Long forgotten today, these raids constituted the first major outbreak of civil disobedience (and sometimes violence) by the nation's first generation of post-war college students. As Beth Bailey reports,

> In the spring of 1952, as the police action in Korea dragged on and as support for Eisenhower's presidential candidacy grew, college campuses throughout the nation erupted in violence. Windows were smashed, buildings were briefly occupied. Students fought police—and one another—while the media breathlessly reported each new riot.

And an eruption it was. At the University of Wisconsin, 5,000 students attacked the women's dorm; at the University of Oklahoma, 2,000 students battled state police; in Missouri, 2,000 students were involved in a raid; at the University of Kansas, over 1,000 students attacked the women's dorm and sorority houses; and other battles took place at Indiana University, University of Alabama and other campuses. Students at Princeton marched through the campus chanting, "We want girls! We want sex! We want panties."[10]

---

* See Chapter 4, A Nation in Crisis, for more on the Tilden scandal.

Sexual panic and legislated criminality crisscrossed over "white slavery." Regular reports of violation of the Mann Act, originally enacted in 1910 to prohibit the transport of women across a state line for the purpose of prostitution and other immoral acts, drew front-page press headlines.* However, as the sociologists Harry Benjamin and R.E.L. Masters warned, "[t]o the extent that 'White Slavery' existed in the West in recent times—and that extent was very greatly exaggerated—the women involved were not necessarily prostitutes."[11] Cumulatively, the effects of the sex panic were profound. As historian Estelle Freedman points out, "… public outrage over rare, serious sexual crimes facilitated the establishment of legal and psychiatric mechanisms that were then used to regulate much less serious, but socially disturbing, behaviors." No less an authority than then-FBI director Hoover warned "depraved human beings, more savage than beasts, are permitted to roam America almost at will."[12]

The panic so disturbed the nation's body politic that, between 1947 and 1955, twenty-one states and the District of Columbia passed laws targeting what Terry calls "sexual psychopaths." According to historian John Loughery, the full effect of this sex panic was dramatic: "the terms sexual psychopath, sex criminal, deviant, and homosexual came to be used almost interchangeably in discussing the situation."[13] George Chauncey is even more to the point:

> Like the term abnormal, the term deviant made any variation from the supposed norm sound ominous and threatening, and it served to conflate the most benign and the most dangerous forms of sexual nonconformity. People who had sex outside marriage, murdered little boys and girls, had sex with persons of the same sex, raped women, looked in other people's windows, masturbated in public or cast 'lewd glances' were all called sex deviants by the press.

In effect, social authority, embodied in legal, medical, religious and civil forums, did not simply demonize the deviant as a threat to male self-identity, but considered all forms of sexual difference challenges to moral and political order.[14]

The most obvious "deviant" was the male homosexual (and, less so, the lesbian). His shameless behavior threatened the masculin-

---

* See Chapter 3, Making of Modern America, for more on the Mann Act.

ity of the deeply insecure heterosexual American male. Loughery notes just how restrictive and repressive was this new, vehemently anti-homosexual civic culture: "In the more sexualized post-war era, even bachelorhood was suspect, and marriage became more than an emotional, economic, and procreative arrangement."[15] For women (and particularly for lesbians), the expanded social freedoms afforded both in the civilian labor market and within the Armed Forces during the World War II years were forcefully curtailed. No wonder, as Lillian Faderman observes, "The 'homosexual' became a particular target of persecution in America." Going further, she pointedly adds: "He or she presented an uncomfortable challenge to the mood that longed for obedience to an illusion of uncomplicated 'morality'."[16]

The social repression of homosexuals during this period took many forms and involved both governmental and civil action. Government repression was implemented in two ways: in actions directed at federal employees (civilian or military) and in actions directed at the American citizenry. Government action took place on many fronts. Congressional and federal officials held hearings and investigations, conducted raids, undertook prosecutions and imprisoned ordinary (and sometimes extra-ordinary) people. Repression was framed as a battle over loyalty and ended in many front-page exposés, with Weegee-esque black-and-white shots that gave the event a tawdry sheen. The social repression of this period represented the profound political instability America was confronting in terms of both domestic capitalism and international power.

Congressional hearings (as well as innumerable local and state government probes) were directed at perverts—homosexuals and pornographers, publishers of pulp fiction, comic books and "adult" photo-magazines. Among these, and probably the most pitiful, was the campaign waged against homosexuals.[17] In 1950, the Nebraska House Republican A. L. Miller helped write special language into that year's Security Act which legitimized the investigation of those identified as "perverts." At the other end of the Congress, the Senate conducted a wide-ranging investigation into the presence of "homosexuals and other perverts" in the federal government. Advocating the removal of all homosexuals from government employment (both civilian and military), the Senate report warned that "perverts"

tend to have a corrosive influence upon his fellow employees. These
perverts will frequently attempt to entice normal individuals to
engage in perverted practices. This is particularly true in the case
of young and impressionable people who might come under the
influence of a pervert. ... One homosexual can pollute a Government office.[18]

Congressional hearings, investigations and legislative actions
served to embolden local police and other moral authorities. The
most publicized assaults on private "association" among consenting adults took place in Washington, DC, when the vice squad informed the public that it estimated that there were some 3,500 "sex
perverts"—i.e., homosexuals—working in the government, three to
four hundred in the State Department alone. As David Cuate notes
in his definitive history of Cold War anti-communism, *The Great
Fear*, "... since 1945 the [State Department's] Foreign Service has been
accorded little support or respect, with its members favorite whipping boys in public debate, depicted as homosexuals, bunglers and
Communists."[19] Between January 1947 and November 1950, some
five hundred and seventy-four civilians were investigated for allegedly being perverts. Things only intensified with the passage
of, first, Truman's Executive Order 10241 (issued in 1951) and, then,
Eisenhower' Executive Order 10450 (issued in 1953), that lead to the
sexual policing of public employees. As a result, between May 1953
and June 1955, some eight hundred and thirty-seven investigations
of alleged sex perverts took place.[20]

The purging of this demonized population went far beyond the
halls of Congress and the Executive Branch. It was formally introduced into the military in 1954 with the establishment of the Armed
Forces Disciplinary Control Board. This agency had the sole purpose
of weeding-out "deviants" from the (nearly) all-male military. During the 1950s, the number of men (and some women) in uniform
discharged for homosexuality skyrocketed. Whereas in the forties,
such discharges averaged annually about one hundred cases, these
actions topped 2,000 per year in the fifties.[21]

The anti-homosexual terror was repeated (and often with far
more malice) at both state and local levels, destroying the lives of all
too many decent people. In Florida, the state legislature established
a special committee to investigate anti-social activities, particularly

conducted by "sex perverts." The focus of its investigation was homosexual encounters at the university and led to the forced resignation of both teachers and students. In Lawrence, KS, investigation of homosexual activities by the university's dean had an equally devastating effect.[22]

\* \* \*

If Hoover's alleged transvestitism remains more myth than corroborated fact, the campaign against reputed homosexuals among well-known celebrities, especially Hollywood movie stars, tended to be equally masked. This campaign took place in parallel to the McCarthyite blacklisting of alleged Communists or fellow-travelers like the Hollywood Ten. However, because stars play such an important role in the economy and popular imagination, much deception was required.

Among stars subject to sexual innuendo were Montgomery Clift, Rock Hudson, Sal Mineo, Roddy McDowell, Tab Hunter and Liberace. Many of the actors, like Clift, Hudson and Hunter, were widely known within the industry as "pretty boys," a common term for "fag." Sexual rumors also circulated about Greta Garbo and Marlene Dietrich, James Dean and Marlon Brando. Under a mounting national sex panic, it was in the interest of the Hollywood studios to present these and other stars in the best light, as upstanding heterosexuals. The studios wanted to safeguard their investments; respectable stars sold tickets. Nevertheless, while they sought to keep private the sexual practices of "deviant" stars, scandals often took place. Many were trumpeted in *Confidential* magazine and other gossip rags known as the "scandal press." These revelations often ruined people's lives.

Clift's acting career was established in 1938 when, at seventeen, he appeared as the lead in the Broadway play, *Fly Away Home*. Hollywood soon called and he debuted in Howard Hawks' 1948 film, *Red River*, followed shortly by an Academy Award nomination for his role in Fred Zinneman's *The Search* (1948). During this period he developed a life-long and genuine friendship with Elizabeth Taylor and, in 1951, costarred with her in George Stevens' *A Place in the Sun*.

Clift's homosexuality was a public secret, known to his friends and much rumored about by gossip columnists. In his biography of Clift, Michelangelo Capua reports:

Everyone knew about his [Clift's] sexual preferences; it was not a secret. In fact, he had a male lover with him on the set [of *The Young Lions*]. According to a cameraman, Duke Calahan, Monty's homosexuality was tormenting him more than ever, which [director Edward] Dmytryk thought he was just plain sick. "The women on the set wanted to meet Marlon [Brando] and Monty, but about Monty they'd say, 'I can't help him,' which was a great mistake. Nobody could help him."

Capua also mentions that Clift, using a duplicate passport, regularly disappeared from the Paris set for days on end, one time turning up in "a third-rate brothel in southern Italy, dead drunk."

Early indications of Clift's sexual proclivities were evident during his adolescence. His mother is reported to have observed, "I knew right away that he was addicted to little boys. It shocked me and I told him so, and I said it would weaken him artistically. His father was furious. 'How can a son of mine stoop to this,' he asked."[24]

In Hollywood, "closeted" gay men like Clift regularly dated and sometimes even married women to conceal their homosexuality. Among the women Clift "dated" was Taylor. In 1954, Clift rented a house in the gay resort of Ogunquit, ME, and spent the summer, according the GLBT Encyclopedia, picking up men on the beach "for SM sex parties." His exploits were apparently well known to studio executives who were unable to keep gossip columnists from telling stories about his sexual exploits. Hedda Hooper went so far as to question whether Clift had been arrested for pedophilia.[25]

Following *The Young Lions*, Clift's career went into decline as he appeared in a series of poorly received films. During this period Clift got involved with Claude Perrin, a young Frenchman who he had met in Paris and who came to live with him in New York. Their relationship was explosive. Clift turned more and more to drink and drugs during his final years. He seemed to give up on his career and considered increasingly unreliable. As his personal and professional life deteriorated he developed, according to Capua, "a compulsion for anonymous sex." Nevertheless, he did find a moment of redemption with his appearance in John Houston's legendary film, *The Misfits* (1961), costarring Cary Grant and Marilyn Monroe. While shooting near Reno, NV, he was reported drunk and on drugs, came close to fighting in local bars and was even stopped one night "sleepwalking naked in [Mapes Hotel's] corridors." He died a few years later a broken man.[26]

Scandal serves to enforce social and personal moral standards. Like Clift, this repression is evident in the life of Rock Hudson. Born Roy Harold Scherer, Jr., in 1925, in Winnetka, IL, and, after his mother's divorce and remarriage, was renamed Roy Fitzgerald. He served in the Navy during World War II and relocated to Los Angeles with demobilization. While holding down various minimum-wage jobs he took acting, singing, fencing and riding lessons and sent his photos to Hollywood studios and casting agents.

During this period he changed his name to Rock Hudson and got his first bit part in Raoul Walsh's 1948 film, *Fighter Squadron*. In the early fifties, Hudson got roles in Sidney Salkow's *Scarlet Angel* (1952), playing opposite Yvonne De Carlo, and in Walsh's *Sea Devils* (1953). He then jumped to leading roles in Walsh's *The Lawless Breed* (1953), Budd Boetticher's *Seminole* (1953) and Douglas Sirk's *Magnificent Obsession* (1954). Hudson was hot, a heartthrob and a homosexual.

Hudson first met the notorious Hollywood agent, Henry Willson, in 1947. As Robert Hofler details in his exhaustive biography, *The Man Who Invented Rock Hudson*, Willson was renowned in the movie community for his stable of "pretty boys" that included Hudson, Tab Hunter and Rory Calhoun. Around the same time he met Phyllis Gates, Willson's secretary. The two stories of their marriage differ significantly.[27]

One story is pure Hollywood. It involves their courtship, Gates' moving in with Hudson and their marriage. "Living with Phyllis helped normalize Rock's reputation in Hollywood," reports Sara Davidson in her quasi-autobiography, *Rock Hudson: His Story*.[28] Their courtship effectively stanched media rumors like the one that appeared in the September 1955 *Life* magazine cover story. Under the headline, "Hollywood's Most Handsome Bachelor," it challenged Hudson: "Fans are urging 29-year-old Hudson to get married—or explain why not."[28] The couple married in early November. Ms. Gates recently died at age eighty and the *Los Angeles Times* reported that she held firmly to the public story. "I was very much in love," she recalled. "I thought he would be a wonderful husband. He was charming, his career was red hot, he was gorgeous. ... How many women would have said no?"[29]

The other story is equally Hollywood, but with a noir edge appropriate to the fifties. When Hudson signed with Willson, he was Hollywood's fastest rising star. Willson believed Hudson had a unique, all-American appeal: "Rock Hudson was a cross between Superman and Clark Kent."[30] Unfortunately, with stardom, his past came out of the closet. Willson bought off a former lover who attempted to blackmail Hudson with incriminating photos. And *Confidential* was rumored to be preparing a tell-all exposé of his homosexual past.

What better way to end such threatening gossip then by a well-publicized love affair and marriage. It would make Hudson an all-American heterosexual man and a giant star. The year after the marriage he costarred with Taylor and James Dean in George Steven's *Giant* (1956). Unfortunately, his marriage lasted only until 1958, when Mrs. Hudson learned that her movie-star husband had been unfaithful while on location in Italy—unfaithful with an Italian actor.

The great secret of Hudson's life could no longer be denied when HIV/AIDS finally caught up with him. In 1984, Hudson came "out" about his AIDS and his homosexuality. He (with Taylor's support) put a new face on a horrible plague. He died the following year.

Like Hudson, the career of Liberace is marked by a closeted life and death due to AIDS. Ironically, Liberace was America's first truly gay entertainer and TV celebrity while denying the very homosexuality that fashioned his public persona. This contradiction affected his personal life, but most acutely defined the American sexual culture in the post-war decades before the sexual revolution of the late-sixties. It was the basis of the scandals that haunted his career.

Liberace was born Wladziu Valentino Liberace in West Allis, WI, in 1919, the child of a respected musical family. Considered a child prodigy, his official biography claims that he received praise from Ignacy Paderewski, the legendary Polish pianist and composer. However, rumors abound that he got his start performing in Milwaukee's gay establishments in the post-Prohibition period.[31] In 1940, he moved to New York and began performing as an intermission pianist at the Plaza Hotel's celebrated Persian Room. Mystery still surrounds the fact that he did not serve in the U.S. military in World War II, a period in which most able-bodied men were called up. Nevertheless, by the late-forties, he had established key features of his entertainer persona: his flamboyant attire and an oversized grand piano with glittering candelabra.

By the 1950s, Liberace was a national celebrity. He made his movie debut as a honky-tonk pianist in H. Bruce Humberstone's *South Sea Sinner* (1950), costarring MacDonald Carey and Shelley Winters. He issued a number of popular recordings through Columbia and made numerous guest appearances on radio and TV programs. His efforts peaked when he secured his own TV series, *The Liberace Show,* in 1952. In 1956, Liberace starred in a sold-out concert at the Hollywood Bowl celebrating his twenty-fifth anniversary in show business. That same year, he was invited to England to give three Royal Command Performances.

In London, rumor became scandal. An entertainment-gossip columnist for the tabloid, *The Daily Mirror,* Cassandra (William Connor) implied that Liberace was gay:

> ...the summit of sex, the pinnacle of masculine, feminine, and neuter. Everything that he, she, and it can ever want... a deadly, winking, sniggering, snuggling, chromium-plated, scent-impregnated, luminous, quivering, giggling, fruit-flavored, mincing, ice-covered heap of mother love.[32]

Liberace sued the newspaper for libel. He testified in court that he was not a homosexual, nor had ever taken part in homosexual acts. He won! Yet, victory need not always bring success. While Liberace fought the good fight in England, he paid dearly in the U.S. He lost personal and TV appearances and his record sales dropped off considerably.

Liberace died in 1987 from cardiac arrest due to AIDS. He never admitted to being homosexual and his foundation and museum continue the fiction. Nevertheless, in 1982, Scott Thorson, Liberace's live-in lover for the previous five years, sued the entertainer for $100 million in palimony. Their acrimonious break-up captured headlines throughout the country. Most of Thorson's suit was thrown out, but he did receive a $95,000 settlement that attests to something about their relationship.[33]

Liberace would never have entered New York's Stonewall Inn, or taken part in the now-legendary 1969 riot by its drag queens and other gay patrons. If the riot marks the beginning of the modern queer movement, Liberace represents the end of pre-politicized homosexuality. His flamboyant femininity was a gay analogy to the blackface performer of American theatre. Both represent a stigmatized expression of public transgression; both are caricatures. When the cultural legitimacy that fosters such representations, homophobia or racism, is socially challenged, caricature can be discarded.

During the post-war period, celebrity scandals were not limited to gay male stars. The grandest scandal of the era involved Ingrid Bergman, the image of virginal innocence. She established herself as an international movie star when she migrated from Sweden and appeared in the Hollywood remake of *Intermezzo* (1939). It was followed by a string of hits that included *Adam had Four Sons* (1941), *Rage in Heaven* (1941), *Casablanca* (1942), *For Whom the Bell Tolls* (1943), *Gaslight* (1944), *The Bells of St. Mary's* (1945), *Spellbound* (1945), *Notorious* (1946) and *Joan of Arc* (1948).

However, when her husband, Dr. Peter Lindstrom, revealed in 1949 that she had left him and their 10-year-old daughter, Pia, an international scandal was underway. It came out that she had become involved with the Italian film director, Roberto Rossellini, and had an out-of-wedlock son with him in February 1950. So enraged were upstanding Americans that, in March, Edwin C. Johnson (D-CO) denounced Bergman on the floor of the U.S. Senate, insisting that her behavior was "an assault upon the institution of marriage" and she a "free-love cultist" and a "powerful influence for evil."[34]

Johnson was not alone in outrage over Bergman's activities. The syndicated gossip columnist Louella Parsons, who originally broke the story of Bergman's affair with Rossellini, joined other Hollywood moralists denouncing the actress' adulterous affair. In the wake of her scandalous behavior, Bergman was essentially blacklisted from Hollywood for seven years. However, as culture norms changed, she made a triumphant return in *Anastasia* (1956) for which she won an Academy Award. Her career continued until the seventies, with her final film *Murder on the Orient Express* (1974).[35]

Another entertainer who scandalized the public during this period was the rock & roll pioneer, Jerry Lee Lewis. He got his big break in a fluke jam session at Sam Phillips' legendary studio, Sun Records, in 1956. As the story goes, Lewis played piano at an impromptu session with Clyde Perkins, Johnny Cash and Elvis Presley that Phillips unexpectedly recorded; this recording was eventually released as the *Million Dollar Quartet*. In '57 he broke out with his two all-time hits, *Whole Lotta Shakin' Goin' On* and *Great Balls of Fire*.

Lewis' pop celebrity was, however, eclipsed in 1957 when it was revealed that he was not only a bigamist, but that his latest wife was a cousin, just thirteen years old. At twenty-two, he had already been through two marriages. While awaiting a formal divorce from his first wife, Dorothy Barton, he married Jane Mitcham. Shortly after their divorce, he married his third cousin, Myra Gale Brown. The press called him a "cradle robber" and a "baby snatcher." This already scandalous state of affairs was further complicated when word got out that his latest marriage occurred, yet again, before the previous marriage was legally finalized. With his marriage and his refusal to accept the social sanction (not the legality) of marrying an under-age girl, his career essentially died. (Ironically, only Elvis, a son of the white South and who would himself fall in love with a 14-year-old girl, Priscilla Beaulieu, supported Lewis.) The cultural and sexual revolution of the sixties helped reestablish Lewis' career.[36]

\* \* \*

Celebrities were not the only fodder for the scandal mill. Just weeks before the momentous 1964 election, President Lyndon Johnson's chief of staff, Walter Jenkins, was arrested engaging in a compromising activity in the men's room of the Washington, DC, YMCA. According to former Supreme Court justice Abe Fortas, "It was common knowledge among Washington attorneys that the YMCA was the home of homos."

As Al Weisel retells the tale, Jenkins, along with his wife, were guests at a celebrity shindig on October 7, 1964, commemorating the opening of *Newsweek* magazine's new corporate headquarters. After sending his wife home, Jenkins left the party and walked around the corner to the YMCA. He made his way to the basement men's room that *Time* magazine described as a "9-foot by 11-foot spot reeking of disinfectant and stale cigars." There he cruised Andy Choka, a 60-year-old divorced Hungarian immigrant and guard at the Army-Navy Club, and the two men entered a pay-toilet stall.

Unbeknownst to them, as Weisel reports, "two policemen were watching them through peepholes; a third policeman had placed a stool outside the door and peered over the transom." He adds, "Within minutes the police burst into the room and led the pair away in handcuffs." Apparently brow-beaten by the police, Jenkins did not contest the arrest, paid a $50 fine and left the police station assuming his story would remain a secret.

Unfortunately, on October 14th, as the Johnson-Goldwater election was coming to a head, the story broke about Jenkins' arrest and quickly became a national scandal. The revelation devastated Jenkins, a father of six. It precipitated an emotional breakdown leading to his admittance to a local hospital where he was sedated and put on a twenty-four-hour suicide watch. It also led to the uncovering of his previous arrest in 1959 for the same offense in the same men's room. However, the revelation had no noticeable effect on the election.

When the story broke, it reverberated through the political elite. Johnson was reported surprised by the revelation. According to former attorney general Ramsey Clark, Johnson sought to distance himself from Jenkins. "I had a profound disappointment in the president," says Clark. "His immediate decision was to completely insulate himself from the issue, to protect the power of his political and presidential position. Nothing should be extended from that to help Walter [Jenkins]." However, Lady Bird Johnson broke with her husband and issued a public statement in support of Jenkins. Perhaps the most surprising response came from none other than FBI-director Hoover. According to Weisel, Hoover and Jenkins had been professional associates and he "behaved with uncharacteristic decency," sending flowers to Jenkins in the hospital.

Upon release from the hospital, Jenkins left government service and returned to Texas where he resumed a career as an accountant. Ironically, he continued to prepare LBJ's tax filings and even visited the Johnson estate. After divorce and his ex-wife's death, he became close to one of his daughters. She admits: "My father never came out." Adding, "I assume he was gay, but it was a different time and a different place. It was nothing we ever discussed. He didn't bring it up and neither did I, in spite of the fact that we were exceedingly close." Putting the best interpretation on the incident, Weisel reflects, "Yet the incident signaled a transformation of public attitudes toward homosexuality—if not outright acceptance, then at least an acknowledgment that gay men and lesbians existed, and even a sympathy for them that would one day make acceptance possible."[37]

The Jenkins affair was more than an individual scandal. It was a crack in the wall of silence that protected presidents and other high officials from public exposure. The mainstream media had long draped the private indulgences of national leaders like Harding, FDR and JFK under a cloak of discreet silence. This wall of public deception slowly crumbled as both media and sexual culture changed and, as with the Clinton sexual peccadilloes, private indiscretion could be used for political purposes.

In the summer of 1963, just months before President John Kennedy's assassination, a truly international sex scandal captured media headlines. John Profumo, the UK's minister of war, was outed in a particularly British affair, an extra-marital indulgence with a high-class call girl, Christine Keeler. However, he lost his position not for his adulterous affair, but because he initially lied about the affair when giving public testimony before the House of Commons. It was further revealed that Keeler was having a simultaneous affair with a senior naval attaché at the Soviet Embassy, Eugene Ivanov. The story crossed the pond when one of Keller's fellow call girls, Mariella Novotny, claimed she had a relationship with both Kennedy and Ivanov. The American media heard about the allegations involving JFK and raised the story with the White House. Robert Kennedy, then attorney general, intervened to keep the story from going public.

After his assassination, rumors about Kennedy's sexual dalliances became fodder for gossip columnists and others. These affairs involved movie stars Marilyn Monroe and Angie Dickinson; Inga Arvad, a Danish journalist; the stripper, Blaze Starr; Judith Exner Campbell, mistress to mob boss Sam Giancana; White House secretaries Priscilla Weir and Jill Cowan, who were referred to as "Fiddle" and "Faddle,"; and Mimi Beardsley Alford, an intern. Today, JFK's affairs have moved from scandal to presidential lore.*[38]

---

* David Friend recently argued in *Vanity Fair* that JFK had an out-of-wedlock "love child," Jack Worthington II, with Mary Evelyn Bibb Worthington. [*Vanity Fair*, April 2008.]

Lyndon Johnson also benefited from media discretion. He once boasted: "I have had more women by accident than he [JFK] has had on purpose." Among his reported conquests were Madeline Brown, who claims that they had an affair that lasted more than two decades and that LBJ fathered her son. Brown insists that their affair was purely physical and remained hidden from Lady Bird.

In his biography of LBJ, Robert Caro revealed that Johnson also had a thirty year affair with Alice Glass. Their friendship began in 1937 when she was living with her common-law husband, Charles Marsh, and their two children. Marsh was a newspaper mogul and one of his papers, the *Austin American-Statesman*, was an influential LBJ supporter. It is rumored that Glass ended her affair with LBJ in 1967 over her opposition to the Vietnam War. She also burned their love letters.[39]

And then there is Richard Nixon. Much gossip circulated about his long-term friendship with Marianna Liu, a Chinese cocktail waitress he met in Hong Kong as vice-president. Nixon first met Liu in 1958 while she was a tour-guide. It is reported that, in the mid-sixties, Liu and a female friend had a party with Nixon and his buddy, Bebe Rebozo, in a suite at the Mandarin Hotel. What gives this scandal a sleazy cast is the alleged role of Hoover in exploiting the affair to gain leverage over Nixon. As the story goes, one of Liu's closest friends was a general in the Communist Chinese army. In 1969, Liu moved to Nixon's hometown of Whittier, CA, and denied that there ever had been an affair.[40]

If the Jenkins scandal hit at the heart of the Washington political elite, then the sad tale of Edward Kennedy's ill-fated car ride with Mary Jo Kopechne, a 28-year-old secretary, on the night of July 18, 1969, marks the gravest moment of this period of renewal. The Kennedy clan gathered to host an intimate barbeque on Chappaquiddick Island, near Martha's Vineyard, MA, in appreciation for six female staffers who had worked in Robert Kennedy's ill-fated presidential campaign. Ted Kennedy had won a special election to finish the final years of his brother John's Senate term, following his election to the presidency.

At around 11:00 pm, Kopechne sought a ride to a nearby ferry and Kennedy give her a lift. As Kennedy later reported, he made a wrong turn onto an unlit dirt road and drove off the Dyke Bridge. The car turned over into the tidal water. The Senator got out of the submerged car, but, he says, failed in his attempts to pull out Kopechne.

Kennedy walked back to the party and, after speaking with some of his closest confidants, returned to the scene of the accident but could not access the submerged car. Nevertheless, neither Kennedy nor his associates called the police that night. Next morning, local Chappaquiddick fishermen found the car, pulled it from the water and notified the police. When local police questioned Kennedy about the accident, he initially denied all knowledge of it, but then admitted his involvement only to refuse further comment until his attorney arrived. Controversy emerged when a witness reported that Kopechne's body was in a position that suggested she had suffocated and had not drowned. This implied that she might have been saved if Kennedy had acted more expeditiously. Others suggested that Kennedy might have been drunk while driving. Still others suggested that he may have made inappropriate sexual advances to Kopechne. However, these issues went unaddressed as the Kopechne family refused to submit her body to an autopsy.

The incident ended with Kennedy being charged with leaving the scene of the accident, for which he received a two-month suspended sentence and one year probation. In a subsequent television interview he called his actions "indefensible" and said he would not run for reelection in 1972. Nevertheless, he reversed course and was reelected. This ugly incident was never quite forgotten but diminishes in significance over his long career.[41]

Ted Kennedy's scandal represented the moral crisis of traditional American political values. This value system found expression not in what occurred, whether an accident or not, but in the need to cover it up in order to preserve a political legacy. It was a value system that would be challenged by the 1960s' cultural revolution and, finally, essentially collapse as untenable under a wave of scandals involving politicians during the 1970s.

Like the sex scandals that befell Republican politicians during the era of George W. Bush, Democratic congressmen were undone by scandal during the mid-seventies. These apparent worthies included Wilbur Mills (D-AK) and Wayne Hays (D-OH) as well as John Young (D-TX) and Allan Howe (D-UT). Their collective tale reveals a pivotal moment in the evolution of scandals in America.

According to *Time* magazine, Wilbur Mills, the 65-year-old chairman of the powerful House Ways and Means Committee, made his unfortunate theatrical debut in December 1974 on the stage of Boston's Pilgrim Theater, "a seedy burlesque house in the city's newly designated 'Combat Zone' for sex films and ecdysiast exhibitions," accompanying the stripper, Fanne Fox. Fox, born Annabel Battistella and popularly known as "the Argentine Firecracker," was a regular performer at Washington's Silver Slipper club when she first met the congressman.

The Boston appearance came only months after the congressman and his companion were involved in a much-publicized scandal that immortalized her as "the Tidal Basin Bombshell." Mills, who had been married for forty years, was the subject of Washington rumors for nearly a year about his infatuation with the stripper. One night, four fun-loving and apparently intoxicated partygoers were stopped by the police in Mills' car at 2:00 am. Fox leapt from the car, ran toward a small estuary of the Potomac River known as the Tidal Basin, and, fully clothed, jumped into the water. She was pulled out by a policeman. Faced with wide-scale criticism, Mills was contrite.

However, in the wake of the Boston episode, he faced a political firestorm. He retreated to the Naval Medical Center in Bethesda, MD, to deal with his alleged medical problems and alcoholism. Mills quickly lost his prized chairmanship and, in 1976, did not seek re-election, his political career over. However, Fox published a tell-all memoir, *The Congressman and the Stripper,* which claimed that Mills had gotten her pregnant and she had an abortion. She eventually returned to Argentina, a celebrity of sorts.[42]

In June 1976, two scandals involving still other congressmen broke within days of one another. In a *New York Times* exposé, John Young's former secretary, Colleen Gardner, revealed that the congressman offered her a pay raise if she would have sex with him. Young denied the charges and won reelection in '76. However, he could never really shake Gardner's accusations and was defeated in 1978. More painful, Young's wife, who had supported him throughout the scandal, committed suicide a few months before the '78 election, contributing to his defeat.[43]

Howe underwent a similar fall from grace. Just two days after the *Times* broke the Young story, on June 13, 1976, police busted the congressman for propositioning two undercover policewomen posing as prostitutes in Salt Lake City's red-light district. Following a jury trial, Howe was found guilty, sentenced to a thirty-day suspended sentence and had to pay court costs. However, in the face of the scandal, the congressman refused to resign. Mounting Mormon fury led to his easy defeat to a Republican opponent in the '78 election.[44]

"I can't type, I can't file, I can't even answer the phone." These are the famous words that brought down Congressman Wayne Hays. As reported in *The Washington Post*, these words were from the congressman's former mistress, 27-year-old Elizabeth "Liz" Ray. According to Ray, as a clerk in Hays' office she had responsibilities other then her secretarial duties, including regularly sleeping with the congressmen once or twice a week as well as with his cronies.

The *Post* also revealed that Ray had worked as a clerk for another congressman, Kenneth J. Gray (D-IL), and had provided similar professional services. According to the *Post*, Ray reported being "frequently given days off to prepare for evenings spent on a date with Gray or favored constituents" on Gray's houseboat. He denied dating her, and said, "I never knew what my employees did after work. Liz was great at greeting people . . . I think she did a little typing." A couple of months after the Hays' scandal broke, the congressman resigned his position. Ray, following Fanne Fox's example, took pen in hand and authored *Washington Fringe Benefit*, a fictionalized account of her adventures. So provocative was her work that it went through four printings and there were even rumors of a movie option. Her celebrity brought her to the pages of *Playboy* and even an attempt at an acting career.[45]

\* \* \*

Few remember just how *shocked*, shocked!, mainstream America of the post-war era was by Alfred Kinsey's revelations about male and female sexuality. His findings are widely accepted today, even though some raise questions about his statistical methodology. When the first volume on male sexuality was published in 1948, his findings precipitated a near crisis of social conscience. The numbers spoke for themselves: 70 percent of men had visited prostitutes; 40 percent of married men were "unfaithful" to their wives; 37 percent of men (and 19 percent of women) had had at least one homosexual contact; and one farmhand in six had sexually experimented with an animal.[46] With the notable exception of the indulgences of farmhands, little seems to have changed over the last half-century other than the acceptance of the obvious.

Based on approximately 18,000 interviews conducted between 1938 and 1953, Kinsey's twin studies, *Sexual Behavior of Human Male* published in 1948 and *Sexual Behavior of Human Female* in 1953, represent a landmark not only in empirical research, but in moral philosophy as well. He sought to apply a research model that he had pioneered as a noted entomologist* to the study of American sexuality. By presenting the findings from a database drawn from detailed sexual histories of a relatively large sample, Kinsey sought to make it impossible to deny the full range—or "individual variation," as he referred to it—of sexual practices engaged in by (white) men and women. His studies provide an invaluable snapshot of pre- and postwar sexual practice as well as insight into the deeper historical forces that were restructuring modern American sexuality. Confronting the dominant sexual standards head-on, Kinsey paints a grim picture of the official sexual culture of the period:

> Specifically, English-American legal codes restrict the sexual activity of the unmarried male by characterizing all pre-martial, extra-marital, and post-marital intercourse as rape, statutory rape, fornication, adultery, prostitution, association with a prostitute, incest, delinquency, a contribution to delinquency, assault and battery, or public indecency—all of which are offenses with penalties attached.

Going further, he reminds his readers that "all intercourse outside of marriage (non-marital intercourse) is illicit and subject to penalty by statute law ...." He stressed that laws "penalize all homosexual

---

* Kinsey was a tenured professor at Indiana University and author of two pioneering works, *The Gall Wasp Genus Cynips: A Study in the Origin of Species* (Bloomington, 1930) and *The Origin of Higher Categories in Cynips* (Bloomington, 1936). For portraits of his scientific background see, Jonathan Gathorne-Hardy, *Alfred C. Kinsey: Sex the Measure of All Things, A Biography* (London, Pimlicio, 1999), 100-19, and James H. Jones, *Alfred C. Kinsey: A Public/Private Life* (New York: W.W. Norton, 1997), 141-47 and 197-226.

activity, all sexual contact with animals; and they specifically limit the techniques of marital intercourse."[47]

In line with his entomological notion of individual variation, he revised the conventional tri-part model of human sexuality—i.e., heterosexual, homosexual and bisexual—into a seven-point range (from zero to six) or heterosexual-to-homosexual rating scale. This scale was based on the reported sexual practices of his subjects. Each point delineated a very imprecise distinction between men engaged in exclusive heterosexual to exclusive homosexual acts and—as with any bell-curve—with the greatest segments of the population clustering somewhere near the center. For Kinsey, there were no "homosexuals" or, for that matter, "heterosexuals"—only men engaged in sexual acts which were labeled the one or the other.

Based on his extensive research and measuring scale, Kinsey found that "37 percent of the total male population has at least some overt homosexual experience to the point of orgasm between adolescence and old age." In addition, he found that "30 percent of all males" between the ages of sixteen and fifty-five have had homosexual "experience or reactions" over a period of three years; and that "18 percent of all males" between the ages of sixteen and fifty-five have had "at least as much of the homosexual as the heterosexual in their histories" over a three year period. Finally, he found that only "4 percent of the white males are exclusively homosexual throughout their lives."[48]

The empirical truths revealed in Kinsey's first study disturbed many and provoked widespread criticism among religious, academic and civic leaders. No less a would-be moral authority than Billy Graham attacked the work, warning, "It is impossible to estimate the damage this book will do to the already deteriorating morals of America."[49] Other religious leaders, like conservative Norman Vincent Peale and liberals Reinhold Niebuhr and Henry Pitney Van Dusen, head of Union Theological Seminary, joined the chorus of criticism. Prominent sex researchers, most notably Gershon Legman, assailed the report. Leading psychologists and psychoanalysts like Lawrence Kubi and Edmund Bergler joined the chorus of criticism. Even progressive thinkers, most notably Margaret Mead, Ashley Montagu and Karl Menninger, challenged the study's findings. There were even calls for a congressional investigation and, following the publication of the 1953 female study, Dean Rusk, head of the Rockefeller Foundation and Kennedy's future Secretary of State, withdrew the organization's financial support for Kinsey's research.*[50]

Nevertheless, moralists, politicians and the medical establishment could no longer conceal the deepest private truths of American male sexual life that Kinsey's research revealed. To everyone's, including Kinsey's, surprise this eight hundred and four-page scientific tome became a best seller, quickly selling over 200,000 copies. It rose to the top of the *New York Times* best-seller list in spite of the fact that the *Times* refused to carry advertisements for the book and failed to review it when it first appeared. One commentary of the day observed, "If present laws concerning sexual crime and misdemeanor were in force, 95 percent of all adults would be or would have been at some time, in prison...."[51]

In 1953, Kinsey and his associates published an even more massive work—eight hundred and forty-two pages—on the sexuality of American white women. Seeking to address a number of the statistical and medical-scientific criticisms raised against the first study, Kinsey subjected his empirical data to far more rigorous analysis. In addition, he paid more attention to the role of biological factors such as neural mechanisms and hormonal factors among females than he had considered when analyzing males. Nevertheless, like the first volume, the focus of this study was the reported sexual practices of his sample, in this case some six thousand women.

Like no other work over the last half-century, Kinsey's twin studies opened up a national debate on a subject that had long been considered to be beyond the boundary of acceptable social discourse.

---

* Kinsey's relationship with the Rockefeller Foundation is a story unto itself. Kinsey, who was first funded by a Rockefeller subsidiary, the National Research Council, in 1941, believed that the Foundation had made a truly long-term commitment to his research effort—sometimes estimated at gaining 100,000 interviews. The Foundation informally notified Kinsey about its plans to cease funding his research before Rusk assumed the directorship; in 1953, when the plug was finally pulled, Kinsey felt his long-term effort being thwarted and, thus, unable to refute his popular and academic critics. [See Gathorne-Hardy, 188 and 407.]

By presenting information about sexual practices—especially as apparently neutral statistical, scientific findings[52]—that had long been denied or simply ignored, these works confronted head-on some of the most deeply-held and popular Judeo-Christian moral verities. In throwing down the gauntlet to a sheepish scientific, moral and political population, Kinsey declared:

> Even some of the most extremely variant types of human sexual behavior may need no more explanation than is provided by our understanding of our process of learning and conditioning. Behavior which may appear bizarre, perverse, or unthinkably unacceptable to some persons, and even to most persons, may have significance for other individuals because of the way in which they have been conditioned. Flagellation, masochism, transvestism, and the wide variety of fetishes appear to be products of conditioning, fortified sometimes by some other aspect of an individual's personality and by inherent or acquired anatomic and physiologic capacities. Sexual reactions to stockings, to underclothing, to other articles of clothing, to shoes, or to long hair may be no more difficult to explain than attractions to the body of a sexual partner, or to particular parts of the body, to the legs of females, to the breasts of females, to male genitalia, to buttocks, or to other portions of the human anatomy.[53]

Kinsey's humanism remains as radical today as when first stated a half-century ago.

*        *        *

Secluded in the hills of Topanga Canyon, just north of Los Angles, the Sandstone Ranch was an epicenter of the 1960s sexual revolution. Founded by John and Barbara Williamson in 1969, it drew a fairly wide and often distinguished following among "free love" advocates and others exploring the vast yet limitedly-charted territory of sexual intimacy. Among those who were regulars at the retreat were the sexologists Alex Comfort and Phyllis and Eberhard Kronhausen, the journalists Gay Talese and Max Learner, the artist Betty Dodson, the performer Bobby Darin, and Daniel Ellsberg, renown for leaking the Pentagon Papers. According to John Heidenry, at "its high point, membership rolls reached two hundred and seventy-five couples ...."[54]

Gay Talese, author of the "sex-posé," *Thy Neighbor's Wife*, provides an invaluable first-person portrait of the setting. In the words of this former *New York Times* reporter:

> After descending the red-carpeted staircase, the visitor entered the semidarkness of a large room where, reclining on the cushioned floor, bathed in the orange glow from the fireplace, they saw shadowed faces and interlocked limbs, rounded breasts and reaching fingers, moving buttocks, glistening backs, shoulders, nipples, navels, long blond hair spread across pillows, thick dark arms holding soft white hips, a woman's head hovering over an erect penis. Sighs, cries of ecstasy could be heard, the slap and suction of copulating flesh, laughter, murmuring, music from the stereo, crackling black burning wood. ...
>
> There were triads, foursomes, a few bisexuals; bodies that would belong to high-fashion models, line-academicians; tattooed arms, peach beads, ankle bracelets, ankhs, thin gold chains around waists, hefty penises, noodles, curly female pubes, fine, bushy, trimmed, dark, blond, red valentines. ...

"It was," as Talese proclaims, "a room with a view like none other in America, an audiovisual aphrodisiac, a *tableau vivant* by Hieronymus Bosch."[55]

Sandstone might well have been the most well-known intentional sex community during the tumultuous age of renewal, but it surely was not the only one. Talese cites a survey reported in the *New York Times* that claimed that there were nearly two thousand "alternative lifestyle communities" in the U.S. during the 1970s. The sixties-seventies period was a unique moment in modern American history—a moment during which nearly all forms of social convention and authority were challenged. Race relations, foreign military interventions, dress codes and musical tastes were but the most obvious points of contestation. Sexuality was another. And under the pressure of this confrontation, sex was witness to an unprecedented expansion in term of both scope and scale.

In 1964, William and Jerrye Breedlove published *Swap Clubs: A Study in Contemporary Sexual Mores*. According to the book's "bio," the couple were married for twelve years, he was a 30-year-old engineer, she was a 29-year-old librarian and mother of four children; they lived in southern California. Their study is based on an extensive series of first-person interviews as well as (although unstated) participatory observation.* If one accepts their findings, the sexual environment of the sixties was in the midst of a much more profound exploration process than is usually acknowledged. Interpolating from alleged Kinsey data, the Breedloves' detail the evolution of the swap club, projecting over the two decades between 1953 and 1973:

> The number of swap clubs in 1953 was probably less than 2 percent of the married couples between the ages of 20 and 45 years. In 1963, it was probably above 5 percent. By 1973, the total will probably reach 15 percent—maybe reaching all the way to 25 percent before leveling off.[56]

However one reads the Breedloves' findings, a distinct sexual subculture existed and, for those who sought it out, could be found and joined.

The Breedloves' study is invaluable for the reports on the swap groups the authors discovered operating throughout the country. Like a travel guide, they report on mate-swapping groups in such likely place such as New York, Los Angeles, Chicago, San Francisco (ninety couples participating), Boston and Miami. But they also found groups operating in Baltimore (thirty-two couples), Denver, Detroit (forty-two couples), Elizabeth, NJ, Kansas City, Las Vegas (ten couples), Milwaukee, Minneapolis-St. Paul, Palm Springs, Philadelphia (more than one hundred couples), Phoenix, Salt Lake City (including Mormons), Seattle (thirty-four couples), St. Louis and Washington, DC (twelve couples), among other cities.

In 1971, Gilbert Bartell published a study of group sex that had been originally commissioned by the Playboy Foundation. He estimated that about one million people were involved in "organized" swinging. He found a particular sexual sociology operating, much of it confirming the Breedloves' findings. First, swinging took one of two forms—either "closed" (i.e., couples in private) or "open" (i.e.,

---

* This is a non-scholarly study with no discussion of methodology; thus, it is impossible to know if this is a work of fiction or really based on primary research.

group play). Second, women tended to be more active than men—women engaged in homoerotic play, it was most often two women in three-somes, and men tended to voyeurism and women exhibitionists in two- or three-way sexual encounters. Third, swingers forged a community outside the confines of mate-swapping get-togethers or clubs, including attending conventions, going on specially-chartered cruises (often sponsored by Lifestyle Tours and Travel) and subscribing to and/or placing personal ads in such publications as *Select* and *Kindred Spirits*. As Bartell found, "Many had taken the [*Playboy*] magazine's philosophy to heart: They would not allow marriage to end sexual exploration."[57]

Another husband-and-wife research team, the anthropologists Charles and Rebecca Palson, undertook primary research to understand the phenomenon. Employing first person, participatory observations of some one hundred and thirty-six swingers, their findings very much confirm those of the Breedloves and Bartell. However, because they were apparently active participants in the scene, the authors note:

> ... swingers consider an ideal gathering one in which everyone can express themselves as individuals *and* appreciate others for doing the same. If ever one person fails to have an enjoyable experience in these terms, the gathering is that much less enjoyable for everyone.[58]

The goal of this form of sexual activity among multiple partners was the giving—and receiving—of a gift, mutually pleasing intimacy among active and equal partners, not merely sexual conquest. Scarred as they were by their predominately heterosexual (and patriarchal) sensibility of the time, these practices nonetheless expressed an effort—however imperfect and compromised—to achieve sexual pleasure without turning either partner into a commodity.

The post-WWII recovery was accomplished through the institutionalization of a new economic-political order, what Eisenhower called in his legendary 1961 Farewell Address, the "military-industrial complex." Eisenhower was not merely pointing out the potential for abuse resulting from the enormous growth of the military, for its new, and historically unprecedented, size was the consequence of having weathered the near-collapse of capitalism and mobilization for world war. More so, he was concerned that the vast resources and power of this gargantuan entity would be unduly guided by what are today called "special interests," especially the career officers at the Pentagon, the corporations that are their principal contractors and the Congress that allocates federal resources. His concerns were—and still are—well founded.

The military-industrial complex facilitated the transition to the "high-tech" society that defines America today. This was accomplished through the significant—and sustained—investments in military-related research at most major universities, government-backed research labs and corporate research-and-development entities. One outcome of this effort became the "computer revolution"—the creation of the "information society," including the Internet—that recast late-twentieth century life.[59] Finally, the creation of the consumer society was facilitated through federal financing of road construction programs, the GI bill supporting college education, home ownership and tax policies favoring home mortgages, and increased personal credit.

In 1964, Herbert Marcuse published *One-Dimensional Man*, a prescient study that analyzed the unfolding twentieth century. He not only identified the forces that drove the transformation, but outlined the social consequence of its triumph. Marcuse grasped the full personal and social consequences of technological rationalization. He never lost sight of what would be lost: in the same way that animals and plants become extinct, so do forms of social relations, the living culture of daily life and the sensuous body. He was concerned about the loss of the progressive features of earlier phases of capitalist development, particularly those related to the development of a humanistic sensibility. Marcuse saw self-hood and sexuality being profoundly changed, with sexual titillation replacing erotic fulfillment as the measure of pleasure.

Marcuse's prophetic insights were made more compelling in light of the fact that only a decade earlier he had penned *Eros & Civilization—A Philosophic Inquiry into Freud*.[60] Published in 1955, the book rediscovered the utopian elements in Freud and remains one of the most visionary works of the post-WWII era. He recognized the great potential inherent in capitalism's industrial and manufacturing capabilities, especially the roles of science and technology, to free people from toil and want. But he was fearful of the resulting "rationality" that capitalism fosters.

Capitalism could, in principle, solve many of the problems associated with human need. Not only could the material conditions of need, like food, shelter and healthcare, be essentially met, but people would no longer be traumatized by the resulting fear, despair, desperation, guilt and other feelings that so contort daily life. Equally critical, the shortening of the work week, together with the emotional security of quality social amenities, especially for one's children, could create what one seventies utopian called a "post-scarcity" society.[61]

At the heart of Marcuse' subsequent despair was the perception that technological and scientific rationalization—the forces that give capitalism the capability to solve some of the basic troubles that haunt human life—fashions a new condition of totalitarianism, one fundamentally different than all pre-existing forms of tyranny. As he warns:

> In this society, the productive apparatus tends to become totalitarian to the extent to which it determines not only the socially needed occupations, skills, and attitudes, but also individual needs and aspirations. It thus obliterates the opposition between the private and public existence, between individual and social needs. Technology serves to institute new, more effective, and more pleasant forms of social control and social cohesion.

The collapsing of the differences between the private and the public, self and other, individual and social creates a "one-dimensional" society. And, at its essence, "as a technological universe, advanced industrial society is a *political* universe, the latest stage in the realization of a specific historical *project*—namely, the experience, transformation and organization of nature as the mere stuff of domination."[62]

For Marcuse, the domination of nature involved two forms of tyranny. First, it involved the destruction of the natural world, that which is traditionally identified as nature, the environment, ecosystem, countryside or other characterizations of the material world. And second, it involved the deformation of human nature, a person's physical and psychological being, her/his body and sexuality, the sense of being alive. The resulting oppression was profound. First and foremost, nature was being transformed from a living—and many would say magical, mythical or sacred—entity into a thing, a commodity of exchange, something that can be bought and sold.

This process also involved a corollary activity: Human domination of nature requires the domination of human nature. This domination requires, first, social domination, the formal structure of hierarchical relations and values, and, second, the tyranny of consciousness over physical being, of rationale calculation over impulse, intuition and wisdom. This process culminates when, as a self-conscious individual, a person actively participates in turning one's very self-hood—one's physical and psychological being—into a thing, a commodity. Self-commodification has become "second nature," something we all do, everyday. Few can imagine a world in which an alternative concept of the valuation of self-hood could exist.

The emerging counterculture, women's and gay movements of the 1960s and 1970s directly challenged capitalist values. Sexism, racism and homophobia are regressive legacies that inhibit the freer functioning of social relations and even the marketplace. Ironically, many of those who championed the most progressive values, particularly social equality irrespective of race, gender, class or sexual proclivity, those who were self-consciously the most critical of capitalism, helped to further rationalize the system. They did this by insisting that all people be treated equally, without prejudice. Unfortunately, and as Marcuse foresaw, capitalism adapted to this challenge, but turned it on its head. The outcome is profound:

> The range of socially permissible and desirable satisfaction is greatly enlarged, but through this process, the Pleasure Principle is reduced—deprived of the claims which are irreconcilable with the established society. Pleasure, thus adjusted, generates submission.[63]

The radical refusal historically inherent in pleasure is absorbed, integrated into the satisfaction derived from consumer purchasing. Is a more subversive sexual pleasure possible?

# References

1 Herbert Marcuse, *One Dimensional Man: Studies in the Ideology of Advanced Industrial Society* (Boston: Beacon Press, 1964), 78.

2 Anthony Summers, *Official and Confidential: The Secret Life of J. Edgar Hoover* (New York: Putnam's Sons, 1993), 254-55.

3 Ronald Kessler, *The Bureau: The Secret History of the FBI* (New York: St. Martin's, 2002), 107-11.

4 John D'Emilio and Estelle B. Freedman, *Intimate Matters: A History of Sexuality in America* (New York: Harper & Row, 1988), 242; Janice M. Irvine, *Disorders of Desire: Sex and Gender in Modern American Sexology* (Philadelphia: Temple University Press, 1990), 71.

5 Jennifer Terry, *An American Obsession: Science, Medicine and Homosexuality in Modern Society* (Chicago: University of Chicago Press, 1999), 333.

6 Mark E. Adams, "The Sexual Criminal in Prison," in *The Sexual Criminal: A Psychoanalytical Study*, ed., Paul DeRiver (Burbank, CA: Blout, nd. [Originally published 1949, revised edition 1956]), 306 and 323.

7 Estelle B. Freedman, "'Uncontrolled Desires': The Response to the Sexual Psychopath, 1920-1960," in *Passion & Power: Sexuality in History*, Kathy Peiss and Christina Simmons, eds. (Philadelphia: Temple University Press, 1989), 205; Benjamin Karpman, *The Sexual Offender and His Offenses: Etiology, Pathology, Psychodynamics and Treatment* (New York: Julian Press, 1954), 22-29; and James P. Petersen, *The Century of Sex: Playboy's History of the Sexual Revolution, 1900-1999* (New York: Grove Press, 1999), 217.

8 de Rivers, xli-xliii and 428-38.

9 John Loughery, *The Other Side of Silence: Men's Lives and Gay Identities — A Twentieth-Century History* (New York: Henry Holt & Company, 1999), 166-69, 241-44; Jennifer Terry, *An American Obsession: Science, Medicine and Homosexuality in Modern Society* (Chicago: University of Chicago Press, 1999), 349; see also John Gerassi, *The Boys of Boise: Furor, Vice and the Folly of an American City* (New York: Macmillian, 1967).

10 Beth Bailey, *Sex in the Heartland* (Cambridge, MA: Harvard University Press, 1999), 45-46.

11 Harry Benjamin and R.E.L. Masters, *Prostitutes and Morality: A Definitive Report on the Prostitute in Contemporary Society and an Analysis of the Causes and Effects of the Suppression of Prostitution* (New York: Julian Press, 1964), 29-30; Benjamin and Masters quote in David J. Langum, *Crossing Over the Line: Legislating Morality and the Mann Act* (Chicago: University of Chicago Press, 1994), 379.

12 Freedman, 200; Hoover quote in Loughery, 168.

13 Terry, 324; Loughery, 168.

14 Chauncey quote in Petersen, 217; Terry, 329-33.

15 Loughery, 159.

16 Lillian Faderman, *Old Girls and Twilight Lovers: A History of Lesbian Life in Twentieth-Century America* (New York: Penguin, 1991), 140.

17 Terry, 338-40; Victor Navasky, *Naming Names* (New York: Hill and Wang, 1991), 75.

18 Senate quote in John D'Emillo, *Sexual Politics, Sexual Communities: The Making of a Homosexual Minority in the United States, 1940-1970* (Chicago: University of Chicago Press, 1983), 228.

19 David Caute, *The Great Fear: The Anti-Communist Purge Under Truman and Eisenhower* (New York: Touchstone Book, 1979), 308.

20 Terry, 242-44; Petersen, 214.

21 Terry, 347.

22 Loughery, 244-48; Bailey, 63-66.

23 Michelangelo Capua, *Montgomery Clift: A Biography* (Jefferson, NC: McFarland & Company, 2002), 113.

24 Ibid, 22.

25 www.glbtq.com/arts/clift_m.html; Bosworth/173

26 Capua, 126 and 137.

27 Rober Hofler, *The Man Who Invented Rock Hudson: The Petty Boys and the Dirty Deals of Henry Willson* (New York: Carroll & Graf, 2005), 7.

28 Rock Hudson and Sara Davidson, *Rock Hudson: His Story* (New York: Morrow, 1986), 89.

29 *Los Angeles Times*, January 13, 2006.

30 Hofler, 162.

31 www.Liberace.org; Darden Asbury Pyron, *Liberacy: An American Boy* (Chicago: University of Chicago Press, Yale, 2000), 79-129.

[32] Pyron, 194-97 and 223-33.

[33] I bid, 370-77.

[34] Donald Spoto, *Notorious: The Life of Ingrid Bergman* (New York: Harper Collins, 1997), 296-96.

[35] Laurence Leamar, *The Kennedy Men: 1901-1963* (New York: Morrow, 2002), 165-208.

[36] Peter Guralnick, *Careless Love: The Unmaking of Elvis Presley*, (Little Brown, 1999), 36-40.

[37] Kim Long, *The Almanac of Political Corruption, Scandals and Dirty Politics* (New York: Delta, 2007), 213; Al Weisel, "LBJ's Gay Sex Scandal," *Out*, December 1999 at http://home.nyc.rr.com/alweisel/outwalterjenkins.htm

[38] Seymour Hersh, *The Dark Side of Camelot* (New York: Little, Brown, 1997), 102-06, 294-325 and 391-98.

[39] Robert Caro, *The Yeas of Lyndon Johnson: Means of Ascent* (New York: Knopf, 1990), 25-26, 58 and 65; Caro, *The Yeas of Lyndon Johnson: Master of the Senate* (New York: Knopf, 2002), 141 and 144-45; see also Madeline Brown, *Texas in the Morning: The Love Story of Madeline Brown and Lyndon Baines Johnson* (Baltimore: Conservatory Press, 1997).

[40] Anthony Summers, *The Arrogance of Power: The Secret World of Richard Nixon* (New York: Viking, 2000), xiii and 269-70.

[41] Theo Lippman, Jr., *Senator Ted Kennedy: The Career Behind the Image* (New York, Norton, 1976), 119-20.

[42] "The Fall of Chairman Wilbur Mills," *Time*, December 16, 1974.

[43] "What Liz Ray Has Wrought," *Time*, June 21, 1976.

[44] Ken Rudin, "Congressional Sex Scandals in History, *Washington Post*, June 13, 1976; http://www.washingtonpost.com/wp-srv/politics/special/clinton/congress.htm.

[45] Marion Clark and Ruda Maza, "Closed Session Romance on the Hill," *Washington Post*, May 23, 1976.

[46] Alfred C. Kinsey, Wardell B. Pomeroy and Clyde E. Martin, *Sexual Behavior in the Human Male* (Philadelphia: W. B. Saunders Company, 1948), 218-62; Alfred C. Kinsey, Wardell B. Pomeroy, Clyde E. Martin and Paul H. Gebhard, *Sexual Behavior in the Human Female* (Philadelphia: W. B. Saunders Company, 1953), 503; Reay Tannahill, Sex in History (New York: Scarborough House, 1992), 404; Irvine, 31-66.

47   Kinsey, *Male*, 263-64.

48   Kinsey, *Male*, 639-59; see especially 650-51.

49   Graham quote in David Halberstram, *The Fifties* (New York: Fawcett Columbine, 1993), 280.

50   Gershon Legman, "Minority Report on Kinsey," in Norman Lockridge, ed., *The Sexual Conduct of Men and Women: A Minority Report* (New York: Hogarth House, 1948), 13-32; Terry, 307-14; James H. Jones, *Alfred C. Kinsey: A Public/Private Life* (New York: W.W. Norton, 1997), 577-80; see also Terry, 305-06.

51   Halberstam, 278; Robert L. Dickinson, "The End of 'Hush and Pretend'," in *About the Kinsey Report: Observations by 11 Experts on "Sexual Behavior of the Human Male,"* Donald Porter Geddes and Enid Curie, eds, (New York: Signet Books, 1948), 163.

52   Paul Robinson, *The Modernization of Sex* (New York: Harper & Row, 1976), 42-119.

53   Kinsey, Female, 645-46.

54   John Heidenry, *What Wild Ecstacy: The Rise and Fall of the Sexual Revolution* (New York: Simon & Schuster, 1997), 175-76; D'Emilio and Freedman, 326.

55   Gay Talese, *Thy Neighbor's Wife* (New York: Dell, 1981), 398-99.

56   Williand and Jerrye Breedlove, *Swap Clubs: A Study in Contemporary Mores* (Los Angeles: Sherbourne Press, 1974), 45.

57   Petersen, 346-47.

58   Charles and Rebecca Palson, "Swinging in Wedlock," in John H. Gagnon and William Simon, eds., *The Sexual Scene* (New Brunswick, NJ: Transaction Press, 1973), 106.

59   Stuart W. Leslie, *The Cold War and American Society: The Military-Industrial-Academic Complex at MIT and Stanford* (New York: Columbia University Press, 1993).

60   Herbert Marcuse, *Eros & Civilization: A Philosophic Inquiry into Freud* (New York: Vintage Books, 1962).

61   Murray Bookchin, *Post-Scarcity Anarchism* (Montreal: Black Rose Books, 2006).

62   Marcuse, xv and xvi.

63   Ibid, 75.

# CHAPTER 6. SEXUAL COUNTER-REVOLUTION

*There is a religious war going on in our country for the soul of America.*
*It is a culture war,*
*as critical to the kind of nation we will one day be as the Cold War itself.*
*[It is a] struggle for the soul of America ...*
Pat Buchanan, 1992[1]

I n May 1979, Jerry Falwell invited a select group of Christian conservative leaders to a strategic planning retreat at his Lynchburg, VA, estate. Falwell, who ran a private Christian academy and hosted a popular televangelist program, "The Old-Time Gospel Hour," gained national prominence in 1977 with his support for Anita Bryant's anti-gay campaign in Dade County, FL. In '78, he generated controversy by encouraging churches to register voters and evangelicals to vote for conservative candidates. Falwell offered a new direction for committed Christians.

Those who attended the Lynchburg conclave included Richard Viguerie, the direct mail fund-raising guru; Paul Weyrich, who helped found the Heritage Society, the Christian Voice and the Free Congress Foundation; Robert Billings, founder of the National Christian Action Coalition; Howard Phillips, chairman of the Conservative Caucus; and Ed McAteer, an influential Christian organizer. According to Deanna Spingola, "their objective was to set up multiple New Right organizations to shape issues, raise money and acquire political power in an effort to restructure America's domestic and foreign policies."[2]

Perhaps more apocryphal than actual, Falwell once recalled that at the 1979 gathering, Weyrich said to him: "Jerry, there is in America a moral majority that agrees about the basic issues. But they aren't organized." Thus was born the nation's religious right.

Looking back three decades later, these religious warriors could legitimately claim that they were instrumental in mobilizing a moral force which forged a political movement leading directly to George Bush's elections in 2000 and 2004. Adopting a Leninist program, these hardcore counter-revolutionaries ultimately seized state power and wielded it for eight gruesome years. They accomplished this through a campaign known as the culture wars.[3]

The 2008 electoral victory of Barack Obama and the Democrats signaled not only a repudiation of the Bush presidency, imperialist misadventure and free-market or "unregulated" capitalism, but the Christian right's culture wars as well. After three decades of growing influence and power, the fierce rightwing assault on popular values, especially sexuality, is in eclipse. This round of the culture wars is over.

Six months after Falwell's conclave, in November 1979, the New York sex club, Plato's Retreat, hosted what was dubbed the Super-marathon, a performance intended to break all sex records. The evening star attraction was Tara Alexander, an occasional porn actress, who, during a nonstop six-hour spectacle, had sex with eighty-six men, often four at a time. The performance was videotaped for posterity and, being so provocative, rebroadcast on a New York X-rated cable show, *Midnight Blue*. It was the scandal of the sexual revolution.[4]

Confirmation of the Christian right's worst fears about America's "degenerating" sexual culture came from an unlikely source—one of its fiercest critics, the historian Lillian Faderman. She observed:

> The decade of the '60s had ushered in unprecedented sexual permissiveness, characterized by mini skirts, the pill, group sex, mate swapping, a skyrocketing divorce rate, and acceptance of premarital sex. The rigidities of the '50s was turned on its head. Heterosexuality began to look somewhat like homosexuality, as nonproductive sex and cohabitation without marriage came to be commonplace.

It was a permissiveness that encouraged not only social egalitarianism, but also sensual hedonism. It was a libido that opposed the war in Vietnam, supported the civil rights movement, empowered the new feminism, infused the spirit of the counter-culture and spawned the gay liberation movement. It was a libido that terrified the Christian right.[5]

The upstanding citizens who gathered with Falwell were shocked by what they perceived as the mounting evidence of America's moral degeneration—rock & roll, the pill, short skirts, petting and premarital sex, pot and pop porn. If this was not sufficient confirmation, they need only recall the Supreme Court's momentous 1973 decision, Roe v. Wade. Only the previous year, California voters turned down the Briggs Amendment, an effort by Christian conservatives to ban homosexuals from teaching in public schools. These actions signified America's moral degeneration and confirmed two assumptions that cut to the heart of the Christian right's belief system. First, women had the right to terminate an unwanted pregnancy and personhood was established at the moment of birth. Second, homosexuality was socially accepted. In the face of such degeneration, these social worthies were determined to do something about it.

These moralists knew all too well that the erstwhile 1960s sexual revolution challenged moral standards. What they considered degeneration affected all social classes, including the political elite. Between 1975 and 1998, there were approximately forty highly publicized sex scandals involving members of the U.S. Congress and culminated in the impeachment of a president. A true accounting of the illicit sexual lives of members of Congress and other political leaders is impossible to determine as the political elite can still effectively conceal much of their private lives. Nevertheless, an unprecedented number of "reported" scandals involving members of the nation's political elite took place during this period. These scandals slowly and steadily built until Clinton's impeachment. Those who gathered at Falwell's estate perceived a profound sexual crisis then underway and that would reverberate through all domains of social life. However, to secure state power, they had to suppress the mounting threat posed by what they identified as sexual degeneration.

\* \* \*

Tara Alexander's performance at Plato's Retreat was one of the many forms of sexual exploration that flourished during the pre-AIDS era. It was a sexuality that scandalized the Christian right and many mainstream Americans. While a profound moment in America's evolving sexual culture that involved millions of people, much like the speakeasy culture of the 1920s, it was short lived. The combined pressures of cultural burnout, rightwing counter-revolution and AIDS killed the sexual revolution. However, the death of the sixties would drag out for decades; it was invoked in the 2008 presidential campaign in attacks against Obama as conservative culture warriors kept it alive like a mythic enemy to rally their troops and cover their own moral, political and intellectual failings.

The men who gathered with Falwell appeared especially troubled by an emboldened women's movement. The start of the "second wave" of feminism is dated to the 1963 publication of Betty Friedan's *The Feminist Mystique*. She gave voice to a profound disillusionment with post-war consumerism that, in the 1950s, began to percolate through society, particularly among women, but also African-Americans, homosexuals and disillusioned beatnik-types. Federal approval of the contraceptive pill in 1961 helped create a new sexual climate; the 1965 Supreme Court ruling, Griswold v. Connecticut, ended legal restrictions on married couples purchasing and using contraceptives. In 1966, the National Organization of Women (NOW) was formed and, two years later, protests against the Miss America contest on the Atlantic City boardwalk gave rise to the apocryphal tale of bra burning that defined a movement. It became an iconic image of the new woman, a woman at once symbolically freed from the restrictions of social convention and physical inhibition, and more sexual in both erotic imagination and sexual practice. This development culminated in the crisis of '73, the year of the Roe decision and the defeat of the Equal Rights Amendment. These countervailing tendencies, one progressive, the other regressive, framed sexual contestation over the following quarter century. They culminated in Clinton's scandal of '98.

Second generation feminism inherited a storied past that built from the abolitionist and suffragist sisterhoods of the nineteenth century, through the birth control activists of the early-twentieth century, the labor organizers of the 1930s and the Rosie-the-Riveters of World War II. These second generation women were "modern"— middle-class, professional, accomplished. They knew how to organize, whether for Kennedy, civil rights, against the war or for a woman's right to terminate an unwanted pregnancy. Unfortunately, as Faderman argues, many of these women were threatened by lesbianism; some even denounced it as the "lavender menace."[6]

Against the changing landscape of sexual politics, an equally important change in America's sexual culture took place. A radical sexual insurgency became more visible after the '69 Stonewall riot. It was especially evident in graphic depiction, the provocative—some would call it "obscene" or "pornographic"—images that appeared in newspapers and magazines, let alone in under-the-counter men's magazines. Its visibility found more "realistic" expression in the emerging medium of video. The old 8mm porn world, a world of the sleazy geezer in a dirty trench coat sneaking out of a decrepit porn theatre, got a facelift. Porn became a high-tech industry, offering better-produced programs that could fulfill a person's (i.e., man's) most personal fantasies. The homevideo revolution owes its success to pornography—and to the Supreme Court's 1973 decision, Miller v. California, that redefined obscenity in terms of the concept of community standards and a work's creative value taken as a whole.

Equally important, visibility took a material form as evident in the increasing number of experiences and venues that encouraged traditional conceived illicit sexuality. These experiences were both noncommercial and commercial. They involved the apparent increase in pre-marital sex and adulterous liaisons as well as an apparent increase in casual encounters with sex workers. But they also included the increasing number of anonymous sexual hookups that took place on street corners, alleyways, public parks and lavatories, and the proverbial backseat. Social visibility included the sex clubs like Plato's Retreat where Tara Alexander performed as well as the bars and other gathering places in which sexual liaisons took place, including massage parlors and gay bathhouses. Together, this expanded ensemble of cultural sexuality gave the era its erotic edge.

The change in popular culture, as both media representation and sexual venue, reflected a change in public morality. It was best captured in the change of (male) sexual fantasy that distinguished the 1970s from the fifties. Against the sexual explicitness of Marilyn Chambers and Linda Lovelace of the seventies, Marilyn Monroe and Bettie Page of two decades earlier seemed quaint and innocent. The seventies and eighties embodied a starker, more explicit sexuality. This explicitness was the public expression of what Faderman identified as cultural permissiveness and found its most radical representation in the depiction of (female) nudity. And nudity, in as seductive, sensuous and explicit representation as possible, radiated throughout society whether as fashions, popular ads, magazines images, movies or Broadway plays. Not since the 1920s' burlesque star had the female form been so erotically displayed.

This new sexuality was also a social practice. College-aged women felt less guilt or shame about their sexual desires—which their parents, and most of mainstream society, feared as "promiscuity." Some of these young women found employment as Playboy bunnies or at the massage parlors and strip joints that operated throughout the country. Many others felt less inhibited about their own sexuality and about making demands for their pleasure in their relations. Men, straight and gay, were overwhelmed by this new hedonism. Even the police and judiciary seemed changed by the new sexual culture; they were either more tolerant or easily bribed, adopting a-wink-and-a-nod attitude toward local prostitution and other sexual practices. However, to flourish, this sexuality had to be off the street, free from public nuisance complaints (e.g., sale of alcohol) and trafficking in hard drugs. No venue better represents the exaggerated sexuality of this era than the massage parlor.

No one provides a better, more accurate if not intimate, portrait of the sexual culture of the massage parlor than Gay Talese. With the same rigor and commitment to first person, participatory-observer research that he applied to the swinging practiced at the Sandstone Ranch, Talese explored the world of massage parlor in *Thy Neighbor's Wife*. He found that "by 1970, however, things began to change in the massage world as this private service went public."[7]

Massage parlors proliferated during the seventies. One of the first to open in New York was the Pink Orchard, on East Fourteenth Street, and its success led to the opening of others. Among these were the Perfumed Garden, on West Twenty-third Street; the Secret Life Studio, on East Twenty-sixth Street, described as "four dimly lit mauve rooms"; the Casbah East and Casbah West, which resembled "an ultramodern cave"; the Middle Earth Studio, on East Fifty-first Street, which resembled "a hippie commune, having beaded curtains, madras pillows, and incense burning in the rooms"; the Stage Studio, on East Eighteenth Street; and the Studio 34, on West Thirty-fouth Street.[8] The most lavish parlor in New York was undoubtedly

Caesar's Retreat, on East Forty-sixth Street.* Opened in 1972, it was, as Talese reports, quite the place:

> Nothing in New York yet compared to Caesar's Retreat, where thousands of dollars had obviously been spent by its owner—a Bronx-born onetime stockbroker named Robert Scharaga—in decorating, the main private rooms, the sauna, the circular baths, the plaster-cast Romanesque statuary and fountain. The customers could drink free champagne in the reception room while waiting for a half-hour massage session done with warm herbal oil. A proper massage cost twenty dollars, but more money could buy more, and for one hundred dollars a customer could have a champagne bath with three liberated ladies.[9]

Massage parlors flourished throughout the country. Atlanta, Charlotte, Chicago (on South Wabash Street and was decorated like the interior of a church), Dallas, Washington, DC, suburbs (the ten-room Tiki-Tiki) sported parlors as did the dozens that operated in Los Angeles, especially along Sunset Strip and Santa Monica Blvd. The most lavish parlor in LA was the Circus Maximus, a three-story house off Sunset Street and founded by Mark Roy. According to Talese, the parlor's décor "sought to suggest Roman hedonism; its thirty masseuses wore mini-togas of purple, gold, or white crepe, and its advertising proclaimed: 'Men haven't had it so good since the days of Pompeii.'"[10]

The young female masseuses at these clubs usually received about one-third of the fee for the session—as well as tips for additional services provided. Most often, the masseuse provided some form of a full-body massage as well as either a "hand-job" (i.e., masturbation) or a "blow-job" (i.e., fellatio). These young women often earned $300 to $500 per week for services rendered, a good salary for the period. The sexual revolution had created an historically appropriate form of prostitution.

During this era, prostitution took still other forms. First, prostitutes became more public. While proletarian streetwalkers and courtesan brothels persisted, more modern sex workers turned to dating

---

* John Heidenry places Caesar's Retreat on East Fifty-fourth Street [John Heidenry, *What Wild Ecstasy: The Rise and Fall of the Sexual Revolution* (New York: Simon & Schuster, 1997), 85.]

or escort services, nude photographic galleries and even sex thera-
pists or surrogates to facilitate commercial encounters. Better than
walking the street in some desperate part of town, more middle-
class sex workers gained easier access to customers by placing ads
in weekly newspapers or other outlets. Nevertheless, prostitution
remained illegal in all states but Nevada. Local police throughout
the country were expected to harass and arrest a certain number
of "hookers" monthly; they also sought to catch a social worthy
or two, be he a local pol, clergyman or country-club grandee, for a
prime-time exposé.

Other venues provided people—mostly men—with opportunities to engage in sexual encounters and often became the subject of
a front-page scandal. They ranged from public restrooms or toilets
(i.e., "tearooms"), truck stops and public parks to the back rooms
of bars, after-hours clubs and porn theatres and bookshops. These
venues were distinguished by two factors—the sexual engagements
were often anonymous and they were often non-commercial. The
participants might well be lovers, random pick-ups or streetwalkers
and johns. While semen and other body fluids often passed between
the participants, cash was not the primary form of exchange. These
encounters were often hurriedly sought to consummate an illicit
sexual liaison.

Heterosexual massage parlors and gay bathhouses shared much
in common as venues of illicit desire. First, both operated as quasi-
healthcare establishments, offering concealed practices that skated
the line between beneficial physical therapy and meeting other,
more genital, needs. Second, both existed in the middle-zone of commercial sex outlets, between an established brothel and a random
encounter, between a sex club and an anonymous hook-up. Finally,
both could, over time and recurring patronage, foster a sense of
"community," where individual participants—customers or workers—could become "regulars," establishing a unique form of friendship, if not intimacy, toward one another. These establishments often
functioned like swinger get-togethers, where for a price participants
could share something more than a commercial encounter, something invoking the possibilities of a gift.

Massage parlors were a venue of sexual engagement incubated
by the sexual revolution of the 1960s and seventies. They emerged

as a legitimate form of physical therapy during the post-WWII era, as many men returned from the war suffering a wide variety of disabilities. During the post-war decades, massage underwent a fundamental split, dividing between those who sought to legitimize their practice through professionalization (including licensing boards, trade associations, conventions, etc.) and those, more enterprising, who saw how providing physical contact and stimulation, including genital release, could be a profitable business. The line between these two tendencies sometimes became difficult to maintain. As Talese notes:

> Visitors were admitted by appointment only, and the masseuses, invariably refined-looking women, often wore starched nurses' uniforms that were covered with a white smock while administering a massage to a naked man on the table. To be fully massaged and finally masturbated by one of these white-gowned professionals was, to many men, a highly erotic experience ...[11]

The increasing split between physical therapy and genital satisfaction would define the evolution of the massage business to this day.

Gay bathhouses were an outgrowth of the progressive era's effort to provide the poor and immigrants of turn-of-the-twentieth-century urban America with public hygiene. It is perhaps ironic that these establishments were the result of a half-century of social struggle to better the life of immigrants and the poor. Municipalities throughout the country built sex-segregated public baths in order to mitigate the poor sanitary conditions and the dearth of indoor plumbing that typified urban working-class life. Ethnic, fraternal, religious and other organizations also set up bathing facilities with similar aims in mind. It was only gradually that these places developed a gay profile. Nor would it be fair to say that they ever lost their social dimension, for as historian George Chauncey points out, "the baths were also important social centers, where gay men could meet openly, discuss their lives, and build a circle of friends," thus creating "a social world on the basis of a shared and marginalized sexuality."[12]

Nearly a century later, gay bathhouses had become modern-day Roman orgies. Bathhouses operated throughout the country during the 1960s and seventies. In 1972, over one hundred were running throughout the continental U.S. and Puerto Rico; by 1980, their number had grown to between one hundred and fifty and two hundred. While many gay bathhouses faced regular police harassment, enough business was generated to encourage more entrepreneurial businessmen to take advantage of the emerging opportunity.[13]

The most famous gay bathhouse of this era was New York's Continental Baths, opened by Stewart Ostrow at the Hotel Ansonia. Its more attractive environment included a large swimming pool, clean showers and steam rooms as well as discrete private rooms for consensual sexual encounters. And it was explicitly "gay friendly." But the Continental added respectability with the performance by stars like Bette Midler (accompanied by Barry Manilow), Cab Calloway, Melba Moore and the Metropolitan Opera's Eleanor Steber, among others. Not unlike the appeal of the famed drag balls of the 1920s and thirties, at the Continental, gay sexuality became respectable. As John Loughery notes, "The unspeakable has become the fashionable to gays and straights, at least in New York."[14]

\* \* \*

Those who gathered with Falwell in 1979 may well have brought with them memories of the recent spate of sex scandals that deeply disturbed the nation. Only a few years earlier congressmen from across the country—Wilbur Mills (D-AK) and Wayne Hays (D-OH) as well as John Young (D-TX) and Allan Howe (D-UT)—were involved in front-page scandals that destroyed their reputations and forced them from office. More recently, in April 1978, New York congressmen Fred Richmond was arrested for soliciting a 16-year-old African-American delivery boy and an undercover police officer. Taking the highroad, Richmond publicly apologized, sought psychiatric counseling and won reelection. For those who joined with Falwell in the formation of the Moral Majority, this result may have been more disturbing than traditional Christian justice, public shaming and a prison sentence: Forgiveness. Sin seemed to have become a public virtue. In 1979, two additional congressmen were outed. Robert Bauman (R-MD) was arrested for soliciting a 16-year-old gay male dancer. Robert Leggett (D-CA) revealed that he had fathered two out-of-wedlock children in an adulterous relation with a congressional secretary. Traditional moral prohibitions were breaking down.[15]

Bauman was the quintessential Christian conservative politician: devoted married man, champion of family values and chairman of the American Conservative Union. He is what today is called within the black community, living on the down-low, playing straight while into gay sex. He was tripped up when the male dancer demanded a cash payment to keep his indiscretion secret. He was outed and, while claiming alcoholism as the cause of his misadventure, was defeated in his reelection bid. (In 1986, Bauman stepped out of the closet and published his autobiography, *The Gentlemen from Maryland: The Conscience of a Gay Conservative*.)

Sin can strike anyone, conservative or liberal. Leggett was a committed liberal who was first elected to Congress in 1962 from the San Francisco suburb of Vallejo and served eight terms. He was an early opponent of the Vietnam War even though serving on the Armed Services committee. However, in '79, he was outed for an affair with Suzi Park Thomson, an aide to then-House Speaker Carl Albert. Additional rumors circulated as to still other of Leggett's extra curricular activities, including having fathered two children with a congressional secretary he financially supported. In disgrace, he resigned his position and became—what else?—a lobbyist. However, in 1981, when the scandal subsided, he married Thomson and they moved back to the Bay area.[16]

* * *

Falwell and his Moral Majority associates may well have been troubled by the increasing incidents of sex scandal among politicians. They were deeply disappointed by the presidency of Jimmy Carter. While a "born again" Christian, Carter represented the liberal wing of the Southern Baptist Convention (SBC), the nation's largest evangelical denomination. (Carter admitted, in a 1976 *Playboy* interview, "I've committed adultery in my heart many times.") In 1979, the year of the Falwell conclave, a profound theological and ideological split wracked the SBC—and the conservative forces won.[17] The split led to organizational changes that remade evangelism into both a more orthodox, formal religious practice and a more political, combative religious movement.

In 1980, Carter's Democrats introduced a gay rights plank in the party's electoral platform. While a brave gesture, it provided the religious right with proof that Carter, even as a Christian, could not be trusted. It was a gesture that contributed to Ronald Reagan's 1980 electoral victory. The Republicans received enormous support from the Christian right, helping an invigorated fundamentalism move closer to securing state power. Reagan, and the Christian right, received unexpected moralistic confirmation as the AIDS crisis deepened during the eighties.

Under the stewardship of Falwell and other Christian conservative leaders, the meaning of religious ecumenicalism changed. Where once it meant one denomination partnering with another religious groups like Baptists or Pentecostals, ecumenicalism now sought to join different (historically often competing) faiths in common cause, whether they be Christian, Jewish or Muslim. The new religious right refocused its effort to unite those who were self-defined conservatives, traditionalists or fundamentalists. The new enemy was identified as not only secular humanists, but also liberal or moderate believers.

During the 1980s, the Moral Majority claimed a constituency of fifty million people and effectively drew upon the energies of what the sociologist Robert Davison Hunter calls "para-church" groups. He claims, based on the scholarship of Robert Wuthnow, that in 1900 only about one hundred and fifty such groups operated in the U.S. However, by 1975, they had grown to four hundred and, by 1987, they totaled nearly one thousand. And Falwell was at the heart of this movement. As reported in *Time* magazine, "By 1985, his operations had budgets of more than $100 million a year, and he was winging round the world in private jets."[18]

The Moral Majority put together a strategic plan, "Top-Secret Battle Plan for 1982," that laid out its political campaign to remake America. Its goals were clear: pass the Human Life Amendment to the Constitution; repress the growing homosexual influence; mount a coordinated fight against pornography; and counter the American Civil Liberties Union (ACLU). Joining with groups like the Christian Voice and the National Conservative Political Action Committee, it mobilized an electorate that defeated the reelection efforts of Senators George McGovern (D-SD), Frank Church (D-ID), John Culver

(D-IA) and Birch Bayh (D-IN). While the organization formally dissolved in 1989, the moral majority hatched by those who attended Falwell's gathering a decade earlier ultimately seized state power a decade or so later.[19]

\* \* \*

For all the efforts of the Moral Majority and other groups committed to uplifting America's moral standing, the 1980s witnessed a flurry of nearly two-dozen major sex scandals involving members of the political elite. They included the usual peccadilloes, heterosexual adulterous affairs, outings of closeted gays, illicit relations with lobbyists and hookups with hookers. They also included revelations about a Supreme Court nominee's alleged sexual harassment of a fellow federal employee, an alleged gay prostitution ring operating out of the White House and sex scandals involving two of the nation's leading pastors.

Adultery is a shadow haunting monogamous marriage. As moralists during the eighties proclaimed the sacredness of marriage and pushed for a Constitutional Amendment sanctifying the family, divorce rates increased and politicians were caught up in numerous adulterous liaisons. These scandals reflected the adulterer's sense of power, especially those involving Sen. Gary Hart (D-CO) and Rep. John Jenrette (D-SC). The illicit affairs involving Sen. Roger Jepsen (R-IA) and Reps. Thomas Evans (R-DL), Sue Myrick (R-NC) and Arlan Stangeland (R-MN) only intensified the era's moral crisis.[20]

Hart's infatuation with Donna Rice, a model and actress, remains one of the great mysteries of modern political history. This popular liberal senator, who had his sights set on the White House, refused to accept the fact that journalistic ethics had changed. The discretion that hid from the electorate the affairs of Harding, FDR, Ike, JFK and LBJ was no longer fully operational. Hart did not recognize that the culture wars fostered an atmosphere that make politicians, along with preachers, athletes, movie stars and other celebrities, fair game for moralists, gossip-mongers and those wanting to "out" ideological hypocrites.

Hart was the perfect target: He wanted to be caught, punished. Like Clinton, he was compelled by a desire to test his power, to see how much he could get away with challenging moral standards before he was caught. Tales of philandering and womanizing dogged his marriage and political career. And, like a moth to a flame, in 1987 in Bimini, he spent a night on the yacht, *Monkey Business*, with Rice. Hart challenged the media to report on his tryst—and they did! While first denying any illicit purpose for being with Rice, his fiction proved untenable as additional stories of his wayward activities came out. Shamefaced and humiliated, as evidence of his sexual misdeeds mounted, Hart fled the Washington spotlight and the '88 presidential race, returning to Colorado to reclaim a more private life.

Measured against the Hart scandal, the other political scandals of the period seem almost banal. Jepsen was outed in 1980 for having visited a call house earlier in his life; his pathetic defense: he thought it was a health club. Myrick, a self-described "devout Christian," was elected to Congress in 1995 after serving two terms as mayor of Charlotte, NC; in 1989, while running for reelection she was outed for having had an adulterous affair with a married man whom she would ultimately marry. Evans succumbed to "Parkinson's disease"—an obsessive fascination with Paula Parkinson. She was an aspiring Washington lobbyist who, as a former bunny at the New York Playboy Club, expanded the scope of her professional services to include private, bedroom activities. Unfortunately, she videotaped some of these liaisons and they became the subject of a Department of Justice investigation into congressmen providing votes for sex. Kiss and tell may be one thing; but kiss and show is a Washington no-no. And Evans paid the price, losing his reelection bid in 1982. Stangeland, an upstanding Christian with seven children, was outed for what he argued was mere indiscretion: he was caught using his House credit card to make hundreds of long-distance phone calls to and from the residences of a female lobbyist. He insisted that the calls—and his presence at the lobbyist's home—were purely professional activities. His constituency did not look so kindly upon his conduct and replaced him with a Democrat.

And then there were the Jenrettes, John and Rita. In Washington, a scandal involving just sex is, well, just so ordinary. However, a scandal with a FBI sting operation and a big bucks pay-off, now that's the real deal. Mrs. Jenrette outed her hubby, the honorable congressman, first in an exposé in *The Washington Post*, then in a follow-up spread in *Playboy* and finally in a tell-all memoir, *My Capitol Secrets*. Commentators were shocked, *shocked*, by revelations about the congressman's adulterous goings-on and stories of other politicians stepping out from the hallowed-halls of Congress for noontime quickies with staffers, lobbyists and hookers. However, amidst these revelations, the good congressman, along with a half-dozen other political worthies, was caught in an FBI sting operation, ABSCAM, accepting a $50,000 bribe. He went to jail and the Jenrettes' model marriage ended in divorce.

Seven years earlier, in the summer of 1983, the House ethics committee censured Gerry Studds (D-MA) and Dan Crane (R-IL) for their sexual conduct with two teenage congressional pages. The Studds incident was in 1973 and involved a male page; the Crane incident was in 1980 and involved a female page. However, the reaction of their respective electoral constituencies illuminated the changing moral climate beginning to redefine the nation. Studds, who came out as gay, was from a liberal Northeast district and was reelected; Crane, married and the father of six, was from a conservative heartland district and lost his reelection bid.

Studds was not the only congressmen to be outed for homosexuality during the eighties. The experiences of Jon Hinson (R-MI) and Barney Frank (D-MA) further illustrate the deepening moral polarization redefining the nation. During his 1980 campaign for reelection, Hinson sought to take the moral high ground by admitting to a number of inappropriate activities. One involved a 1976 incident in a Virginia gay bar, another concerned a 1977 escape from a fire in a gay porn theatre. Running in a conservative southern district, he swore that he was not gay and, surprisingly, won reelection due to a three-way split. However, shortly after taking office in 1981, he was arrested in a House restroom and charged with attempted oral sodomy. He resigned in disgrace; in 1995, he died of AIDS.

Frank's homosexuality was one of the most public secrets in Washington. However, he seemed as surprised as everyone else when it was revealed in '89 that his live-in "personal assistant" during the 1985–1987 period, Stephen Gobie, was a prostitute who ran a male escort service out of his apartment. The House ethics committee reprimanded Frank for his poor judgment (including attempts to fix his lover's parking tickets) and he has been reelected ever since.

Sexual harassment scandals captured national attention during the late-eighties as the woman's movement fought the legitimacy of traditional male abuse, making it finally into the bad conduct, if not crime, it really is. Revelation about the misconduct of Sen. Brock Adams (D-WA) as well as Reps. Ernie Konnyu (D-CA), Jim Bates (D-CA), Gus Savage (D-IL) and Donald "Buzz" Lukens (R-OH) raised the issue of harassment to national prominence. However, it was the confrontation between Supreme Court nominee Clarence Thomas and Professor Anita Hill, at Thomas' 1991 Senate confirmation hearings, that brought sexual harassment to national attention.

In September 1988, *The Seattle Times* broke the story of Kari Tupper's complaint aginst Adams. The former congressional aide was twenty-four years old and her parents were the senator's family friends. She claimed that in '87 she had gone to the senator's Washington, DC, home to confront him over his ongoing sexual harassment only to be drugged and molested. The senator fiercely denied the charges. She originally brought her claim to the U.S. Attorney for Washington who spent a year and a half "investigating" her charges, but never acted. A few weeks after the original story appeared, the paper reported that "eight women—as well as others not willing to sign statements but insisting that they, too, were his [Adams] victims" of sexual molestation over the previous two decades. Confronted with these stories, the good senator ended his reelection effort.[22]

Enbolden by a growing feminist sensibility, more women came forward with claims of congressional misdeads. Like Tupper's story in *The Seattle Times*, they often turned to the media to publicize their claims, knowing that powerful congressmen are protected by certain privileges. The media, however, like a good scandal, it sells papers, especially if it is corroborated or raises reasonable doubts about an elected official. This approach is based on an unstated media assumption that the local electorate should decide for themselves if the claims they publish are legitimate. For example, in August 1987, the *San Jose Mercury News* broke the story of two former aides who charged Konnyu with sexual harassment; the one-term congressmen was defeated in his reelection bid.[23] The following year, *Roll Call*, the Capitol Hill newspaper, reported accustions by female staffers about sexual harassment by San Diego's Bates.[24] The congressman denied the accusations, apologized for inappropriate conduct and insisted that the scandal was a Republican smear camapign. He was reelected for the next term. In June 1989, *The Washington Post* reported that Savage had fondled a Peace Corps volunteer while on an official visit to Zaire; Savage, who is black, initially called the charges a racially motivated attack but later, after a House ethics committee investigation determined that the incident took place, formally apologized—and was relected.[25]

In February 1989, Lukens was outed by an Ohio TV station reporting on a Columbus woman's charge that he had been paying her daughter for sex over the past three years. The girl, Rosie Coffman, was only thirteen years old when the affair with the congressman began. Lukens was eventually indicted and found guilty, not for rape but for contributing to the delinquency of a minor and given a slap-on-the-wrist sentence of thirty days in jail. Refusing to resign in the face of scandal, he was defeated in his reelection bid. While completing his lame-duck term in Washington, Lukens was accused of inappropriate sexual conduct, this time fondling a Capitol elevator operator. He resigned in disgrace.[26]

One of the biggest—and least reported—scandals of the late-eighties was broken by *The Washington Times*, the conservative, Moon or Unification Church-backed newspaper. The first inkling of a scandal was a report about a male prostitution ring operating in the DC area. Additional reports kept expanding on the story. The paper claimed that Craig Spence, a Republican lobbyist, took youthful prostitutes (one fifteen years old) and clients on late-night tours of the White House. It claimed that Reginald de Gueldre, a Secret Service agent, arranged the tours; it also reported that the Secret Service "furloughed" three White House guards tied to the episode. It reported that Spence hosted lavish parties for the Washington rich and powerful at which cocaine and other illicit pleasures were provided. Also named in the scandal were Paul Balach, White House political personnel liaison for Labor Secretary Elizabeth Dole, and Charles Dutcher, the Reagan Administration's associate director of presidential personnel; both charged prostitute services to their credit cards.

However, the story took a bizarre twist when the paper linked the Washington goings-on to a ring that was trafficking children from Nebraska orphanages for sex orgies with Republican officials and other social worthies. It identified Lawrence King, Jr., an African-American Republican who operated the Omaha-based Franklin Community Credit Union, and Harold Andersen, then publisher of the *Omaha Herald*, as the ringleaders. The scandal reached its "climax" when Spence, who had been indicted on cocaine and gun possession charges, was found dead in a Boston hotel room.[27]

It was, however, the 1991 revelations about Supreme Court nominee Clarence Thomas' questionable behavior toward Anita Hill that became the nation's most controversial sexual harassment scandal. A leaked FBI report alleged harassment of Hill, Thomas' former colleague at the Department of Education (DOE) and the Equal Employment Opportunity Commission (EEOC) and a law professor at the University of Oklahoma. It nearly sank his nomination. Before a national TV audience, Orrin Hatch [R-UT] turned the Senate hearing into the soap opera it really is: "[D]id you ever say in words or substance something like there is a pubic hair in my Coke?" and "Did you ever use the term Long Dong Silver in conversation with Professor Hill?" The candidate, with questionable qualifications and less credibility, denied all accusations. Failing to substantiate Hills' claims, Thomas was confirmed by the Senate with a 52–48 vote, the closest confirmation vote for a Justice in the twentieth century.[28]

If the questionable behavior of a Supreme Court nominee could stir a national scandal, then the documented adulterous activities of two of America's leading religious leaders, Jim Bakker and Jimmy Swaggart, proved that no one was above sexual scandal. In 1988, revelations about the illicit sexual lives of the two preachers captured the nation's attention. Both were charismatic televangelists, happily married family men with large congregational followings.

Bakker, married to the irrepressible Tammy Faye, started his evangelical career working with Pat Robertson on his Christian Broadcasting Network. He became leader of the popular Praise the Lord (PLT) ministry and was caught up not only in an adulterous liaison, but in a bribery scandal as well. Bakker found the new PLT secretary, Jessica Hahn, an actress and model who ultimately posed for *Playboy*, irresistible. To hide his indiscretions, he bribed Hahn with church funds and, eventually, ended up in jail for fraud, racketeering and tax evasion.

As the Bakker scandal unfolded, his fellow TV evangelist, Swaggart, spoke out against his fallen brother-in-ministry; earlier, in 1986, Swaggart joined the growing chorus denouncing another TV evangelist, Martin Gorman, for "immoral dalliances"—Gorman was defrocked for his conduct. Unfortunately, this morally upstanding minister was caught with a prostitute in a seedy Louisiana motel. In a now-famous TV broadcast, Swaggart, crying and beating his chest, apologized for his "moral failing" to his wife and congregation, begged for their forgiveness and resigned his ministry.[29]

Word about America's gravest religious sex scandal involving Catholic priests began to emerge in the mid-eighties, but did not fully grip the nation's attention until the early-twenty-first century. Sexual abuse of women and youthful male and female parishioners by the clergy has taken place since time immemorial. However, with the rise of post-sixties political environment, abuse finally came under intense public scrutiny. According to journalist Carl Cannon, Louisiana writer Jason Berry was the first to begin to raise the issue of sexual abuse by priests and the Church's cover-up. The issue began to generate national attention when "The Phil Donahue Show" covered it on St. Patrick's Day, 1988. By the early-nineties, momentum was building when indictments were handed down against John Porter for molesting twenty-eight boys in Fall River, MA, and John Geoghan, who molested young boys from at least 1972 but was not defrocked until 1998. In 2001, Kristen Lombardi, writing in the *Boston Phoenix*, directly tied Geoghan to the local Catholic hierarchy, naming Boston Cardinal Bernard Law as complicit in the cover-up. Geoghan was eventually convicted of child molestation and, in 2003, was murdered in prison.[30]

Pope Benedict XVI visited the U.S. in the Spring of '08, the first visit by a Pope since the Church pedophile scandal broke. He came, in part, to reassure the millions of American Catholics who were deeply disturbed by the Church hierarchy's role in the cover-up. At a well-publicized but private get-together, he met with victims of the abuse who came from two groups, Survivors Network of those Abused by Priests (SNAP) and Voice of the Faithful. According to Edward Lozzi, "the meeting was forced upon the Pope by the victims." He adds:

Pope Benedict was very uncomfortable meeting with the five representative victims who had been raped by priests and had their lives and families changed forever. This was a private meeting of course. The Pope was visibly embarrassed and in agony throughout the whole encounter.

He concludes, quite pessimistically, "... Ultimately that April meeting was just a publicity stunt by Benedict."[31]

Estimates of the full consequence of the scandal are difficult to determine. In 2004, the U.S. Conference of Catholic Bishops published a study, *A Report on the Crisis in the Catholic Church in the United States*, that notes the following: 10,667 parishioners made accusations against priests; 81 percent of victims were male, 19 percent female; and that more that half (55.7 percent) of the accused priests had one victim, one quarter (26.9 percent) had two or three victims, 14 percent had four to nine victims and 3.5 percent (one hundred and forty-nine priests) were accused of abusing ten or more victims. The Hartford Courant estimated that by 2004 the total liability cost to Catholic dioceses and religious orders topped $572 million. This estimate does not include subsequent settlements, including the $660 million paid by the Los Angeles Archdiocese in 2007. The true consequences of Church pedophile abuse on the lives of the victims, let alone the full costs, will likely never be known.[32]

\* \* \*

Bill Clinton's sex scandals dominated the period from 1992 to 1998. Like bookends, they started with Gennifer Flowers' revelations of a twelve-year affair with the governor and ended with his impeachment by the House over his liaison with Monica Lewinsky. Clinton's conduct captured so much media attention that people tend to forget the scandals involving still other politicians and celebrities that occurred during the 1990s. Together, they reflected the changing nature of scandal. While still a form of public spectacle, sex scandal was morphing from a shaming ritual to a form of popular entertainment, a process facilitated by political theatre. Clinton's peccadilloes, while much in line with those of Harding, FDR and JFK, became fodder of a Republican campaign to discredit and defeat an elected president. While failing to force him from office, the right's campaign helped bring Bush to power in 2000.

A number of scandals broke before Clinton took center stage. One involved Ronald Reagan. In 1991, *People* magazine published a story charging the former president with raping an actress four decades earlier. The story was put forward by the gossip-journalist Kitty Kelley in her unauthorized biography of Reagan's wife, Nancy. As champion of the conservative ascension to federal power, Reagan had come under Christian scrutiny because he was the first, and only, divorced man elected president. He married Jane Wyman in January 1940, her third husband; she filed for divorce in 1948. In 1952, he married the actress Nancy Davis.

More importantly, Kelley uncovered a long forgotten episode that shocked many. In 1952, Reagan, then president of the Screen Actors Guild, visited the home of Selene Walter and, she insisted, overpowered and raped her. In the *People* magazine story, Walters stated: "I opened the door, then it was the battle of the couch. I was fighting him. I didn't want him to make love to me. He's a very big man, and he just had his way." (Kelley also reported, without substantiation, that the Reagans smoked pot with Jack Benny and George Burns and that Frank Sinatra had an affair with Nancy Reagan. It should be noted that no legal actions were taken by the Reagans against Kelley.)[33]

Also in '91, Senator Charles Robb (D-VA) was caught-up in the scandal spotlight. Rumors circulated on Capitol Hill about an adulterous affair between LBJ's son-in-law and the former Miss Virginia USA, Tanquil "Tai" Collins. A producer for the NBC-TV show, "Exposi," cornered the senator and pointedly questioned him about his alleged use of cocaine and extra-marital affairs. In an effort to contain the scandal, Robb setup a preemptive TV interview in which he claimed that he was innocent, having only shared a bottle of wine and receiving a friendly massage from one of his constituents. Unfortunately for Robb, like all such cover-ups, the truth eventually came out. This time it was in the form of a cover spread in *Playboy*. Collins revealed that she provided the senator with a "nude massage" at New York's Hotel Pierre and had been giving him massages and a lot more for years. The senator, with the support of his wife, survived the scandal and beat Oliver North in the 1994 election.[34]

Under the shadow of the Clinton-Lewinsky affair, a host of affairs took place and were either minimized or failed to gain much media attention. These involved Senators Daniel Inouye (D-HI) and Bob Packwood (R-OR) and Representatives Ken Calvert (R-CA), Charles Canady (R-FL), Mel Reynolds (D-IL), Helen Chenoweth (R-ID) and Dan Burton (R-IN). Under the Clinton halo, these scandals if known at all are now long forgotten.[35]

During the '92 campaign when the first allegations about Clinton's sexual dalliances appeared, a Republican opponent raised a story about Inouye's conduct. The Republican placed an ad in a Hawaii paper based on secretly taped revelations of Lenore Kwock, the senator's long-time hairdresser. Unknowingly, she divulged that he had sexually assaulted her more than fifteen years earlier and regularly made unpleasant overtures toward her when she cut his hair. The ad was pulled when Kwock objected that her privacy had been violated. Nevertheless, the story led to reports by still other women regarding Inouye's inappropriate conduct. None of the women would provide depositions about their mistreatment, so the story died.

The story about Packwood, however, did not die, but grew over a two-year period until he was forced from office in 1995. In the weeks following the '92 election and the senator's reelection to his fifth term, both *The Washington Post* and Portland's *Oregonian* admitted that they had sat on stories about Packwood's sexual dalliances because of his strenuous denials. Fearing to contaminate the election with unsubstantiated gossip, the papers held off. While many, including the *American Journalism Review* (AJR), criticized their decisions, the story slowly gained credence as more and more female lobbyists and staffers came forward with similar revelations. One staffer, Julie Williamson, claimed that such behavior took place as early as 1969. Another tale involved an *Oregonian* reporter, Roberta Ulrich, who, according to the AJR, "had been kissed on the lips by Packwood in his office eight months [April 1992] earlier." Ultimately, twenty-six complaints were filed against Packwood.

The good senator might have fought off these acquisitions if it was not revealed that he kept an oral diary in which, each morning, he would recount for posterity the previous day's—and night's!— occurrences. The Senate ethics committee requested Packwood turn over transcripts (estimated at 8,200 pages and dating from the early sixties) of the diary but he refused, insisting that it covered only consensual relations and was his private property. Packwood fought the case to the Supreme Court and lost. The diary revealed far more misdeeds then sexual indiscretions, including under-the-table political horse-trading with lobbyists, businessmen and fellow senators. Faced with mounting evidence of scandalous, if not criminal, conduct, the committee contemplated expelling Packwood—who resigned to avoid further embarrassment and prosecution.[36]

Hypocrisy was one of the social virtues that underscored the Clinton era and no one better expressed it than Calvert. A tireless supporter of the Christian Coalition and "family values," he took a principled stand against Clinton: "We can't forgive what occurred between the President and Lewinsky." However, in 1993, this upstanding citizen was caught naked in his car getting a blowjob from a hooker, only to be apprehended by the police when he attempted to flee. He later pleaded for mercy, complaining that his father had recently committed suicide, his wife had left him and he did not know that the woman was a sex worker. Adding insult to injury, his ex-wife denounced him for refusing to meet his child-support payments. He was nevertheless reelected to office. Canady, another upstanding conservative, was outed in an adulterous affair with Sharon Becker, but survived the scandal and, in '08, was appointed to the Florida Supreme Court.

Chenoweth, a conservative Republican, also railed against Clinton and called for his resignation: "I believe that personal conduct and integrity does matter." However, she admitted in 1995 to a six-year affair with a married associate; she claimed her case was different from Clinton's indiscretions in that she was, at the time, single and had received a pardon from a higher authority: "I've asked for God's forgiveness, and I've received it." Burton, a born-again Christian, supporter of "family values" and fierce Clinton opponent (he denounced the president as a "scumbag") was outed for sexually harassing female lobbyists, staffers and constituents; for repeated adulterous affairs; and for fathering an out-of-wedlock child. His conservative electorate was forgiving and reelected him.[37]

Democrats other than Clinton were not immune to sex scandal. Shortly before the '94 election and while he was campaigning for reelection, Reynolds was indicted for having sex with a 16-year-old campaign worker, Beverly Heard, and then pressuring her to lie about it. The congressman, an African-American, denied the charges, insisting they were part of a Republican dirty-tricks campaign. He was reelected. However, the following year he was charged and convicted of twelve counts of sexual assault, soliciting child pornography and obstruction of justice and sentenced to five years in prison. He resigned. In 1997, he was convicted of a separate set of criminal charges involving bank fraud, wire fraud and lying to the Federal Elections Commission and sentenced to a prison term of six-and-a-half years. He received a pardon from Clinton.[38]

* * *

In January 1992, just weeks before the all-important New Hampshire primary, *Star*, the gossip tabloid, published an exposé claiming that Gennifer Flowers, an Arkansas state employee and cabaret singer, had had a twelve-year affair with the governor. Moving quickly to counter the scandalous claim, Bill Clinton, joined by his wife, Hillary, appeared later that week on CBS's "60 Minutes" immediately following the Super Bowl, thus ensuring a huge national audience. The couples' denial, offered with a sincerity not seen since Nixon's famous Checkers speech of a half-century earlier, was so convincing that it helped him defeat the incumbent president, George H.W. Bush, in a three-way race with Ross Perot.[39]

Clinton's victory was seen by many as illegitimate, an electoral anomaly. Republicans, religious conservatives and other right-wingers started gunning for him from day one of his presidency. Early in 1994, conservative gossipmongers started spreading stories about Paula Jones, an Arkansas state clerical worker, who claimed that she was sexually assaulted by then-governor Clinton. As she later detailed in a formal deposition, she insisted that in 1991 state police escorted her to a Little Rock hotel room where Clinton dropped his trousers and asked her to perform a sex act. Clinton initially denied the charge, his supporters dismissing her as "trailer park trash." However, later in '94 Jones filled a civil lawsuit against Clinton seeking $700,000 in damages and a personal apology. Many credit the Flowers and Jones scandals with helping the Republicans win their '94 "revolution" and capturing both Houses of Congress.

The '92 presidential conventions were noteworthy for two reasons. First, the Democrats nominated Clinton; second, the Republicans formally launched the culture wars. Pat Buchanan, Nixon's loyal foot soldier, drew upon the sociologist Robert Davison Hunter's recently published study of religious politics in America, *Culture Wars*, to lament before a national TV audience: "There is a religious war going on in our country for the soul of America," he ranted. "It is a culture war, as critical to the kind of nation we will one day be as the Cold War itself. [It is a] struggle for the soul of America...."[40]

In early-'97, rumors began to circulate in Washington about the president's fascination with a young intern. According to a detailed chronology of the Clinton-Lewinsky scandal compiled by CNN, the first formal discussion took place in October 1997. Linda Tripp, Lewinsky's fellow employee at the Defense Department and confidante, met with *Newsweek's* Michael Isikoff and Lucianne and Jonah Goldberg at the Goldbergs' apartment in Washington, DC, and listened to a tape of the Tripp-Lewinsky conversations.[41]

Slowly, word started to get out about the affair. Conservative Christians and Republicans believed that Clinton's compulsive desire for sex in the White House Oval Office confirmed Buchanan's warning and indicated that America needed to be cleansed of its moral rot. This legitimized a Republican witchhunt that culminated in the president's impeachment by a vindictive Congress—and contributed to Bush's presidential victory in 2000. More compelling, it precipitated a national sex panic that lasted for more than a decade.

The 1998 revelations of Clinton's illicit liaison with a 22-year-old intern marked the zenith of the culture wars. For half a century, presidential pecadillos remained private indulgences, discreetly ignored or minimized by the press. Press discretion ended with Clinton. His affair, which lasted for more than two years, fueled the nation's grandest sex scandal since World War II. His actions, especially his rhetorical question, when is "is" *is*?, confirmed the Christian right's worst fears of secular, baby-boomer liberals.

Clinton trysts with Lewinsky, Flowers, Jones, Juanita Broaddrick and possibly others defined sex scandals during the nineties. While he is the only president to be impeached for oral sex, he was not the only public personality to be caught up in scandal during that period. The popular media made much of Hugh Grant being busted in 1995 for picking up prostitute Divine Brown in L.A.; he paid a fine and was sentenced to two years' probation. In 1996, Clinton advisor, Dick Morris, captured national attention when his sexual liaison with the courtesan, Sherry Rowland, and his particular shoe fetish were discovered and he was forced to resign. While driving in 1997, Eddie Murphy was pulled over by the L.A. police at 4:45 am and his passenger, a transsexual, was seized and arrested for outstanding prostitution charges. As CNN reported, "A spokesman for the actor maintained Murphy was just being a 'good Samaritan' by offering the transsexual a ride."[42]

These scandals, however fascinating, pale before the scandals involving the leading political moralists who assailed Clinton. Innumerable political hypocrites like Calvert, Canady, Chenoweth and Burton were outed as the Clinton scandal unfolded. Nevertheless, a second group of hypocrites, including Reps. Newt Gingrich (R-GA) and Henry Hyde (R-IL), were outed long after Clinton had left the White House. Their prior sexual liaisons seem to have compromised their high-minded moralistic opposition to the president. Truer hypocrites never walked the halls of Congress.[43]

Gingrich masterminded the '94 Republican revolution and was one of the driving forces behind the campaign to oust Clinton. In 2007, he acknowledged that, in 1977 and while still married to his first wife, he forced one of his campaign workers, Anne Manning, to give him a blowjob. As reported in *Vanity Fair*, Manning claimed, "we had oral sex. He prefers that modus operandi because then he can say, 'I never slept with her.'" In 2007, and in anticipation of a possible presidential run, Gingrich had one of those scripted heart-to-heart sit-downs with James Dobson, founder of Focus on the Family. When asked if he'd had an affair during the impeachment scandal, "The honest answer is yes," he admitted. And added: "There are times that I have fallen short of my own standards. There's certainly times when I've fallen short of God's standards."[44]

Gail Sheehy revealed Gingrich's 1977 affair with Manning while he was married to his first wife.[45] However, in 1981 Gingrich divorced his first wife, Jackie Battley, while she was in the hospital undergoing cancer treatment; he divorced his second wife, Marianne Ginther, on Mother's Day 1999, when his long-running affair with Callista Bisek, a congressional aide, was exposed. Seeking absolution, Gingrich confessed his sins to Dobson, who, along with Jerry

Falwell, forgave him. Rumors also circulated that *Hustler* had credit card receipts of him paying for hookers. No scarlet letter for this worthy.

Henry Hyde was another Republican stalwart who was upended by sexual scandal. In 1998, he admitted to having had an extramarital affair with Cherie Snodgrass, lasting from 1965 to 1969. When the story broke, Hyde admitted that he and Snodgrass were "good friends" but claimed the statute of limitations had passed on his "youthful indiscretions." While formally offering to resign, he continued to serve until he retired in 2006.

And then there is Robert Livingston. He was expected to replace Gingrich as Speaker of the House in the wake of his sexual scandal. However, a major scandal brewed amidst rumors that Larry Flynt had the testimony of four women, and perhaps more, who claimed to have had adulterous liaisons with Livingston over the previous decade. As the story goes, Livingston's wife apparently pleaded with Flynt that if he wouldn't publish the claims, the congressman would resign.[46]

* * *

The culture wars were a conservative counter-revolutionary rebellion against the sixties. A Christian-Republican alliance turned a host of important sex-related personal and social issues into a moralistic crusade. Drawing inspiration from a fundamentalist religious fervor rooted in the Puritans, the movement sought to police the sexual life of its fellow citizens. The arc of the conservative religious-political ascendancy is clear. It emerged with Nixon's 1972 presidential run; gained momentum with Reagan's victory in 1980; Buchanan placed it on the national agenda in 1992; it reached its zenith with the 1998 revelations about Clinton's illicit liaison with Lewinsky; achieved state power with Bush's 2000 victory; first started to sputter with the congressional elections of 2006; and was defeated with Obama's 2008 victory.

America suffers from sexual schizophrenia. On one side, innumerable politicians, clerics and much of the media decry what they see as the threat of illicit pleasure. On the other side, consenting adults, young people and the popular culture push for increased sexual explicitness. And in the middle, a growing and diverse assortment of ordinary Americans challenges restrictions on acceptable pleasure. Since the Puritans settled New Jerusalem nearly four centuries ago, American sexual life has embodied this tension. The nation has never dealt comfortably with human sexuality, including those practices like homosexuality long decried as immoral or illicit. This unresolved tension haunts American sex culture today.

The culture wars were propelled by a powerful, right wing populist rage expressing another Christian "great awakening." It played a pivotal role in the 2000 and 2004 elections, but was eclipsed in the 2006 congressional elections, its moral fervor spent. With the exception of abortion and gay marriage, other "hot-button" sex issues were all but absent from the 2008 national presidential campaign, replaced by immigration as the "red meat" issue. In 2008, the economy, along with the Iraq war, healthcare and energy costs, determined the election outcome.

The religious right's effort to restrict sexual experience was motivated by a number of factors. Many Christians were deeply troubled by the sexualization of society. Fashion, advertising, TV and movies were promoting an ever-increasing display of sexually suggestive (and often prurient) messages of word, image and sound. This sexualization was targeted to the young. And no one, least of all limousine liberals, challenged the intensifying media tyranny of erotic titillation.

The media is but one domain of social life that Christian conservatives felt challenged their deeply held traditions, their "family values." These values are based on hallowed beliefs in the family (the father's hierarchical relations to "his" wife and children), religion (the person's adherence to selective passages from the Bible) and sexuality (the man's monogamous heterosexuality for procreation and, secondarily, pleasure). Together, these values were the core of a traditional notion of moral authority that modern, secular society challenged.

At the heart of this belief system is a commitment to—wish for?—an unchanging and predetermined moral order. It is a moral order grounded upon biblical myth, Adam and Eve. The sociologist Hunter calls this belief "natural and divinely mandated sexual relations among humans." This is the sexual relationship "between male and female and this relationship is legitimate only under one social arrangement, marriage between one male and one female." Sin is understood as a violation of this order, especially involving unacceptable sex practices like premarital relations, extra-marital adultery and homosexual encounters.[48]

The religious right's efforts were an attempt by sizeable segments of (white) America to preserve privilege (particularly racial) and to maintain patriarchy (family structure and sexual relations). The religious right's growth and eventual political triumph bears witness to the challenge posed by the earliest phase of globalization. Nixon's abandonment of the gold standard, the military failure in Southeast Asia and the institutionalization of the permanent war economy set the stage for the social destabilization that marked the last quarter of the twentieth century.

A growing number of ordinary Americans, including many Christian fundamentalists, were experiencing an increasing sense of powerlessness. The revolt of Christian fundamentalists started as a rejection of the hedonism unleashed by the post-war consumer revolution. The Christian movement got enmeshed in a false war against New Deal liberalism, policies that significantly benefited them. And now, as the Bush administration exited the political stage, Americans, including many of the Christian right, find themselves left holding the proverbial bag of empty promises, fiscal crisis and foreign-policy disasters that the culture warriors bequeathed the nation.

## References

[1] www.buchanan.org/pa-92-0817.

[2] www.spingola.com/rise_of_the_religious_right.

[3] *New York Times*, May 16, 2007.

[4] Jon Heidenry, *What Wild Ecstacy: The Rise and Fall of the Sexual Revolution* (New York: Simon & Schuster, 1997), 263.

[5] Lillian Faderman, *Old Girls and Twilight Lovers: A History of Lesbian Life in Twentieth-Century America* (New York: Penguin, 1991), 201; see also Heidenry and David Allyn, *Make Love, Not War — The Sexual Revolution: An Unfettered History* (New York: Routledge, 2001).

[6] Faderman, 212.

[7] Gay Talese, *They Neighbor's Wife* (New York: Dell, 1981), 305.

[8] Ibid, 307-08 and 311-14.

[9] Ibid, 314.

[10] Ibid, 315-16.

[11] Ibid, 303.

[12] Chauncey, 224.

[13] John Loughery, *The Other Side of Silence: Men's Lives and Gay Identities — A Twentieth-Century History* (New York: Henry Holt, 1999), 259-60; Allyn, 238.

[14] Loughery, 358-60.

[15] Sources for these scandals are drawn from: John W. Dean, *Chronology of Congressional Sex Scandals*, http://writ.news.findlaw.com/dean/congsexscandals.html; George Kohn, ed., *The New Encyclopedia of American Scandal* (New York: Checkmark Books, 2001); Barbara Feinberg, *American Political Scandals: Past and Present* (New York: Watts, 1992); Stanley Hilton, *Glass Houses* (New York: St. Martins, 1998); Chadwick Matlin, *The Map of Shame* (www.slate.com/ id/2186335, posted March 11, 2008); and www.dkosopedia.com/wiki/Republican_Sex_Scandals.

[16] Robert Bauman, *The Gentlemen from Maryland: The Conscience of a Gay Conservative* (New York: Arbor House, 1986); see also Footnote 15.

[17] Elizabeth Ann Oldmixon, *Uncompromising Positions: God, Sex and the U.S. House of Representatives* (Washington, DC: Georgetown University Press, 2005), 85-86.

[18] James Davison Hunter, *Culture Wars: The Struggle to Define America* (New York: Basic Book, 1991), 89 and 90; Time, May 15, 2007.

[19] Moral Majority, http://rightweb.irc-online.org/gw/2803.html.

[20] See Footnote 15.

[21] Rita Jenrette, *My Capitol Secrets* (New York: Bantam Books, 1981).

[22] Duff Wilson, "The Kari Tupper Interview She Says Senator Pursued Her for Two Years," *Seattle Times*, 2, September 30, 1988.

[23] See Footnote 15.

[24] Susan F. Rasky, "Washington Talk," *New York Times*, April 11, 1989.

[25] See Footnote 15.

[26] See Footnote 15.

[27] Paul M. Rodriguez and George Archibald, "'Call-boy' Service Prospers Using High Finance, High Tech," *Washington Times*, June 20, 1989; Michael Hedges and Jerry Seper, "Power Broker Served Drugs, Sex at Parties Bugged For Blackmail," *Washington Times*, June 30, 1989; Paul M. Rodriguez and George Archibald, "RNC Calls Scandal a 'Tragic Situation," *Washington Times*, June 30, 1989; Frank Murray, "White House Mute on 'Call Boy' Probe," *Washington Times*, July 7, 1989; Michael Hedges and Jerry Seper, "Secret Service Furlough Third White House Guard," *Washington Times*, July 26, 1989; Michael Hedges and Jerry Seper, "In Death Spence Stayed True to Form," *Washington Times*; November 13, 1989; and Karlyn Barker, "Sex and the Capital," *Washington Post*, July 24, 1990.

[28] Richard Berke, "The Thomas Nomination," *New York Times*, October 12, 1991.

[29] Wayne King, "Swaggart Says He Has Sinned; Will Step Down," *New York Times*, February 22, 1988; Joanne Kaufman, "The Fall of Jimmy Swaggart," *People*, March 7, 1988.

[30] Carl M. Cannon, "The Priest Scandal," *American Journalism Review*, May 2002.

[31] Edward Lozzi, "Papal Bull: Sex, Lies and Vatican-tape," *Huffington Post*, July 15, 2008.

[32] www.usccb.org/nrb/nrbstudy/nrbreport.pdf; "4,500 Priests Accused of Abuse, Draft Says," Associated Press, Hartford Courant, February 17, 2004; Gillian Flaccus, "L.A. Archdiocese Agrees to $600 Million Settlement," Associated Press, *Washington Post*, July 15, 2007.

[33] "Meow, Meow!," *People*, April 29, 1991.

[34] Playboy, October 1991; Jack Tapper, "Dead Senator Running?," Salon, November 17, 1999.

[35] See Footnote 15.

[36] Cheryl Reid, "A Newspaper Confesses: We Missed the Story," *American Journalism Review*, January-February 1993; Nina Burleigh, "The Fall and Rise of Bob Packwood," *Time*, April 3, 1995.

[37] Susan Lehman, "Media Circus," Salon, October 15, 1998; David Neiwert, "Lives of the Republicans," Salon, September 16, 1998.

[38] "Ex-Congressman Reynolds & Wife Indicted for Fraud," CNN, November 7, 1996; Tim Graham, "ABC Ignored Teen-Sex Scandal

of Democrat Mel Reynolds Until 1995 Convention," *USA Today*, October 5, 2006.

[39] "The 1992 Campaign; Clintons to Rebut Rumors on '60 Minutes," *New York Times*, January 25, 1992.

[40] www.buchanan.org/pa-92-0817.

[41] www.cnn.com/ALLPOLITICS/1998/resources/lewinsky/timeline.

[42] "Transsexual Prostitute Arrested in Eddie Murphy's Car," CNN, May 2, 1997.

[43] See Footnote 15.

[44] Ben Evans, "Gingrich Had Affair During Clinton Probe," Associated Press, *Washington Post*, March 8, 2007.

[45] Gail Sheehy, "The Inner Quest of Newt Gingrich," *Vanity Fair*, September 1995.

[46] David Talbot, "This Hypcrite Broke Up My Family," Salon, September 1998; see also Footnote 15.

[47] See Footnote 15.

[48] Hunter, 122.

# CHAPTER 7. AMERICA'S SEX WARS

*Emperor's Club vip is the most preferred international social introduction service for those accustomed to excellence. ...*
*We specialize in introductions of: fashion models, pageant winners and exquisite students, graduates and women of successful careers (finance, art, media etc...) to gentlemen of exceptional standards*[1]

On April 3, 2008, Texas state moral enforcement authorities, including members of the Texas Rangers, Family and Protective Services, local police and the FBI, raided a compound of the Fundamentalist Church of Jesus Christ of Latter Day Saints (FLDS), a dissident Mormon sect, located near Eldorado, TX. An estimated five hundred and thirty-four people (four hundred and one girls and boys as well as one hundred and thirty-three women) were removed from the colony. News coverage of the scandal dominated national and international media headlines for months. Stories of young girls being forced to "marry" and have sex with Church male elders was the centerpiece of a media circus. After two months of bitter legal contestation, the Texas Supreme Court ordered the children removed from the state custody and returned to their parents.[2]

When the story about the alleged sexual abuse at the FLDS compound first broke, people were scandalized. The media camped out near the religious group's compound, telling and retelling any tidbit of gossip that would capture and keep the public's attention. However, other than demonizing the "cult" and its mysterious founder, Warren Jeffs, little information about what took place at the compound, the group's beliefs or the legal issues involved was presented. This typifies how sex scandal had evolved from a spectacle of shame to a form of entertainment distraction.

181

Sex played a decisive role in the 2000 and 2004 presidential elections, but was eclipsed in the 2006 midterm election, the religious right's moral fervor spent. Abortion and gay marriage were the only sex issues to be raised in the 2008 national presidential campaign, but played a minor role in rallying the conservative faithful. Efforts to outlaw gay marriage were successful in Arizona (Proposition 102), California (Proposition 8) and Florida (Marriage Protection Amendment) as was Arkansas' Proposed Initiative Act No. 1 that prohibits co-habiting couples of the same sex, whether gay or straight, from either adopting a child or serving as foster parents. These ostensible victories signal the eclipse of the culture wars, the Christian right's dwindling power over public life.

The once-powerful Christian Republican movement is in retreat. After more than a quarter-century of growing influence, the fierce right wing assault on popular values, especially sexual freedom, is in decline. The Christian-Republican alliance turned a host of important personal and social issues into a moralistic nightmare. Personal health, family life, sexual relations, scientific knowledge and popular culture became battlegrounds of the culture wars. This round of the culture wars seems over.

The culture wars were a conservative counter-revolutionary rebellion against the progressive gains of the 1960s. The conservative religious-political alliance emerged with Richard Nixon's 1972 presidential run, gained momentum with Ronald Reagan's victory in 1980, reached its zenith with the 1998 revelations about Bill Clinton's illicit liaison with Monica Lewinsky and achieved state power with George Bush's victory in 2000. Now, it is in eclipse.

In addition to the FLDS affair, a host of other sex scandals took place amidst the 2008 electoral season. They included the outing of New York governor Eliot Spitzer and Democratic presidential-contender John Edwards as well as Representatives Vito Fossella (R-NY) and Tim Mahoney (D-FL). In each case, the scandal led to the politician's departure from public life. Both 2008 presidential candidates, Barack Obama and John McCain, were subjects of sex scandal during the campaign, but the accusations against them proved unsubstantiated and easily dismissed.

The *New York Times* sparked a scandal about journalistic integrity when it ran a front-page exposé implying that McCain had had an affair with lobbyist, Vicki Iseman. She is a partner with Alcalde & Fay, representing telecommunications companies that contributed tens of thousands of dollars to his campaigns. After extensive denials, the story disappeared; in December 2008, Iserman brought a $27 million defamation suit against the *Times*. A scurrilous rumor was floated by the Drudge Report and other right wing sources about Obama. It reported that Larry Sinclair claimed that, in 1999, he had sex and took drugs with then-state representative, Obama. In a video posted on YouTube, "Obama's Limo Sex and Drug Party," he claimed that they partied twice, once in a limo and the other at a hotel. However, WhiteHouse.com paid Sinclair $10,000 to take a polygraph test which, it claims, he failed.[3]

Sexual politics matter. Issues like the economy, Iraq and healthcare were at the top of the voting public's list of concerns in '08. Culture war issues were not central to voters' worries. Sex-related issues, nevertheless, set the moral agenda of each presidential administration. The moral hypocrisy that defined the Bush administration's repressive domestic and international policies was expressed in the innumerable sex-related scandals that took place during its tenure.

* * *

George W. Bush's presidency was a political disaster. His leadership failures, from the illegal invasion of Iraq and the Katrina catastrophe to the ever-expanding financial disaster to the overwhelming healthcare crisis, marked his administration—and him personally!—as the worst presidency in the nation's history.

During the '04 presidential election mention was made of "W's" dubious participation in the National Guard, as little mention was made of his alcohol and cocaine problems during the 2000 campaign. However, in the 2000 run, even less attention was paid to a series of alleged sex scandals that took place while he was Texas governor. If his handlers could manipulate a more-than-willing media into a war with hyped intelligence and sanctimonious calls of patriotism, it's easy to hide a sex scandal or two.

Bush is haunted by two sex scandals that have been successfully dismissed as crank complaints, effectively swept under the proverbial rug. The first involved a criminal complaint and lawsuit of rape by Margie Schoedinger, who later committed suicide; the second was an accusation by Tammy Phillips, a former stripper, of having an affair with Bush that ended in 1999.

In 2002, Margie Denise Schoedinger, a 38-year-old African-American woman who lived in the Houston suburb of Missouri City, TX, filed a lawsuit against Bush alleging that he had raped her in October 2000. In her suit she alleged, "race based harassment and individual sex crimes committed against her and her husband." It adds:

> On or about, October 26, 2000, an attempt was made to abduct Plaintiff (Schoedinger) by three unknown assailants. Because of the actions of these assailants, Sugar Land [TX] police officers were dispatched to the scene. In the end, no report was taken. The assailants were treated respectfully and allowed to go free while Plaintiff (Schoedinger) was repeatedly and aggressively questioned. After filing a lawsuit, the Plaintiff's family and past contacts were questioned and harassed.

The compliant also states:

> Throughout this conversation, she learned that there was no time that the Defendant (Bush) ever stopped watching Plaintiff, nor did he stop having sex with Plaintiff. The sole concern of the Defendant and his representatives was whether Plaintiff could actually recall, the individual sex crimes committed against Plaintiff and Plaintiff's husband, utilizing drugs.

There was no substantiating evidence for any of her claims.

Schoedinger claimed Bush also raped her husband, Christopher. At the time, he was a 33-year-old white man who apparently served a year in prison after pleading "no contest" to assault charges against his wife. He later filed for divorce. Her claims against Bush were dismissed as the publicity-seeking ravings of a disturbed woman. Only one U.S. newspaper seems to have covered the case, the local *Fort Bend Star*. It quoted a Sugar Land police captain saying his department had no record of any complaint by Schoedinger. (At the time, the complaint was on the Fort Bend County's civil court records website.) Its editor is said to have off-handedly smirked, "I had heard she was a nut case." Schoedinger died on September 22,

2003, of a gunshot wound to the head, nine months after filing the suit. The Harris County, TX, Medical Examiner's office ruled the death a suicide.[4]

Tammy Phillips, a 35-year-old partner in a gym in Carrollton, TX, and (based on some accounts) an Austin exotic dancer or stripper, reported an affair with W that ended in June 1999. She claims her uncle, a prominent Republican, introduced her to then-governor Bush in December 1997 during a political function at a hotel in Midland, TX. Reports differ as to whether the alleged affair lasted nine or eighteen months. The scandal did get some initial traction with reports in the *National Enquirer,* Slate, *New York Post* and on Fox News, but disappeared as the 2000 campaign got underway. One local politico expressed surprise about Bush's alleged affair with Phillips, "It means that he stopped fooling around just prior to announcing his presidential run." Phillips seems to have disappeared and not pursued the accusation.[5]

A peculiar sexual perversion marked George Bush's presidency. The Bush administration began auspiciously when Attorney General John Ashcroft draped two semi-nude statues, "Spirit of Justice" (female) and "Majesty of Law" (male), in the Justice Department auditorium. It gained momentum with the obscenity scandal involving Janet Jackson's now-infamous nipple, forcing a reluctant FCC to stand up for moral rectitude and slap a stiff fine of $550,000 against a contrite (if dumbfounded) CBS. It achieved its clearest absurdity in the scandal involving Jeff Gannon, the Republican White House blogger who, after-hours, turned out to be James Dale Guckert (aka "Bulldog"), operator of a gay website with U.S. Marine Corp themes for the solicitation of male prostitutes.

However, it is hard to forget the disturbing photographs of tortured prisoners at Abu Ghraib and Lynndie England's seductive leer to the camera—the moment when the perversion of sadism became the pathology of empire. Former-Rep. Chris Shays (R-CT) warned America that Abu Ghraib "ain't torture, it's a sex ring."[6] But the most perverse moment surely was when (to use the author Arundhati Roy's wonderful term) Bush-the-Lesser jumped from the cockpit of a Navy S-3B Viking fighter and, posing against a banner proclaiming "Mission Accomplished," strode assertively across the deck of the USS Abraham Lincoln. Like the super-stud captain of a small town

Texas high school football team, Bush symbolized unchallenged power.

At that moment, Bush had pulled off what appeared to be a slam-dunk military victory. He, along with the others who had taken part in the conspiracy of false intelligence about Iraqi weapons of mass destruction, thought that they had gotten away with the greatest deception in American history: They manipulated the nation into an illegitimate and failed war. It was an exercise of absolutist power. And power, as Henry Kissinger knew so well, is the ultimate aphrodisiac. Bush's strutting on the Lincoln was a demonstration of his full masculine, imperial potency for the entire world to see. It was an erotic moment few experience.

Each presidency is marked by a sexual dark side. This is especially true among recent presidents who have come to resemble the hottest rock and movie stars. Jimmy Carter suffered from lust in his heart; Ronald Reagan, a divorcee, was plagued by the denial of AIDS and rumors that his son was gay; Bush-the-Elder's administration was shadowed by rumors (instigated by the Moon-backed *Washington Times*) of gay and pedophile rings operating out of the White House; and Clinton's trysts bespoke a sexuality of excess, of a passion that comes when an oversized ego fuels an unquenchable libido.*

Bush's public sexuality seemed centered in a Christian zeal that rejects sexual pleasure as an end in itself, erotic fulfillment beyond the requirements of procreation. Like the Puritans of old and subsequent evangelicals, he seemed to take literally the notion of original sin, in which the most intimate human relation is contaminated, forever scarring all subsequent generations. His sexuality seemed to be one of prohibition, a sexuality infused with a shame of the physical body and its deepest passions. One can only suspect that this repression is rooted in a deep, personal knowledge—and fear—of the excesses of self-indulgence, an outgrowth of his equally threatening experiences with alcohol and cocaine. The Bush presidency was an incarnation of America's long-festering Puritan curse.

But in keeping with the times, Bush's public sexuality embodied a highly fetishized imagery, replete with all kinds of symbolic mean-

---

* See Chapter 7, Sexual Counter-Revolution.

ing. Strutting about in his "Top Gun" uniform or with his sleeves rolled up while ineptly asserting command amidst the debacle of Hurricane Katrina, Bush was a fetishist's dream come true. He understood (if only unconsciously) that the trappings of power, the costumes, the proclamations, the public presentations, are as essential as its exercise, the wars conducted, the deals cut, the legislation passed. Whether in a Top Gun outfit, a business suit or swaggering in a cowboy getup, Bush's uniforms codified a fetishistic representation of power.

The Top Gun outfit that Bush wore on the Lincoln is but one option for those seriously into uniform fetishism. While his was a high-tech nylon-poly jumpsuit, others favor leather, latex/rubber, spandex, denim or silk. A man can choose from many uniforms, whether serviceman, policeman, fireman, cowboy, deliveryman, wrestler or priest. With our new gender-neutral military, a woman has her choice of the services to find that special uniform which is truly her or such old favorites as a French maid, nurse, waitress, hooker or nun. Anyone can choose a diaper.

Unfortunately, when private sexual fantasy confronts the forces of moral rectitude, the pervert often gets screwed. Nothing captures the lingering unacceptability of illicit sex more than what befell the 2004 Illinois GOP senatorial candidate, Jack Ryan, a millionaire playboy. Drawing upon previously-sealed divorce papers, the *Chicago Tribune* reported that Ryan's ex-wife, the TV actress Jeri Ryan, star of "Star Trek" and "Shark," "accused him of taking her to sex clubs in New York and Paris, where he tried to coerce her into having sex with him in front of strangers." The revelations forced Ryan to withdraw from the election, leading to Obama's victory. And, as the saying goes, everything else is history.[7]

\* \* \*

The Seventh Commandment states: "Thou shalt not commit adultery."[8] Soon after Bush took office, in May 2000, one of his most ardent supporters, Rudi Giuliani, held an outrageous press conference to publicly announce his intention to divorce his second wife, actress Donna Hanover. Surprised, Hanover held a follow-up press conference in which she declared, "I had hoped that we could keep this marriage together. For several years, it was difficult to participate in Rudy's public life because of his relationship with one staff member." The soon-to-be-former Mrs. Giuliani was referring to Cristyne Lategano-Nicholas, Giuliani's former communications director. Giuliani and Lategano-Nicholas denied allegations of a sexual liaison. Giuliani was also accused of having an ongoing, if discreet, sexual liaison while married to Hanover with his current wife, Judith Nathan, herself a survivor of two previous marriages.[9]

Giuliani's antics would be the first, but not the last, of the headline-grabbing scandals that marked the Bush era. Many were adulterous or out-of-wedlock affairs and involved leading politicians and clergymen. They are best divided between those occurring during the period of 2000 and the 2006 congressional election and the subsequent period through the '08 election. While the first phase saw the outing of many leading Republican and Christian worthies, the second period witnessed Democrats, most notably Spitzer and Edwards, fall under the specter of sex scandal.

Adultery is an all-American sin. Nathanial Hawthorne's classic tale, *The Scarlet Letter*, was published in 1850, one hundred and fifty years after the colonial witchcraft trials. Among early New England colonialists, adultery was a capital crime punishable by hanging or being branded with an "A" on the forehead. Other sexual practices denounced as sins included premarital sex, bestiality, masturbation, fornication, incest, rape, polygamy, interracial sex and sodomy as well as temptations like carnality, licentiousness, lust and seduction. While Hawthorne's character, Hester Prynee, suffered public ridicule and the shame of wearing a scarlet "A," early colonial women often met far worse fates. Two women, Elizabeth Seager and Rachel Clinton, were charged with witchcraft and adultery; their lives were spared. However, three women (Alice Lake, Martha Corey and Suzannah Martin) were accused of witchcraft and having illegitimate children; they were executed. Ten other women were accused of having sex with Satan and their individual fates vary.*

Since Independence, adultery by leading political figures has been an ongoing scandal. In the 1828 presidential election, Andrew Jackson was assailed for marrying a bigamist, Rachel Donelson Robards; their marriage occurred before her divorce was legally fi-

---

* See Chapter 2, Birth of a Nation.

nalized. In 1874, Grover Cleveland was confronted by newspaper reports claiming he had an affair with Mrs. Maria Crofts Halpin, who accused him of fathering her illegitimate 10-year-old son, Oscar Folsom Cleveland. Warren Harding had an affair for fifteen years with Carrie Fulton Phillips, the wife of a friend, James Phillips, and Nan Britton, thirty years his junior; he had sexual liaisons with Britton in the White House and fathered an out-of-wedlock daughter, Elizabeth Ann, with her. And then there are the extra-marital relations of FDR, Ike, JFK, Clinton and, lest we forget, the reported indiscretions of Bush-the-Lesser.

Estimates range widely as to the current rate of adultery in America. For example, a 1991 survey conducted by the University of Chicago's National Opinion Research Center found that 10 percent of married women reported that they had engaged in extramarital relations; in a 2002 follow-up study, 15 percent of women reported that they had engaged in such relations; in both studies, 22 percent of the male respondents reported engaging in such relations. A 1997 Ball State University study found that women eighteen to forty years are just as likely to commit adultery as men of comparable age. Reports in *Men's Health* place the husband's infidelity at one in twenty (5 percent) and the wife's infidelity at one in twenty-two (4.6 percent); *Oprah* magazine found that a wife's infidelity was at 15 percent. However, researchers Joan Atwood and Limor Schwartz estimate that, in 2002, 45–55 percent of married women and 50–60 percent of married men engage in extramarital sex during their marriage.[10]

While popular sexual practice is changing and martial infidelity appears more widespread and more tolerated, in 2004, twenty-four states still outlawed adultery; ten states had anti-fornication statutes prohibiting sex before marriage. States define adultery differently, the laws vary considerably and prosecution is arbitrary. For some states, adultery involves sexual intercourse outside marriage; for others, it occurs when a married person lives with someone other than his or her spouse. In West Virginia and North Carolina, for example, it involves "lewdly and lasciviously associate" with anyone other than one's spouse.

Adding more confusion, individual states prosecute adultery differently and punishment varies. It is a felony in Idaho, Massachusetts, Michigan and Oklahoma, but a misdemeanor everywhere else. Most states litigate both people involved, but Colorado, Georgia, Nebraska, North Dakota and Utah only punish the married person. However, states rarely enforce adultery laws. The most recent prosecution appears to have taken place in Virginia in 2003–2004. It involved John R. Bushey, Jr., a 66-year-old attorney for Luray, VA, who had an affair with Nellie Mae Hensley, a 53-years-old "other woman." While Hensley was divorced, Bushey was married and, when the affair ended, the spurned lover complained to the police who brought a misdemeanor adultery charge against him. He accepted twenty hours of community service as punishment.[11]

\* \* \*

At the time of his death in June 2003, the long-rumored story of the committed racist Strom Thurmond's youthful sexual liaision with his family's African-American maid, Carrie Butler, became a public scandal. Among the many unanswered question to be raised is whether Ms. Butler was a consenting partner or the victim of rape; another is her age at the time of sexual engagement, whether she was fifteen or sixteen years and, thus, whether the future senator was guilty of violating age-of-consent laws and, therefore, a pedophile. This part of Thurmond's past only became public when the daughter of his ill-fated liaison, Essie Mae Washington-Williams, brought it to public attention. Further complicating Thurmond's darker past is the revelation that, genetically, he and the civil rights activist, Rev. Al Sharpton, share the same family line.

Other revelations added to the Bush-era parade of scandals. The sexual exploits of Congressmen Mark Foley (R-FL) and Don Sherwood (R-PA), Reverends Paul Crouch and Ted Haggard, and pundit Bill Bennett undermined Bush's "compassionate conservative" moral posture and contributed to Democratic electoral victories in '06. When the Foley scandal broke in the fall of '06, many worried that sex predators were prowling the halls of Congress. Foley's rapid resignation and departure to a rehab center failed to sweep the growing scandal under the proverbial rug. While many in Florida's Sixteenth District and Congress seemed to have known that Foley was gay (and is reported to have had a lover for many years), no one wanted to out him, least of all the Republican Party or the local press. ABC News broke the story when it reported on a series of sexually suggestive emails Foley sent to a congressional page, thus undercutting the wink-and-a-nod morality that characterized Republican politics. As long as he stayed in the closet—and his particular predilection remained hidden—the party supported him.

The media seemed especially captivated by Foley's peculiar sexual inclination, an erotic fascination with adolescent youths. Most disturbing, they didn't know how to make sense of it. Media thugs like MSNBC's Tucker Carlson labeled him a "child molester" and others called him a "child predator" and a "pedophile."[12] However, his particular sexual obsession may be what psychiatrists identify as ephebophilia, the adoration of youthful lads—and which may or may not involve sexual contact. Foley rationalized his inappropriate behavior by hiding behind the self-denier's trifecta: being drunk, being sexually assaulted as a youth by a priest and being gay. However, following the law of unintended consequences, the Republican leadership, most notably Speaker of the House J. Denis (Denny) Hastert (R-IL), was aware of Foley's inappropriate proclivities from at least 2000. The Florida electorate took their revenge by voting in a Democrat in the '06 election; in keeping with Washington's merry-go-round of scandals, Foley's replacement, Tim Mahoney, would himself become the subject of a sex scandal two years later and lose his reelection bid.[13]

The Foley scandal placed in stark relief the moral hypocrisy that underscored Republican attitudes toward sexuality and power. Don Sherwood was the next hypocrite to take the hit. In 2004, Cynthia Ore called the police to Sherwood's DC apartment, claiming she was a victim of a physical attack from the congressman and was hiding in the bathroom. Follow-up headlines revealed they had a five-year extra-marital affair. In 2005, Ore filed a $5.5 million suit against the congressmen, insisting that he repeatedly struck her, pulled her hair and strangled her. The congressman denied all accusations. Like Foley, he lost his seat to a Democrat.[14]

Amidst the Foley scandal, CBS's Gloria Borger broke the story of what became known as "The List," a group of well-placed gay congressional staffers who regularly met for friendship and to compare notes about life on the Hill. A few days later, *New York Times* reporter Mark Leibovich added fuel to the fire by making public that every month or so, ten top Republican congressional staff members got together for dinner. Referring to themselves as the "P Project," a nod to P Street that cuts through DC's version of boy's town, they met to discuss their experiences as gay Republicans.[15] The group included nine chiefs of staffs, two press secretaries and two directors of communications. If accurate, it shows that some of the Christian right's favorite Washington legislators, including Senators Bill Frist, George Allen, Mitch McConnell and Rick Santorum and Representatives Katherine Harris, Robert Dornan and Henry Hyde, knowingly hired gay staffers.

These insiders joined a growing gay caucus within the Republican orbit that included Rep. Jim Kolbe (AZ), the retiring (and only "out") Republican; Rep. Bob Allen (R-FL), outed in July 2007 for soliciting an undercover male officer inside a restroom and offering to perform oral sex for $20; the retired—and disgraced—Rep. Ed Schrock (R-VA), a virulent right-winger forced to resign when his secret homosexuality was made public; and David Dreier (R-CA), about whom rumors of his sexuality circulated in the Los Angles gay press. This orbit also included two legislative players central to the Foley affair, Jeff Trandahl, a former House clerk, and Kirk Fordham, a former aide to Foley and Tom Reynolds (R-NY). (Rumors have long circulated in Florida as to Governor Charlie Crist's sexual orientation.) Most disturbing, against a background of Christian fundamentalist denunciation of homosexuality as a sin, a value embraced by the Republican Party, none of these upright political figures appear to have repudiated the party's homophobic belief, let alone left the party.

Simultaneous to the sex scandals disrupting Washington, a second set of scandals befell the Christian evangelical community. In 2004, the televangelist and former president of Trinity Broadcasting Network (TBN), Paul Crouch, was outed in an adulterous affair with a former TBN employee—unfortunately, this employee happened to be a male, Enoch Lonnie Ford. As revealed in a *Los Angeles Times* exposé, the evangelist had the affair at a TBN-owned cabin at Lake Arrowhead, CA. Making matters worse, Crouch siphoned off $425,000 of TBN funds to bribe his lover to keep their affair a secret.[16]

However, it was the outing of "Pastor Ted" Haggard in 2006 that put the nail in the coffin of the Christian right. A week or so before the election, Haggard, a devoutly married father of five children, was caught with his proverbial pants down in a gay scandal. Mike

Jones, a male prostitute from Denver, claimed that he had had many drug-fueled trysts with Haggard over the previous three years. Haggard initially denied ever having met Jones, taking illegal drugs or having a homosexual liaison. He insisted that he "[n]ever had a gay relationship with anybody, and I'm steady with my wife, I'm faithful to my wife. So, I don't know if this is election year politics or if this has to do with the [gay] marriage amendment or what it is."

Over the next few days, Haggard's story unraveled. First, he acknowledged meeting Jones, but only as a masseur. As for the drugs, "I was tempted, but I never used it," he claimed, insisting that he had bought methamphetamine only to flush it down the drain. Finally, the ugly truth came out: "There is part of my life that is so repulsive and dark that I've been warring against it all of my adult life." In a letter to his congregation, Haggard confessed that he was "a deceiver and a liar" and begged for forgiveness.

Haggard was a leading light of the evangelical movement and, ironically, was considered a moderate. He was the founder and head of the 14,000-member New Life Church, based in Colorado Springs, CO, and president of the National Association of Evangelicals, a group that claims thirty million members. He advocated against global warming, poverty and the genocide in Darfur. He enjoyed considerable influence on Capitol Hill and was a regular participant in the Monday-morning White House conference call to religious leaders. He condemned both homosexuality and gay marriage, insisting, in a scary YouTube video, "We don't have to debate about what we should think about homosexual activity, it's written in the Bible." In disgrace, Haggard resigned his ministry and, with wife and kids in tow, withdrew from public life.[17]

A homosexual scandal also befell Jim McGreevey, the former New Jersey governor. Elected in 2002 as a Democratic reformer, he unexpectedly resigned in August 2004 as news spread that he was the subject of a sexual harassment suit brought by a former security aide, Golan Cipel. McGreevey, a father of two, announced at a news conference accompanied by his wife, "And so, my truth is that I am a gay American." After a bitter divorce, McGreevey turned to the priesthood to reclaim his life.[18]

Finally, we have the example of William Bennett, the self-serving, self-righteous hypocrite who, as the author of *The Book of Vir-*

*tues*, turned "virtue" into a dirty word. This devout Catholic, former drug czar under Bush the First and outspoken critic of drinking, gay marriage and wife swapping, was one of Clinton's most unrelenting detractors during his impeachment hearings. However, as reported in *The Washington Monthly* and other sources, over the previous decade Bennett made dozens of trips to casinos in Atlantic City and Las Vegas where, as a "preferred customer," his total losses topped $8 million. It was also reported that he maintained a clandestine liaison with a buff Las Vegas dominatrix, Mistress Lee, his "beautiful domme muse mistress." In his best seller, Bennett wrote: "We should know that too much of anything, even a good thing, may prove to be our undoing... [We] need ... to set definite boundaries on our appetites." In the face of such self-serving hypocrisy, one should never forget Mae West's memorable rejoinder: "Too much of a good thing can be wonderful." (Not surprising, while an on-screen commentator for the '08 election, this aspect of Bennett's life was effectively air-brushed out.)[19]

\* \* \*

The object of Bennett's sexual obsession was the dominatrix, Mistress Lee. Better known to Las Vegas regulars as Leola McConnell, Mistress Lee is an up-scale sex worker. She, like Sherry Rowland who fulfilled Clinton-aide Dick Morris' shoe fetish and Ashley Alexandra Dupre who was the focus of Spitzer's attention\*, provided high-priced services to a discriminating clientele. These women recall the age-old male fantasy of the courtesan.

The courtesan is the symbol of up-scale (male) pleasure, a sexuality that seeks to overcome the contradiction between sexual commerce and erotic affection. Traditionally, she functioned as the sex worker who was seen as not being a prostitute. She embodied the highest expression of the alienation of commercial exchange, but represented (for her male customer) the fantasy of sensual intimacy. It was an intimacy of mutual choice, without obligation or strings. The fantasy of the courtesan remains a defining feature of patriarchy, of male heterosexual sexual culture.

The courtesan operates at the top of the commercial-sex food chain. Mostly women, but some men, like Mike Jones who serviced

---

\* Spitzer episode discussed below.

Rev. Ted, ply this trade. They are far removed from the proletarian streetwalkers, pole dancers, massage parlor attendants and those who advertise through craigslist and weekly newspapers. They range from those available through escort services to those truly upscale professionals who operate anonymously in Washington, New York and cities throughout the world. The most super-discreet sex workers don't have websites advertising their services and fees. Rather, they benefit from word-of-mouth referrals and, as the old saying goes, if you have to ask you can't afford them.

Mistress Lee is such a sex worker. According to Mike Knapp, a Las Vegas columnist, not only is she a successful dominatrix, but a body builder who hopes to become the next Ms. Natural Olympia. Besides Bennett, she claims to know other conservative politicos. One, a Texas Republican with close ties to the Bush clan, is reported wearing woman's clothes in a photo. There are also the congress-man who had her facilitate a homoerotic encounter and another she caught on tape calling a gay chat line. She has been a busy bee, penning a self-published tell-all, *Lustful Utterances*.[20]

The most tragic courtesan of the Bush era was Deborah Jeane Palfrey, of Vallejo, CA. She ran an up-scale escort service, Pamela Martin & Associates (PM&A), and was dubbed by the tabloids, the "DC Madam." Among her most memorable clients were Dick Morris and Sen. David Vitter (R-LA).* Another client was Randall Tobias, the head of the U.S. Agency for International Development (USAID), who, in the wake of his outing, abruptly resigned his position for "personal reasons." Tobias was the former chairman and CEO of Eli Lilly and AT&T International as well as chairman of Duke University. He was also a Republican Party stalwart and major fundraiser; his "ambassadorship" was awarded for services rendered. However, in his role as the first U.S. Global AIDS Coordinator, he led the Bush-administration's PEPFAR campaign insisting on abstinence-only sex education and opposing support for prostitutes.

Ms. Palfrey operated, as her website stated, "a high-end adult fantasy firm which offered legal sexual and erotic services across the spectrum of adult sexual behavior." If one can believe Tobias,

---

* Vitter episode is discussed below.'

our hardworking public servant was busted for using the Madam's services only for massages, not for sex. Sure.

When the story first broke, the DC Madam held a press conference on the steps of Congress and announced that she had turned over some forty pounds of her private billing records (including phone and credit card numbers) to ABC to ferret out high-ranking customers. To kick-start the investigation, she identified another Washington insider who patronized her services, Harlan K. Ullman, an associate with the Center for Strategic and International Studies. His main claim to fame was a scholarly paper he wrote more than a decade earlier on the military strategy known as "shock and awe." Ullman rejected her claims, insisting: "It doesn't deserve the dignity of a response."[21]

The DC Madam got her start in the adult-sex business in San Diego. In court papers, she acknowledged that she was "appalled and disgusted" by how "seedy, lazy and incompetent" were the local escort agencies. An avowed teetotaler, she said she was most upset by the drug-related atmosphere promoted by the services. Palfrey's first escort service collapsed in 1990 when she was arrested. She employed about a dozen women and claims that she would have made $100,000 that year had not an employee's angry mother apparently tipped off the police. She served eighteen months in prison after her 1991 conviction and, while on probation in 1993, started her Washington business.

Palfrey's website noted that services were pegged at $300 for a ninety minute session. A help-wanted ad published in DC-area college- and weekly-papers sought attractive women over twenty-three with at least two years of college. According to court records, the women sent roughly 50 percent of the money they made to her PO box in Vallejo. Authorities claim that she amassed upward of 15,000 customers between 1993 and 2006.

In 2004, the Internal Revenue Service and the U.S. Postal Service launched a joint investigation into Palfrey's business activities. In March 2007, the feds seized Palfrey's assets, including her home valued at $500,000. Palfrey speculated that the federal indictment against her came as fallout from the investigation into former congressman Randy "Duke" Cunningham. While she does not claim a direct link to Cunningham, she suggests that federal authorities were investigating charges that a defense contractor provided hookers to Cunningham as part of an influence-peddling scheme. Palfrey believes that the federal probe of her business "had solely to do with some Duke Cunningham-type bigwig client that got caught up in something and started to say, 'Do you know this?' and 'Do you know that?' And that he might have been able to lead them to somebody." All this caught up with Paltry in May 2008 and she committed suicide, fearful of spending years in prison.[22]

Mistress Lee and the DC Madam were not the only courtesans operating during the Bush era, particularly out of the national spotlight in towns and suburbs throughout the country. In the tony Westchester, NY, town of New Bedford, the hometown of Martha Stewart, Ralph Lauren and George Soros, Sandra Chemero, a 46-year-old woman, was busted for running a successful sex club. On her website, Chemero identified herself as a professional dominatrix catering to men seeking a highly specialized kind of pleasure or, as she advertised, "where submissives and slaves are immersed in training." Her club, "The Sovereign Estate," operated out of a mansion owned by K'hal Adas Kashau, an ultra-Orthodox rabbinical school. (A school's representative bemoaned, "It's against our religion. It's against the Bible. We've never even heard of such a thing.")[23]

Not far from New Bedford, in Greenburgh, NY, Erik Ward, a local police officer, was fired after being acquitted of having a tryst in the woods with a 32-year-old dominatrix, Gina Pane. On her website, she called herself "angelabella" and offered her services for a variety of sadomasochistic fantasies. Ms. Pane had been stopped for marijuana possession, but the officer was willing to exchange favors for services rendered. Ward insisted his actions were above suspicion; all he was trying to do was "turn" Pane into a confidential informant in order to get to her dope supplier. Pane testified that she and Ward drove off to a secluded spot and that he masturbated while she squatted on a tree branch and defecated to satisfy his sexual fetish.

In Boston, wife, mother of two and dominatrix, Paula Webb was arrested following disclosures by her husband, who was upset with her after a fight. Mrs. Webb's website listed services including corporal punishment, humiliation and role-playing. According to the police, a detective posing as a customer responded to one of the ads and, when the detective and Webb met, she told him that she offered oral sex for $150. Her basement dungeon was equipped with an assortment of whips, chains, ropes and other items.

In San Francisco (only San Francisco!), a former dominatrix and current employee at the U.S. Treasury Department, Susan Peacher, won a sexual harassment and retaliation lawsuit against her office manager who was a former client. She complained that he wouldn't leave her alone. She went to court to stop him from sexually harassing her, attempting to kiss her in the elevator, telling her she had "luscious lips" and repeatedly asking for "sessions."

A Columbus, Ohio-based dominatrix, "Lady Sage," ran a website and private service, "Through the Looking Glass." Sessions cost $275 an hour and, according to the site, "are about good people having great fun." She was the subject of a federal embezzlement case involving Abraham Alexander, an accounts-payable executive at the Manhattan Cardiovascular Research Foundation. He was sentenced to two to six years for stealing $237,162 to cover Lady Sage's unique services.

In Santa Ana, CA, Betty Davis, a 60-year-old great-grandmother dominatrix won a court ruling that forced the Orange County Sheriff's Department to return $20,000 worth of bondage items, including whips, chains and other toys, seized during a raid on her private dungeon. Davis, who says she has twelve grandchildren and two great-grandchildren, was arrested for allegedly soliciting prostitution after an undercover sheriff's deputy answered an ad in a bondage magazine and was led, blindfolded, to her dungeon. According to Davis' lawyer, she offered a therapeutic service that didn't include sex.

In Dedham, MA, a dominatrix, Barbara Asher, fifty-six, was acquitted of manslaughter charges in the death of Michael Lord, a man who allegedly suffered a fatal heart attack while strapped to a contemporary version of a "medieval torture device." During his closing argument, the prosecutor, Robert Nelson, re-enacted the bondage session: Donning a leather mask and speaking to the jury through the zippered mouth, he said Asher did nothing to help Lord as he flailed about and died while strapped to the rack in a makeshift dungeon. "She did nothing, nothing for five minutes," Nelson yelled, his voice muffled through the mask. The jury found her not guilty of involuntary manslaughter and dismemberment.[24]

In today's post-sex revolution America, the grand courtesan has been replaced by the banality of the escort service and the oh-so-conventional dominatrix. Sexual fantasy has not merely become the fodder of marketing and advertising, but one can only wonder if the quality of pleasure has accordingly degraded. One need only consult google, craigslist or a free local newsweekly to find the sex worker of one's (male) choice. Today, Heidi Fleiss, the so-called Hollywood Madam, represents high-end sexual indulgence. Unfortunately, while the popular media presents her as a mysterious sex charmer, closer examination reveals her to be a far less grand figure of style and taste, functioning more like a switchboard operator with a rolo-dex that could supply a caller with a female prostitute who would service his specialized fantasy or fetish.

Once upon a time the courtesan's allure, her claim to overcome alienation, might have been believed like so many other social fictions. While never true, it was wrapped in enough mystery and social stigma to suggest an alternative value system. This fiction was a negation to the dominant Christian value of de-eroticized sexual propriety that defines America's heterosexual patriarchy. Now, as its mirror-image otherness, the courtesan's fiction only serves to reinforce sexual repression.

\* \* \*

The pace of sex scandals seemed to quicken as America moved into the '08 electoral season. The first series of outings took place during the summer of '07 and involved conservative senators David Vitter (R-LA) and Larry Craig (R-ID). These were followed by embarrassing revelations involving leading Republican and Democratic presidential candidates, including John McCain, Rudi Giuliani, Fred Thompson and Mitt Romney as well as John Edwards. In the shadow of these revelations came the exposés involving Eliot Spitzer, Vito Fossella and Tim Mahoney.

Vitter was outed by *Hustler* publisher, Larry Flynt, as part of the DC Madam scandal.[25] He had been a model conservative Christian, a Republican with a pure pedigree: He is white, attractive and articulate, a married family man, a Harvard graduate, attended Tulane law school and was a Rhodes scholar. Most importantly, he has long taken strict moral positions. As a Republican state representative in

1998, Vitter spoke out forcefully in support of the impeachment of Clinton for lying about his illicit sexual affair. Writing an opinion piece for the *New Orleans Times-Picayune*, he argued that impeachment "is a process of removing a president from office who can no longer effectively govern; it is not about punishment."[26]

While running for the Senate in 2004, Vitter issued a position paper, "Protecting the Sanctity of Marriage," decrying the impact of gay marriage and other social "ills" on society. As it stated,

> The Hollywood left is redefining the most basic institution in human history, and our two U.S. Senators won't do anything about it. We need a U.S. Senator who will stand up for Louisiana values, not Massachusetts's values. I am the only Senate Candidate to coauthor the Federal Marriage Amendment; the only one fighting for its passage.

He went so far as to compare the effect of gay marriage on society to the devastation inflicted by Hurricanes Katrina and Rita.[27]

In the first few years he was in Washington, he was a model Republican foot soldier. He opposed healthcare reform, opposed family planning efforts, opposed federal support for housing and education, resisted all calls for improved human rights and civil liberties, opposed labor rights and stalled all environment efforts. He joined other right wing Republicans opposing the McCain-Kennedy Immigration Bill. And, of course, he steadfastly backed mad king George's Iraq war folly.

Revelations about the DC Madam came amidst still other disclosures about Vitter's past. He appears to have been a regular at the New Orleans' Canal Street Brothel run by Jeanette Maier, a former madam, and had an ongoing relationship for nearly a year with a New Orleans prostitute, "Wendy Cortez," with whom he allegedly had an out-of-wedlock child. (He vehemently denies these allegations, insisting: "I think you know that that allegation is absolutely and completely untrue. ... I have said that on numerous occasions.") These stories add to other rumors circulating for years about Vitter's questionable sexual practices. It is rumored that Louisiana's former Republican governor, Mike Foster, encouraged Vitter not to run for governor in 2001 because of his extramarital affairs. In 2002, a Louisiana GOP official, Vincent Bruno, publicly raised questions about his affairs.

Following Flynt's disclosure, Vitter issued a public apology that stated:

> This was a very serious sin in my past for which I am, of course, completely responsible. Several years ago, I asked for and received forgiveness from God and my wife in confession and marriage counseling. Out of respect for my family, I will keep my discussion of the matter there—with God and them. But I certainly offer my deep and sincere apologies to all I have disappointed and let down in any way.

The question not addressed, of course, is not whether Vitter was forgiven by his wife or his God, but by the Louisiana constituency. He comes up for reelection in 2010. In 2000, a reporter asked Vitter's wife, Wendy, if her husband was as unfaithful as former president Clinton, would she be as forgiving as Hillary Clinton? "I'm a lot more like Lorena Bobbitt than Hillary," she replied. "If he does something like that, I'm walking away with one thing, and it's not alimony, trust me." It remains to be seen, then, whether the latter-day Lorena Bobbitt will slice and dice her adulterous hubby.[28]

While the Vitter scandal was subsiding, *Roll Call*, the Capitol Hill newspaper, broke the sad tale of the questionable behavior of an aging senator—and offered a rare glimpse into the secret world of sexual solicitation that goes on in men's public restrooms. In June, Craig was apprehended by an undercover officer, Sgt. Dave Karsnia, who was checking out complaints about lewd conduct at the Minneapolis-St. Paul International Airport men's room. Airport police had previously made numerous arrests in the restroom (often called a "tearoom") in connection with illicit sexual activity.

As *Roll Call* retold Karsnia's official report, the policeman entered the bathroom at noon and hung out for about thirteen minutes before taking a seat in a stall. He reported that he saw "an older white male with grey hair standing outside my stall." The older man, who was later identified as Craig, lingered in front of the stall for two minutes. "I could see Craig look through the crack in the door from his position. Craig would look down at his hands, 'fidget' with his fingers, and then look through the crack into my stall again. Craig would repeat this cycle for about two minutes," the report states.

Kasnia reports that Craig then entered the stall next to his and placed his roller bag against the front of the stall door. "My experience has shown that individuals engaging in lewd conduct use their bags to block the view from the front of their stall," Karsnia reports. "From my seated position, I could observe the shoes and ankles of Craig seated to the left of me," he adds. Craig was wearing dress slacks with black dress shoes. Karsnia adds:

> At 12:16 hours, Craig tapped his right foot. I recognized this as a signal used by persons wishing to engage in lewd conduct. Craig tapped his toes several times and moves his foot closer to my foot. I moved my foot up and down slowly. While this was occurring, the male in the stall to my right was still present. I could hear several unknown persons in the restroom that appeared to use the restroom for its intended use. The presence of others did not seem to deter Craig as he moved his right foot so that it touched the side of my left foot which was within my stall area.

Craig then swiped his hand under the stall divider several times. The officer noted that "... Craig had a gold ring on his ring finger as his hand was on my side of the stall divider." Karsnia then held his identification down by the floor to notify Craig that he was a police officer. He continues:

> With my left hand near the floor, I pointed towards the exit. Craig responded, 'No!' I again pointed towards the exit. Craig exited the stall with his roller bags without flushing the toilet. ... Craig said he would not go. I told Craig that he was under arrest, he had to go, and that I didn't want to make a scene. Craig then left the restroom.

Once placed under arrest, Craig challenged the officer's account of the events. He repeatedly said that he "either disagreed with me [Kasnia] or 'didn't recall' the events as they happened." Craig stated "that he has a wide stance when going to the bathroom and that his foot may have touched mine." Craig insisted that he reached down with his right hand to pick up a piece of paper on the floor. The officer noted that "there was not a piece of paper on the bathroom floor, nor did Craig pick up a piece of paper." On August 8th Craig accepted a guilty plea for disorderly conduct.

After the scandal broke and the full consequences of his actions dawned on him, Craig attempted to rewrite history and withdraw his guilty plea. He initially agreed to pay $500-plus in fines and fees, and receive a suspended ten-day jail sentence plus one year's probation. However, as the story escalated, Craig insisted that he was innocent and would not have accepted the plea if he'd had a lawyer. (He must have missed his buddy Fred Thompson on "Law & Order.") Under pressure, he resigned his position as Senate liaison to the Romney campaign. However, holding to his denials, he refused Republican Party pleas to resign his Senate seat. He did not run for reelection in '08. In December '08, his appeal to overturn his original guilty please was denied. (It should be noted that in 2006, the gay activist website—blogactive.com—outed Craig as a closeted gay man. Craig's office denied the allegation, claiming that the accusation was "completely ridiculous" and with "no basis in fact.")[29]

Once upon a time in America presidential peccadilloes were off-limits to the snooping eyes of the media and the public.[30] However, in the wake of Clinton's impeachment, presidential candidates have become fair game for exposés. And no candidate was beyond the prying eyes of hungry journalists looking for a good story or publishers seeking headlines that would sell papers. Obama was even the subject of a scurrilous scandal meant more as a trial balloon to test the candidate's resolve than the truth of the purported incident—and it failed.

Another failed effort involved McCain. As mentioned above, the *New York Times* took off the gloves when it went after McCain for his alleged affair with a lobbyist. *Times* editorial writer Nicholas Kristof added to the McCain's bashing when he reported that in 1979, and while still married, he aggressively courted Cindy Hensley, a 25-year-old woman from a well-to-do family. McCain then divorced his wife, Carol, who had raised their three children while he was a prisoner-of-war in Vietnam, married Ms. Hensley and launched his political career bankrolled by his new wife's family fortune. It's hard to know if this part of McCain's past mattered to the majority of voters who backed Obama, so many more pressing issues influenced most people's decision making.[31]

Giuliani came under similar scrutiny. Rudi was initially endorsed by Christian conservative leader Pat Robertson. The endorsement drew much attention due to the odd-couple nature of their alignment. It was a political marriage few anticipated and exposed the deeper crisis faced by the Christian-Republican coalition in the '08 election. It represents a pragmatist's bet on "who could beat Hillary," thus dropping any pretense to the higher moral calling that, for more than a quarter-century, fueled Robertson's opportunistic career. Most remarkable, the two old-time artful dodgers skillfully sidestepped any mention of abortion and gay rights, issues that for Robertson and the Christian right were cornerstone concerns during the two previous presidential cycles. Equally surprising, no mention of Giuliani's adulterous past found its way into the orgy of backslapping revelry. While the announcement gained media attention and provoked considerable commentary, it quickly dissipated as Giuliani's protégé in strong-arm deception, Bernie Kerik, was slapped with a sixteen-count federal indictment.[32]

Thompson, the former senator turned actor turned presidential aspirant, was assailed by James Dobson, founder of ultra-conservative Focus on the Family, for being "wrong on issues dear to social conservatives." Dobson was offended by Thompson's opposition to a constitutional ban on same-sex marriage and his support of the McCain-Feingold campaign finance reform legislation. Unstated, but not far from Dobson and other Christian fundamentalist resentment of Thompson, was his trophy bride, his second wife, Jeri Kehn, whom he married in 2002. He divorced his first wife, Sarah Lindsay, in 1985.[33]

Romney's role as a closet pornographer surfaced as his prospects for securing the Republican presidential nod increased. Amidst contestation for the Iowa Republican caucuses rumors spread among the local press and Christian groups of Romney's complicity in offering pornographic programming while serving on the board of the Marriott hotel chain. "Mitt Romney regularly denounces the 'cesspool' of pornography on the campaign trail," wrote Ben Weyl in the *Iowa Independent*. "But recently," he added, "those would-be supporters have been grumbling that Romney did not do enough to shut down hardcore movie options in Marriott hotels while he was on the company's board for nearly a decade."

Glen Johnson, an Associated Press (AP) reporter, first linked Romney to porn programming in July 2008. He pointed out that while

Romney served on the Marriott board, from 1992 to 2001 as chairman of its audit committee, the hotel chain contracted with On Command to provide in-room television services, including adult programming; in 2006, On Command was acquired by LodgeNet. When questioned by AP, Romney claimed that the issue of pornography never came up at board meetings and insisted that he did not know how much money porn generated for the hotel. Ignorance is bliss.

Romney received an annual fee of $25,000 and stock options while serving on the Marriott board. He also received a campaign contribution of $80,000 arranged by J.W. Marriot. When the story broke, the Christian right was up in arms. Tony Perkins, president of the Family Research Council, denounced the Marriott board and, indirectly Romney: "They have to assume some responsibility. It's their hotels, it's their television sets." Kim Lehman, president of the Iowa Right to Life Committee, warned: "If he [Romney] had the opportunity to protect families and didn't take the opportunity, he's going to be viewed as a hypocrite." She added, "[i]f it's true if he could have, but chose not to ... and to say you're for families and for children, when you have a tremendous opportunity to take, these are all issues he's going to be faced with." Daniel Weiss, media analyst for Focus on the Family, added to the rancor: "If [Romney] made money off pornography in the past, is he going to turn a blind eye to it if he's president? Because as chief executive of the nation, it's his responsibility to make sure our nation's obscenity laws are efficiently and vigorously enforced." It's unclear if this played any role in Romney's failed effort to secure the Republican nomination, but it sure didn't help.[34]

Scandal did not only befall Republican candidates. As the *National Enquirer* announced in December 2007: "Presidential candidate John Edwards is caught up in a love child scandal, a blockbuster ENQUIRER investigation has discovered." Its coverage included a photo of a very pregnant Rielle Hunter, the woman with whom Edwards had the adulterous affair. The initial story had a bizarre twist when an Edwards aide, Andrew Young, claimed to be the father. However, in August '08, Edwards, with his wife, Elizabeth, at his side made a formal apology and bowed out of public life.[35]

As the Edwards story was playing out, New York governor Spitzer stepped in it ... big time. He was outed for retaining the services of a "female companion" through the Emperor's Club VIP, a call-girl ring operating in New York, Washington, Miami and other jet-set cities. In keeping with the scandal involving Vitter and the prostitution ring run by the DC Madam, this scandal captured immediate media attention. Spitzer (known as Client 9) was allegedly unwittingly caught up in a federal wiretap probe of the Emperor's Club. He apparently retained the prostitute's services for the night of February 13th while visiting Washington, DC.[36]

According to the federal affidavit, he met the hooker at the Mayflower Hotel in room 871. As reported by the AP and the *New York Times*, federal authorities claimed that the Emperor's Club took in more than $1 million in profits over the previous four years. A session could run from $1,000 to $5,500 per hour and, as an efficient post-modern service, gentlemen could pay with cash, credit card, wire transfers or money orders. Spitzer apparently spent $80,000 on services rendered; most troubling, the object of his affection, Ashley Alexandra Dupre, strikingly resembled one of his daughters. The Emperor's Club website promoted its services:

> Emperor's Club VIP is the most preferred international social introduction service for those accustomed to excellence. Introducing the most impressive models to leading gentleman of the world is our expertise. We specialize in introductions of: fashion models, pageant winners and exquisite students, graduates and women of successful careers (finance, art, media etc...) to gentlemen of exceptional standards. When seeking an evening date, a weekend travel companion, or a friend to accompany you during your next business / social function our models are the perfect preference.[37]

The FBI apparently pulled Spitzer's solicitation from a grab-bag of 5,000 intercepted telephone calls and text messages.

However, as information about the case came out, more seemed to have been involved than chance. Federal investigators from the Justice Department, FBI and IRS were involved. They used search warrants and wiretaps to monitor bank records and wire transfers, including more than 5,000 phone calls and text messages, 6,000 or so e-mails, and travel and hotel records. Some have charged the Bush administration with releasing the damning information to discredit Spitzer as part of an election-year smear campaign against the Democrats.

Spitzer offered a public apology for his action, trying to contain it by labeling it a "private matter." Joined by his wife Silda, Spitzer admitted, "I have acted in a way that violates my obligation to my family and violates my or any sense of right or wrong." He added, "I apologize first and most importantly to my family. I apologize to the public to whom I promised better." However, what galled many was that Spitzer, as New York's attorney general, repeatedly busted call-girl services. In short order, he resigned his position and, in time, was cleared of all criminal charges.[38]

New York governors have long been among the most celebrated sexual characters, so Spitzer should feel in good company. The most outrageous was Lord Cornbury (Edward Hyde), the governor-general of New York who allegedly opened the General Assembly of 1702 in an exquisite, formal gown. Some insisted that he dressed in drag to better represent Queen Anne, but few believed him. He may well have been the nation's most famous drag queen.* However, the most notorious philanderer was Nelson Rockefeller who, while governor and before his appointment as vice president under Gerald Ford, is rumored to have had many extra-marital liaisons. He died of a heart attack in January 1979, naked, having sex with his 27-year-old mistress, Megan Marshak. She was pinned underneath him and had a hard time getting out from under the 71-year-old overweight statesman. For all her pain and suffering, Rockefeller left Marshak the deed to the mid-town Manhattan townhouse in which he died and $50,000.[39]

Adding still more front-page scandal to '08 political season were the outings of Representatives Vito Fossella and Tim Mahoney. Fossella was arrested on May 1st, in Alexandria, VA, and charged with driving while drunk. However, a relatively modest crime of DWI quickly escalated when it was revealed that he called Laura Fay from the police station. Fay, a retired Air Force lieutenant colonel, was the mother of his out-of-wedlock daughter, unknown to his wife and family in New York, his constituency and his fellow congresspersons. Embracing wisdom rather than folly, Fossella chose to not run for reelection; a Democrat won his former House seat. In December '08, he was sentenced to five days for the DWI conviction.[40]

---

* See Chapter 1, Birth of a Nation.

Only weeks before the '08 election, ABC News outed Mahoney for paying a reported $121,000 to a former mistress, Patricia Allen, to hush-up their adulterous affair. When the scandal broke, Mahoney's campaign ads showed the congressman with his wife, Terry, boasting the slogan: "Restoring America's Values Begins at Home." In February '08, Allen filed suit against the congressman due to (in the words of ABC) "sexual harassment, intimidation, humiliation and charged that the Congressman's behavior masked a 'dark and depraved personality'." As only American political hypocrisy would have it, the affair began two years earlier while he was running to replace the discredited Foley. He lost his reelection bid.[41]

## References

[1] See www.theemperorsclub.com.
[2] David Rosen, "The New Texas Two-Step: Polygamy & State Regulation of Sexual Life," *CounterPunch*, April 19-20, 2008; Elissa Wall, Warren Jeffs' FLDS Church and What I Left Behind," *Huffington Post*, May 17, 2008.
[3] Jim Rutenberg, et. al, "For McCain, Self-Confidence on Ethics Poses Its Own Risk," *New York Times*, February 21, 2008; Seth Colter Walls, "Obama Accuser Larry Sinclair Holds Stupefying Press Conference," *Huffington Post*, June 18, 2001; "Sleaze charge: 'I Took Drugs, had Homo Sex with Obama," *WorldNetDaily*, February 17, 2008, http://www.wnd.com/index; deathby1000papercuts.blogspot.com /2008/02.
[4] Barbara Fulenwider, "Who Who Filed Law Suite Found Dead, *Fort Bend/Southwest Star*, December 24, 2003.
[5] Evan Smith "W is for 'Whew!' *Texas Monthly*, February 2002.
[6] Zachary A. Goldfarb, "In Tight Race, Republican Shays Takes a Less Measured Tone," *Washington Post*, October 14, 2006.
[7] Rick Pearson and Liam Ford, "GOP Leaders Say They Felt Misled by Ryan File," *Chicago Tribune*, June 22, 2004.
[8] Exodus 20:14.
[9] Abby Goodnough, "The Mayor's Separation," *New York Times*, May 12, 2000.
[10] "Extramarital Affairs are Not so Common," *USA Today*, May 1, 1998; Rodale Press, *Men's Health* "Best Life," 2003; per *Oprah* magazine, 2004, see Stephany Alexander, "Why Men Are Prone

To Adultery" at www.infidelity.com; Joan Atwood and Limor Schwartz, "Cybersex: The New Affair Treatment Considerations," *Journal of Couple and Relationship Therapy*, vol. 1, no. 3, 2002.

11 Franklin Foer, "Adultery," Slate, June 15, 1997; Jonathan Turley, "Of Lust and the Law," *Washington Post*, September 5, 2004.

12 Katha Pollitt, "Foley's IMbroglio," *Nation*, October 5, 2006.

13 http://thinkprogress.org/2006/09/30/foley-coverup-timeline.

14 http://www.scrantontimestribune.com/projects/lawsuit.pdf.

15 Brian Montopoli, "Foley, Gay Republicans, and The List," CBS News, October 5, 2006; Mark Leibovich, "Foley Case Upsets Balance of Gay Republicans," *New York Times*, October 7, 2006.

16 "Is Charlie Crist Gay?", *Orlando Weekly*, September 21, 2006; William Lobdell, "Televangelist Paul Crouch Attempts to Keep His Accuser Quiet," *Los Angeles Times*, September 12, 2004.

17 David Rosen, "Those Who Preach in Glass Cathedrals: Rev. Ted Haggard & the Eclipse of Evangelical Fury," *CounterPunch*, November 15, 2006.

18 "New Jersey Governor Quits, Comes Out as Gay," CNN, August 13, 2004.

19 George Knapp, "Dominatrix Redux," *Las Vegas Mercury*, July 15, 2004.

20 George Knapp, "Knappster," Las Vegas City Life, June 9, 2005.

21 "'D.C. Madam' Names a Purported Customer," CNN, April 13, 2007.

22 David Rosen, "Moral Hypocrisy on the Hill, Again: The Christian Right, Sexual Scandal and the Sexual Pleasures of the Courtesan," *CounterPunch*, July 17, 2007; Paul Duggan and Amy Shipley, "Operator of D.C. Call-Girl Ring Is Dead in Apparent Suicide," *Washington Post*, May 2, 2008.

23 Jennifer Fermino and Lorena Mogelli, "'S&M' Marriage from Hell," *New York Post*, March 5, 2007.

24 Pane at www.nyinquirer.com, November 30, 2006; Webb at wbztv. com, Apr 7, 2007; Peacher at *San Francisco Chronicle*, April 10, 2005; "Lady Sage" at www.cfo.com, April 10, 2005; Davis at *San Francisco Examiner* at www.sfgate.com (no date); Asher at *USA Today*, January 30, 2006.

25 Adam Zagorin, "Did Senator Vitter Get Hustled?" *Time*, July 10, 2007.

[26] Kate Moran and Martha Carr, "Madam: Vitter a Client at Canal Street Brothel," *Times-Picayune,* July 10, 2007.

[27] http://www.vitter2004.com.

[28] "Sen. Vitter Apologizes for Number Showing Up on Phone Records of Alleged Prostitution Ring," Fox News, July 10, 2007.

[29] John McArdle, "Craig Arrested, Pleads Guilty Following Incident in Airport Restroom," *Roll Call,* August 27, 2007; October 17, 2006, blogactive.com; William Yardley, "Ex-Senator Ends Effort to Withdraw Guilty Plea," *New York Times,* January 8, 2009.

[30] John H. Summers, "What Happened to Sex Scandals? Politics and Peccadilloes, Jefferson to Kennedy," *Journal of American History,* December 2000, vol. 87, issue 3.

[31] Nicholas Kritof, "McCain and His First Wife," *New York Times,* July 11, 2008.

[32] William K. Rashbaum, "Federal Prosecutors Plan to Seek Charges Against Kerik," *New York Times,* November 7, 2007.

[33] "Dobson: Thompson Must Express Faith," CNN, March 30, 2007.

[34] Glen Johnson, "Mitt Draws Flak Over Marriott Porn," *Associated Press,* July 5, 2007; Desert News, July 6, 2007.

[35] "Presidential Cheating Scandal! Alleged Affair Could Wreck Edwards' Campaign Bid," *National Enquirer,* October 10, 2007; and "Update: John Edwards Love Child Scandal!" *Enquirer,* December 19, 2007.

[36] Danny Hakim and William K. Rashbaum, "Spitzer is Linked to Prostitution Ring," *New York Times,* March 10, 2008.

[37] See www.theemperorsclub.com.

[38] Danny Hakim and William K. Rashbaum, "No Federal Prostitution Charges for Spitzer," *New York Times,* November 7, 2008.

[39] Corky Siemaszko, "Spin R.I.P Nelson Rockefeller; 1979," *New York Daily News,* November 6, 1998.

[40] Johnathan P. Hicks, "Fossella Admits to Extramarital Affair," *New York Times,* May 8 and Raymond Hernandez, "Fossella Sentenced to 5 Days in a Virginia Jail for Drunken Driving," *New York Times,* December 12, 2008.

[41] Emma Schwartz, Rhonda Schwartz and Vic Walter, "Congressman's $121,000 Payoff to Alleged Mistress," ABC, October 13, 2008.

# AFTERWORD:

## SCANDALS & 21ST CENTURY AMERICA

One of the most popular campaign buttons at the '08 Republican National Convention read: "Hottest V.P. from the Coolest State." And Alaska's governor, Sarah Palin, was hot. Like an electric jolt reinvigorating a comatose patient, she rejuvenated a frumpy granddad into a barnstorming populist. She gave John McCain's faltering presidential campaign new life, especially among dedicated "values voters" who were long suspicious of his true beliefs.

Unfortunately, only a few weeks after her bombastic introduction, the heat faded from the Klondike queen. Poor showings in TV interviews, Trooper-gate and other episodes raised questions about her competency and her fitness to govern. It became increasingly evident that she was a dubious VP choice. In the face of the mounting crisis of capital that gripped the nation in the months preceding the election, glib one-liners and folksy asides didn't cut it.

Palin exemplifies what conservative analysts call "red-state feminism." She represents a generation of conservative white women who share qualities of their progressive sisters. They are self-assured, many are college educated, with professional careers and often married with children. However, in distinction to modern "blue-state" feminists, many of these women embrace "traditional" (and often fundamentalist religious) values. These values seek to preserve the fading myth of the patriarchal family and the economic and sexual prowess of the husband.

Palin presented herself as an anti-choice, anti-gay marriage, anti-evolution and pro-guns "gal"—a name she proudly embraced. (In her defense, she claims to eat what she kills.) As a candidate, she insisted on moral absolutes, especially when it came to abortion, whether or not the girl or woman was a victim of incest or rape. She also opposed pre-marital sex, opposed in-school comprehensive sex ed and championed abstinence-only programs for teens, including for her own children. Unbeknownst to Palin, the consequences of her stance came back to bite her. A couple of weeks into the campaign, the media revealed that her unmarried 17-year-old daughter, Bristol, was pregnant.

Politicians from both major parties regularly run from embarrassing scandals. During the recent electoral season, when exposed, Eliot Spitzer and John Edwards as well as Vito Fossella and Tim Mahoney fled the political scene. Probably pushed by the McCain campaign that feared an electoral debacle, Palin stood her ground. In fact, she embraced the scandal, accepting the challenge posed by her daughter's pregnancy as an affirmation of her religious certainty. While Bristol's pregnancy was a public secret in the family's hometown of Wasilla, rumors nevertheless circulated that the teen was the mother of Palin's fifth child, Trig, who suffers from Down's Syndrome. At the time of the Republican Convention, the *National Enquirer* broke the story with a front-page headline screaming about Palin's "dark secret." Given the *Enquirer*'s track record outing Bill Clinton and Edwards, the story quickly was picked up by the major media. It became big news in an increasingly competitive (and often vicious) electoral campaign. The *Enquirer* also alleged that Palin had an affair with a business associate of her husband and he fathered her son, Trig.[1]

Palin stood her ground amidst a flood of innuendo and back-biting. She refused to either condemn her daughter for getting pregnant or withdraw from the campaign. She refused to accept both the real and implied social shaming directed at her. Palin and her husband issued a press release that stated, in part, "We're proud of Bristol's decision to have her baby and even prouder to become grandparents. As Bristol faces the responsibilities of adulthood, she knows she has our unconditional love and support." The Palins said that their daughter would shortly marry the child's father, fellow high-school townie, 18-year-old Levi Johnson.*[2]

The Christian right quickly came out in support of the decision. James Dobson, head of Focus on the Family, declared: "That is what

---

* The marriage plans formally ended in March 2009.

the Palins are doing, and they should be commended once again for not just talking about their pro-life and pro-family values, but living them out even in the midst of trying circumstances." Charmaine Yoest, head of Americans United for Life, said, "We join them in welcoming this new life." Ignorance about one's body and sexuality might be bliss, but in a big family one more mouth to feed was no problem.[3]

Unfortunately, neither Palin nor her supporters in the Christian right dared address the fundamental hypocrisy that undermined her moralistic commitment. By failing to educate her daughter, the young woman and her soon-to-be-husband were going to be unintended parents. The issue is not about the morality of two young people having sex, parenting a child or marrying; nor is it about the efficacy of abortion or adoption as options to address an unwanted pregnancy. In 2005, there were over 400,000 pregnancies among teen girls fifteen to eighteen years of age.[4]

Palin's hypocrisy concerns the consequences of ignorance and personal disempowerment, of a daughter (and the child's father) remaining prisoners of bankrupt traditional values. The two young people were passive victims of nature's chance rather than active subjects of human choice. Each forfeited the power of their individual (self) consciousness. They never could make an informed decision about having a child or about marriage. Whether they remain married or not, they were forced into a relationship through the pure chance of an unintended pregnancy and not the love of a conscious decision.

* * *

A new Obama presidency and Democratic Congress have taken state power amidst the worst economic crisis since the Great Depression. America's sex panic is over; the culture wars are in decline. Equally important, after a quarter-century of growing influence and power, the fierce rightwing assault on sexual freedom is in eclipse. Personal health, family life, sexual relations, scientific knowledge and popular culture were battlegrounds of the culture wars. This conservative counter-revolution got started in the 1970s as a rebellion against the sixties; by 2006, it had overplayed its hand, undone as much by the failure of its policies as by the hypocrisy and sexual scandals that upended many of its strongest proponents. With the election of 2008, the once-powerful Christian Republican moralist movement was in retreat—at least for now. Today, a new era of sexual freedom may emerge as Americans have more pressing issues to deal with than policing other people's private sexual lives.

The likely forthcoming change in America's sexual culture will take a variety of forms. These range from a change in the popular experience of pleasure; the lowering of the rate of teen pregnancy and unmarried birth rate; an increase in commercial sex; a growth in the popularity of "fetish" play; and, unfortunately, a rise in sexual violence as the economic crisis deepens and people (especially men) act out their rage. It will also likely involve a change in the role played by scandals in politics and popular culture.

Hopefully, the new sexual culture will be marked by less hostility toward a woman's right to an abortion and the repeal of numerous federal restraints imposed by the Bush administration on choice. More states might adopt same-sex civil unions and some might legalize same-sex marriages. The Christian right's failed abstinence-only policy will likely be scrapped and teens will receive more informed and sex-positive sex education as well as medical care, condoms and other assistance essential for them to develop a better sense of themselves. The military might drop its ineffective policy of "Don't Ask/ Don't Tell," thus finally freely accepting homosexual citizens into the armed services. The FCC may well embrace a two-pronged strategy with regard to obscenity: (i) permitting more explicit materials for adults; and (ii) educating parents and children in cyber-literacy so as to be able to better recognize inappropriate (if not worse) contacts from a child predator or sexual exploiter. We are also likely to see the decriminalization and/or regulation of prostitution, like that which is already operational in Nevada and Rhode Island, and in other states and select sites around the country. Finally, we will likely see a greater commitment to the international fight against HIV and AIDS through an extension and better funding of the PEPFAR [President's Emergency Plan for AIDS Relief] initiative.

As the long-term impact of the current economic crisis deepens, however, these likely developments in sexual culture may be hamstrung. In particular, the potential impact of anti-immigrant xenophobia may precipitate a new witchhunt targeting undocumented immigrants. The economic panic may also lead to the targeting of sex offenders who, for many, seem more threatening than a jihadist terrorist. Such a witchhunt could be reinforced by the puritanical urges of the Obama administration's and the Democratic Congress' desire for political correctness.

Political correctness, however, can be turned on its head—with unintended consequences. Palin's stand against an alleged scandal involving her teenage daughter was an act of political self-defense. The pregnancy indirectly questioned her competence as a parent and, therefore, raised concerns about her candidacy: Could voters trust her being one heartbeat from the presidency? Palin's stand challenged the moralistic shaming that defines sex scandals in America. Once upon a time unacceptable activities, like a premarital pregnancy or an interracial sexual relationship like that involving Obama's parents, would have driven a candidate from office or from an electoral contest. In '08, politically-motivated rumors about both Obama and McCain failed to catch fire. However, an adulterous relationship drove Edwards from the presidential quest; revelations about Mitt Romney's business interests serving "pornographers" haunted his campaign; and Rudi Giuliani's divorces discredited his claim to moral standing. In '08, sex scandals played a modest role in shaking up the political contest.

In the past, vice presidents and veep candidates like Palin have succumbed to scandal. Most famously, vice president Spiro Agnew resigned in 1973 in the wake of a tax-evasion scandal. Revelations that Thomas Eagelton, the other half of George McGovern's 1972 electoral ticket, had undergone electroshock therapy forced him to withdraw. Richard Nixon's Checkers scandal in 1952 threatened to undo his candidacy with Ike. However, in '08, Palin (along with the McCain campaign leadership) faced a major political scandal in which she either had to be removed from the ticket, like Eagelton, or stand with her daughter, like Nixon, and accepting the full consequences of the young couple's action. She made her decision and she, with McCain, lost their electoral bid.

\* \* \*

Palin took a strong, unwavering stand in support of her beliefs and her daughter's behavior. However, this forthrightness may have unintended consequences. Other people, including fellow politicians, celebrities and ordinary citizens, might also stand fast against socially- or politically-motivated shaming. Where the Palins' embraced religious beliefs to legitimize their acceptance of what many other moralists, including Christian evangelicals, might see as immoral behavior, others might take the same stand but base their positions on different ethical or moral beliefs.

As the history of scandals in America shows, public shaming, especially directed toward political and cultural figures, has been a powerful force to impose and maintain social control. Nearly all politicians caught in compromising, and often hypocritical, scandals succumb to public shame and quickly retreat from the media spotlight. However, in the 1970s, Congressmen Alan Richmond and Barney Frank refused to be shamed when exposed about their homosexuality. After being outed in headline-grabbing scandals, they both secured reelection, a vote of acceptance by their respective constituencies.

What if public figures reject the moralist accusations associated with, for example, adultery? What if they reject the hypocrisy of traditional marriage vows, vows based on property or ownership relations? What if, for example, they endorsed the mutuality of an "open" marriage? What if both partners (but especially the politician) agreed to replace noncommercial or other illicit affairs with mutually-agreed-upon erotic friendships?

Once upon a time in America, sex with the devil was a hanging offense. Interracial sexual relations, what used to be called miscegenation, was illegal in many states until the Supreme Court's 1967 Loving decision. Prostitution is legal in two states, accepted, with a wink-and-a-nod illegality, as a form of adult commercial exchange throughout the country. Sexual relations among consenting same-sex adults were decriminalized by the Court's 2003 Lawrence decision. So, why is adultery still a criminal offense in approximately half the states of the union and stigmatized by most moralistic groups? What if, like sex with the devil, miscegenation, prostitution and homosexuality, adultery disappeared as a moral category? What would happen to the sex scandal?

A scandal gains much of its power to enforce sexual discipline by the shaming directed at those who partake in unacceptable indulgences. Such indulgences are at once sexually illicit and alluring, something forbidden yet desired. Scandals delineate the boundary of the socially acceptable.

In America, the ritual of public shaming dates from the country's founding. As Richard Godbeer explains, "Public shaming, the Puritans believed, could play an important role in prompting or reinforcing contrition." He adds:

> The judicial process itself, involved appearance in court as an indicted criminal, presentation of evidence, and admonition by the magistrates, must have been mortifying for most offenders. Judges often required as part of the sentence that those convicted of sex acts confess their transgression not only in court but also in some public setting. ... If they failed to do so [make a public confession] within a month, they would be whipped. Corporal punishment was both physically painful and a humiliating form of exposure, literally so if the whipping was administered on the bare back.

He concludes, "Public shaming would hopefully deter onlookers from following in the malefactor's footsteps."[5]

We've come a long way from the early days of colonial settlement and the nature of public shaming has been transformed. Long gone are most court trials (except for criminal offenses) and corporal punishment, replaced by public spectacle and nonstop media hounding. A form of "reintegrative shaming" is advocated by John Braithwaite and others advancing "restorative justice," shaming remains a minor aspect of the justice system.[6]

Today, there are two different types of perpetrators who get caught up in sex scandals: Those caught living a lie and those caught living out a lifestyle. The vast majority who get outed fall into the former category. Because they have something to hide, they are deeply shamed and socially stigmatized by the scandal. The upending of a public figure's personal reputation, of concealing hypocrisy, is nearly always the death knell of his or her political career. However, those who have less (or nothing) to hide can overcome the (momentary) hounding by the morality police, the vulture media, and resume a more-or-less normal life.

The long arm of puritan moral vengeance hovers over public life today. Social shaming continues as the price paid by those caught refusing to abide by moral conventions. This vengeance has a particular meaning for those holding public office or are in the public eye. A revelation about a heretofore secret sexual indulgence makes the perpetrator not only subject to shame and ridicule, but unfit for public service. One pays a stiff price for keeping a secret. For those in the public eye, only those who reject (self- and public-) deception can escape the glare of the media hunt and thus refuse the centrifugal force of the scandal.

Sex scandals have occurred in America since the days of Pocahontas. Historically, they have served as a form of public spectacle with two increasingly contradictory social functions. First and foremost, a scandal is a morality tale, intended to punish or shame the perpetrator. Second, over the last century, the scandal has changed, becoming a form of entertainment, intended to distract or fascinate the public. The shift in the social function of the scandal is a measure of how moral values of the secular marketplace have mostly replaced the power of religious tradition. In our new twenty-first century America, with a new president, Congress and historical reality, the role of the scandal will likely persist but have far less moral—and entertainment—sway over political and cultural life. Americans have too many more important issues to deal with.

## References

[1] "Palin War: Teen Prego Crisis," *National Enquirer,* September 3, 2008; "Palin Family Shockers: What Sarah's Really Hiding," *National Enquirer,* September 12, 2008; and "Sarah Palin Lover Revealed," *National Enquirer,* September 26, 2008.

[2] Michael Cooper, "Palin Family Welcomes McCain to Twin Cities," *New York Times,* September 3, 2008.

[3] "Statement from Dr. Charmaine Yoest," Reuters, September 1, 2008.

[4] CDC, National Center for Health Statistics, 2005.

[5] Robert Godbeer, *Sexual Revolution in Early America* (Baltimore: John Hopkins University Press, 2002), 100.

[6] See www.restorativejustice.org.

# INDEX

## A

ABC News 190, 208
ABSCAM (sting operation) 162, 163
Abraham Lincoln, USS 185
Abu Ghraib (prison) 185
Academy Awards 122, 127
*Adam had Four Sons* (1941) 127
Adams, Abigail 36, 38
Adams, Brock 164
Adams, John 36
Adams, Mark 117
Adams, Maude 61
Addams, Jane 67
Adler, Polly 77
Adultery 9, 17-18, 20, 26-27, 29, 47, 61-62, 117, 135, 159, 161, 177, 187, 188-190, 209, 216
*Adventures of Robin Hood, The* (1938) 109
Agnew, Spiro 215
AIDS 125-126, 151-152, 160, 163, 186, 195, 214
Albert, Carl 159
Alexander, Abraham 199
Alexander, Tara 150-151, 153
Allen, Bob 192
Allen, George 192
Allen, Patricia 208
Allen, Paula Gunn 22, 31
Allen, Robert 73, 98
American Civil Liberties Union (ACLU) 160
*American Journalism Review* 170, 179
American Vigilance Association 67
*Anastasia* (1956) 127
Andersen, Harold 166
Andrews, Stephen Pearl 43

Appearance industry 92
Arbuckle, Roscoe "Fatty" 15, 105
Argall (aka Argyall), Samuel 25
Ariston Baths (New York bathhouse) 81
Arlington, Josie 77
Armed Forces Disciplinary Control Board 121
Arthur, Chester A. 60
Arvad, Inga 12, 130
Ashcroft, John 26, 185
Asher, Barbara 198
Assing, Ottilie 37
Associated Press (AP) 179-180, 204, 210
Atwood, Joan 189, 209

## B

*Babbitt* (Lewis) 90
Bailey, Beth 118, 145
Baker, Jean 46
Bakker, Jim 15, 69, 166
Bakker, Tammy Faye 166
Balach, Paul 165
Ball State University study 189
Ball, George H. 58
Baltimore, Lord 21
Bancroft, George 29
Bara, Theda 101
Barnum , P.T. 52, 101
Barry, Joan 109
Barrymore, John 103
Bartell, Gilbert 140
Bartiromo, Maria 13
Barton, Dorothy 128
Bates, Jim 164
Bates, Ruby 107
Bathhouses 72, 81, 153, 156-158

219

# C